Puerto Rico

The Trials of the Oldest Colony in the World

José Trías Monge

Yale University Press

New Haven and London

*In memory of my son, José E. Trías
(1944–1994).*

Published with assistance from the Louis Stern Memorial Fund.
Copyright © 1997 by Yale University. All rights reserved.
This book may not be reproduced, in whole or in part, including illustrations, in any form
(beyond that copying permitted by Sections 107
and 108 of the U.S. Copyright Law and except by reviewers
for the public press), without written permission from
the publishers. Designed by Rebecca Gibb.
Set in Ehrhardt and Meta types by
The Composing Room of Michigan, Inc.
Printed in the United States of America by
Edwards Brothers, Ann Arbor, Michigan.

Library of Congress Cataloging-in-Publication Data

Trías Monge, José
Puerto Rico : the trials of the oldest colony in the world / José Trías
Monge
p.   cm.
Includes bibliographical references and index.
ISBN 0-300-07110-8 (cloth : alk. paper)
0-300-07618-5 (paper : alk. paper)
1. Puerto Rico—Politics and government. 2. Self-determination,
National—Puerto Rico. 3. Puerto Rico—Relations—United States.
4. United States—Relations—Puerto Rico. I. Title.
F1971.T75 1997
320.97295—DC21
97-8965 CIP

A catalogue record for this book is available from the
British Library. The paper in this book meets the guidelines
for permanence and durability of the Committee
on Production Guidelines for Book Longevity of
the Council on Library Resources.

10 9 8 7 6 5 4

Contents

Chronology

This selected list of events pertains mainly to the history of Puerto Rico's relations with the United States.

1493, November 19
Columbus becomes the first European to land on Puerto Rico.

1508
Ponce de León founds the first permanent Spanish settlement.

1521
Transfer of the present capital, initially named Puerto Rico and by 1531 known as San Juan, to its present site.

1532–1595
Initial fortification of San Juan.

1587
Mexican treasury sends the first situado, an annual sum to assist Puerto Rico.

1595
A British fleet, led by Sir Francis Drake and John Hawkins, tries to take over San Juan.

1596
Another British fleet, under the Earl of Cumberland, takes San Juan and brings Puerto Rico under British jurisdiction for sixty-five days.

1625
A Dutch fleet attacks San Juan and, after a siege, fails to capture it.

1634
Construction starts on the massive walls around San Juan, unique in the New World.

1797
A large British fleet attacks San Juan and is repelled.

1810
Beginning of the Wars of Independence of the Spanish continental New World colonies.

1812
The first Spanish constitution, the Cádiz Constitution, is extended to Puerto Rico, which becomes a province of Spain with the same rights as other provinces.

1814
The Cádiz Constitution is repealed.

1820
The Cádiz Constitution is restored and remains in effect until 1823.

1824
The Spanish governor is again given absolute powers over Puerto Rico.

1868
A group of Puerto Ricans revolts at Lares and proclaims the Republic. The insurrection is quelled.

1869
Adoption of a new liberal constitution, which restores Spanish citizenship to Puerto Ricans, as well as the right to be represented in the Spanish Parliament and universal male suffrage. Political parties are allowed to be established.

1870
Liberal Reformist party founded.

1871
Conservative party (later renamed the Unconditionally Spanish party) founded.

1887
Autonomist party founded.

1897, November 25
Autonomic Charter proclaimed.

1898, April 25
United States declares war on Spain.

1898, July 25
American troops invade Puerto Rico.

1898, August 12
Armistice of the Spanish-American War proclaimed.

1898, October 18
Military government established in Puerto Rico.

1898, December 10
Signing of the Treaty of Paris, wherein Spain ceded Puerto Rico to the United States.

1899
Republican party founded.

1900, May 1
Civil government established. The first organic act, the Foraker Act, comes into effect.

1904
Unión party founded.

1915
Socialist party founded.

1917, March 2
The second organic act, the Jones Act, comes into effect. Puerto Ricans become American citizens.

1919
First formal petition for a plebiscite on status, filed by the Resident Commissioner, Félix Córdova Dávila.

1919
First elective Governor bills filed.

1922
Bills filed for the creation of the Associated Free State of Puerto Rico.

1922
Nationalist party founded.

1928
First request in Congress by the Resident Commissioner, Félix Córdova Dávila, for Puerto Rico to adopt a constitution of its own.

1934
First statehood bill, filed by the Resident Commissioner, Santiago Iglesias.

1935–36
Official repression of the independence movement increases. Members of the Nationalist party are involved in several violent incidents. The American chief of police is killed.

1937, March 21
Ponce Massacre, in which police fired into the crowd during a Nationalist party march. Nineteen people were killed, and more than a hundred were wounded.

1938
Popular Democratic party founded.

1946
Independence party founded.

1947, August 5
Puerto Rico receives the right to elect its own Governor.

1949, January
Luis Muñoz Marín is sworn in as the first elected Governor.

1950, July 30
Public Law 600 is approved, giving Puerto Rico the right to adopt its own constitution and to establish a relationship with the United States "in the nature of a compact."

1950, October 30
The Nationalist party reacts by assaulting several towns in Puerto Rico and attempting to kill Muñoz Marín. On November 1, Nationalists attempt to assassinate President Harry Truman in front of Blair House in Washington, D.C.

1952, July 25
Commonwealth of Puerto Rico is established under its own constitution.

1954, March 11
Nationalists open fire on a session of the United States House of Representatives.

1959, March 23
Fernós-Murray bill is filed, aiming to reform the Federal Relations Act.

1963, April 30

Aspinall bill is filed, calling for a commission to draft a compact of permanent union between the United States and Puerto Rico. Instead, a Status Commission is set up by Congress to study all status alternatives.

1967, July 23

Upon the recommendation of the Status Commission, a plebiscite is held to determine which status Puerto Ricans want among Commonwealth, statehood, and independence. Commonwealth is preferred by over 60 percent of voters.

1968

New Progressive party founded.

1975

A new United States–Puerto Rico Commission, set up by President Richard Nixon and Governor Hernández Colón, drafts a Compact of Permanent Association to improve Commonwealth status. President Gerald Ford took no action on it.

1989–91

All parties in Puerto Rico petition Congress to authorize a plebiscite among the status formulas that Congress is willing to offer Puerto Rico. The bills fail.

1993, November 14

The Governor and Legislative Assembly of Puerto Rico go ahead and hold a new plebiscite. Enhanced Commonwealth wins again, this time by a thin margin.

About the Author

José Trías Monge has been an eyewitness to the events narrated here since the 1930s and a major participant in the key constitutional developments that occurred after 1947. A native of Puerto Rico who received his M.A. and LL.B. from Harvard University and his S.J.D. from Yale Law School, Mr. Trías soon became (both in and out of government service) chief legal adviser and part of the inner circle of Luis Muñoz Marín, head of the governing party of Puerto Rico from 1940 to 1964 and powerful elder statesman until his death in 1980. Mr. Trías was one of the chief architects and drafters of Commonwealth status, a member of the Constitutional Convention of Puerto Rico which drew up the present constitution for the island, Attorney General, a member of the group which defended Commonwealth status at the United Nations in 1953–54, and a participant in official discussions in San Juan and Washington, D.C., on the possibility of further developing Commonwealth status. Mr. Trías was twice appointed by President Eisenhower to serve as United States representative to the Caribbean Commission (1954–60), and was sole United States representative in President Johnson's administration to the Inter-American Juridical Commission of the Organization of American States (1966–67). After many years teaching law and in private practice, Mr. Trías was in 1974 appointed Chief Justice of Puerto Rico, a position he occupied until 1985.

Since his retirement from the bench, Mr. Trías has been active in Puerto Rican public affairs, including the effort of all parties in Puerto Rico in the late 1980s and early 1990s to obtain from Congress a commitment to honor whatever political status is chosen by the people of Puerto Rico.

Mr. Trías is the author of many books on legal and historical matters, including a five-volume constitutional history of Puerto Rico, the final volume of which was published in 1994.

Introduction

The United States took over Puerto Rico from Spain, together with the Philippine Islands, about a century ago. Those were the heady days when American dreams of empire were rampant, later to become nightmarish. After some fifty years the Philippines were cut loose. Puerto Rico was more of a problem. Through Americans' feelings of humanity or the desire to do right or just plain confusion, Puerto Ricans were made United States citizens in 1917 through a process of collective naturalization. The native leadership, solidly in power since 1904, pleaded not to be overwhelmed with such a blessing, but Congress knew best. As for the recipients, they disagreed with their leaders. Whether grace or gaffe, the splendid gift was happily accepted.[1]

Congress granted Puerto Ricans American citizenship without a clear notion about what to do next. Neither independence nor statehood seemed the right way to go. Puerto Rico was seen as different from both the Philippines and the statehood-bound territories of Hawaii and Alaska. While the U.S. government waited for a policy miraculously to reveal itself or for the problem to disappear, it spent increasingly large sums of money in Puerto Rico. This did not work, although conditions improved considerably. Per capita personal income rose from a dismal $121 in 1940 to $1,169 in 1969 and $6,835 in 1993 at current prices.[2] Illiteracy decreased, reaching 10.6 percent in 1990, although there are municipalities where illiteracy runs nearly three times as high. The death rate plummeted. The contribution of the manufacturing and services sectors to the economy rocketed. Still, unemployment worsened. In 1947, at the start of remarkable local efforts to industrialize Puerto Rico, unemployment stood at 11 percent; in 1994 it was 16 percent.[3] Since the 1960s not only have personal savings declined, but the economy has been further weakened by Puerto Rico's marked tendency to consume more than it produces.[4] The public sector is also unable to generate savings. In 1960 the gross public debt amounted to $476.7 million. It rose in 1990 to over $12.5 billion and to more than $15.2 billion in 1994.[5]

United States generosity has indeed been great. Federal grants and other aid to the government of Puerto Rico amounted to $8.3 million in 1940 and climbed swiftly to $5.8 billion in 1990.[6] Federal transfers to individuals, in the form of Social Security, nutritional assistance, Medicare, and other payments, rose in like manner; all federal aid in 1993 represented close to $9 billion, which amounted to 50 percent of personal income in Puerto Rico. The island has become frightfully dependent on United States munificence, but over fifty years of largesse, and considerable local efforts, have not had the desired effect. More than 60 percent of Puerto Rican families live below the poverty level, slightly less than in 1940, as compared to 7.6 percent in Vermont and 19.9 percent in Mississippi, the poorest state in the Union. The distribution of wealth has in effect grown worse.[7] The few rich have become wealthier and the poor more destitute. As health conditions improved and the mortality rate was lowered, a population explosion occurred, and Puerto Rico is now one of the most densely populated places on earth. This small island, some 3,600 square miles in area, has a population over 3.7 million, larger than that of twenty-five states of the Union and growing fast, as the birth rate stands at 17.3 per thousand and the death rate at 7.9.[8] It has often been remarked that only if all the people in the rest of the world moved to America, would the United States have a population density similar to that of Puerto Rico.

Puerto Rico used to be primarily rural. In 1900 only 8.7 percent of its inhabitants lived in towns with a population over 8,000 people. By 1940 the percentage of people living in urban areas rose to 30.3 percent and by 1970 to 58.1 percent. Urbanization took its toll. Crime has risen steeply. In 1940 there were only 1,432 major (type I) crimes. By the 1990s the number increased close to a hundredfold. Since the 1930s many Puerto Ricans, exercising their right as American citizens to travel freely, fled the island in search of a better world. The number of Puerto Ricans or persons of Puerto Rican descent now living in the United States totals about 75 percent of the current population of Puerto Rico. A worsening of local conditions normally triggers massive emigration to the United States.[9]

For a long time Puerto Rico has been touted as a showcase of democracy and a model for other underdeveloped areas. For a period it certainly was so. A closer look now gives pause. Per capita income in Puerto Rico is still only about one-third of that of the United States and half that of Mississippi. In the Caribbean, eleven other areas enjoy a higher per capita income: the Cayman Islands, Aruba, Montserrat, the Bahamas, Martinique, the American Virgin Islands, the British Virgin Islands, the Netherlands Antilles, Guadeloupe, French Guiana, and Barbados.[10] The per capita income of the poorest of these areas is 20 percent higher than that of Puerto Rico.

In political terms, at the end of the Second World War Puerto Rico had the most self-governing powers of the non-Hispanic Caribbean. It is now one of the most backward in the light of the traditional decolonization options. Twelve former British colonies and one former Dutch colony have achieved independence, whereas Puerto Rico continues to be subject to the almost unrestricted will of Congress. From the point of view of statehood, Martinique, Guadeloupe, and French Guiana have achieved full integration with France, yet Puerto Rico is far from the status of an American state. As regards an autonomous form of government, Puerto Rico's powers pall before those the Netherlands has recognized in the Dutch Antilles.[11]

How have we come to such a pass? After all, the United States has been the champion of liberty in the Caribbean and other areas. How is it possible that Puerto Rico has been kept, in spite of its constant clamor for greater freedoms, as one of the few remaining colonies in the world, a source of unending embarrassment in the yearly debates on decolonization matters at the United Nations? Why is it chugging along with a severely outdated economic model, and why is it lagging to such a degree in political freedoms?

The shocking truth is that for many years now Puerto Rico has not been the subject of a serious look by the United States. On the surface, there appears to be an American policy on the political question. For some time now the Wilsonian rhetoric about self-determination, which has had such devastating effects when ethnicity has come into play, has dutifully been used. Puerto Ricans have been traditionally torn, as have been many other societies in the same quandary, between seeking independence from the metropolis (or colonial power), complete integration to the metropolis, or full autonomy in association with it. Let the Puerto Ricans choose, it is grandly said. Choose what? At some time or other parties favoring each of those formulas have been in power in Puerto Rico, and their pleas in favor of the status of their choice have been studiously ignored. In the past thirty years two formal plebiscites have been held for the people of Puerto Rico to choose among Commonwealth status, statehood, and independence. In the first, in 1967, the people of Puerto Rico reaffirmed their preference for Commonwealth status and petitioned for greater powers of self-government in permanent association with the United States. Congress looked the other way. All Puerto Rican parties joined in 1989–91 to ask Congress to let them choose between such formulas as Congress would approve beforehand. The effort failed. A second plebiscite in 1993 also favored enhanced Commonwealth status, but nothing has changed in its aftermath.

So, what should be done? The answer is that the policy of self-determination, in the manner that it has been used in Puerto Rico, is not a coherent policy at all and something should be done about it. How can a people exercise the right to self-determination if they do not know what their choices are? The United States has to realize that it is rightfully part of the equation. Is it in the interest of the United States to grant Puerto Rico statehood by return mail if Puerto Ricans just ask for it? Is it ready to increase Puerto Rico's self-governing powers within its association to the United States, and if so, to what extent? On what terms would it be willing to grant Puerto Rico independence? The unceasing debate about the island's political status and the uncertainty about its future is sapping Puerto Rico's strength to stand on its own feet and deal with its severe economic problems. Keeping Puerto Rico in a state of subjection does not serve any perceivable United States interest and is seriously out of line with developments in the rest of the world.

There is an urgent need for the United States to take a new look at its relationship with Puerto Rico, and that is what this book is about. The elements of a new policy will be discussed against the backdrop of how Puerto Rico has reached its present predicament—how it has become, to its embarrassment and that of the United States, the oldest colony in the modern world.[12]

1

Puerto Rico Under Spanish Rule

Puerto Rico has had more than half a millennium of recorded colonial history. On November 19, 1493, in the course of his second voyage, Columbus was the first European to land on Puerto Rico. The smallest of the Greater Antilles, Puerto Rico was then peopled by *taínos*, a third wave of Amerindians. The first wave probably reached the Caribbean around 2300 B.C. A second wave, the *igneris*, originally from the Orinoco Valley in South America and as far north as the Guianas, preceded the taínos. The taínos, who were Arawak Indians, had a hierarchical political structure and organized agricultural techniques and hunted and fished for their subsistence. They had no calendar or writing system, and could count only up to twenty, using their hands and feet. They had not discovered the uses of the wheel. The taínos offered little resistance to the Spaniards.[1]

When colonization started in earnest in 1508, the Spaniards, undoubtedly for evangelical reasons, distributed the Indians as slaves among themselves (the *encomienda* system). Being unaccustomed to good, Christian hard work, the taínos died in great numbers; those who survived fled to the hills or left the island. The taínos disappeared, but not their contribution to the culture. They had mixed with the *colonizadores*, and their influence left its imprint. Many place-names and words for various trees, fruits, vegetables, and other items in Puerto Rico and the other Greater Antilles are Arawak. Many English words, including *tobacco, barbecue, canoe,* and *hammock,* as well as many Spanish words, are of taíno origin.

Soon, the Spaniards had to resort to African slavery, and their attention turned to saving the souls of the blacks. Things did not go very well. Puerto Rico was not Mexico or Peru. A 1530 census on the island showed a total of 327 white families owning 2,292 black slaves and 473 Indians. Indians outside the encomienda system, probably still a majority (but not for long), were not counted.

By 1587 Puerto Rico's economy depended to a large extent on Mexican governmental yearly subsidies—the *situado*—the start of a long history of dependence which unfortunately has so far proved hard to shake. By 1765 the population of Puerto Rico stood only at 44,883, of which 5,037 (11.2 percent) were black slaves—a very low ratio, if not the lowest for the Caribbean.[2]

San Juan, originally known as Puerto Rico, moved to its present site in 1521. Because San Juan was for a long time the first port of call of Spanish vessels sailing to the Caribbean and later a prime target of English, French, and Dutch pirates and privateers, fortification was begun soon after its founding and continued for two hundred years. Much of the impressive walled city remains today.

Puerto Rico's geographical position made it, until the end of the eighteenth century, basically a garrison or *presidio*, standing guard over other Spanish possessions in the area. Its economic status did not start to improve somewhat until the nineteenth century.[3]

Spain kept its empire in the New World on a short leash. The Crown itself, assisted by the Council of the Indies—the Real y Supremo Consejo de Indias—ruled on all legislative, executive, judicial, military, commercial, and even ecclesiastical matters. All laws were drafted by the council, initially composed of four members appointed by the king, and presented to him for his approval. All colonial officials were appointed by the king, upon advice of the council. The council was also in charge of approving the budget for every colony and provisioning the fleets; in its spare time it served as the supreme court for the whole empire.[4]

The king's power went unchecked for many centuries, with no parliament to meddle in the kingdom's affairs. A parliament existed on paper, the Cortes, but from 1521 to the early nineteenth century it was convened only four times.

Such concentration of power created, of course, enormous delays in acting upon the simplest matter. In practice the Governor, who in Puerto Rico also carried the military title of Captain General since 1580, could do pretty much as he pleased.

Puerto Rico, together with the rest of the Antilles, was technically a part of the viceroyship of Mexico, but in reality the viceroy rarely intervened in Puerto Rican affairs. The Governor was both the chief representative of the king and the head of the colonial government. The Captain General headed both the army and the fleet, supervised expenditures, presided over the municipal councils or *cabildos*, confirmed the election of the mayors or appointed them, and appointed the minor officials. He also controlled the police, enacted ordinances and decrees (subject to approval of the distant king), could suspend the execution of any royal order (also subject to the king's decision), and was in charge of land grants.

The Captain General also held the highest judicial office on the island, subject to appeal to the Real Audiencia of Santo Domingo, the highest colonial court, from which appeals could be taken to the Council of the Indies only in civil cases where a large amount of money was involved.[5] The Real Audiencia, which also exercised a degree of administrative power, theoretically was one of the chief safeguards against gubernatorial despotism. Puerto Rico, however, did not rate an Audiencia of its own until 1832, and from then until 1861 it was presided over by the Captain General.[6]

Prior to the establishment of the Audiencia, Puerto Rico did not have courts as such. The judicial power was wielded by the mayors or *alcaldes,* who headed the larger municipalities, and by the *tenientes a guerra,* the mayors of the smaller towns, all untrained in the law. Their decisions could be appealed to the Captain General.[7] The cabildos (municipal councils) were composed of *regidores* (councilmen) chosen by the Captain General. The practice of selling these offices to the highest bidder became widespread early on. The regidores selected the alcalde in the larger towns.

The mayors of the smaller towns exercised military and police functions and were appointed by the Captain General, normally from the ranks of men of substance, *hacendados* and *ganaderos* (owners of sugar and cattle estates). The only offices open to Puerto Ricans until the nineteenth century were those of regidor, alcalde, or teniente a guerra, and even those were strictly limited to the moneyed elite and were often given to deserving Spaniards. Under the Spanish constitution of 1812 the alcaldes were elected, but most of the time the Governor appointed them and, in any case, had the power to dismiss them. As late as 1891 the Governor appointed the alcaldes in all of the towns but five.[8]

Puerto Rico had no legislature until the end of the 1800s. When advocates of a constitutional monarchy were in power during parts of the nineteenth century, there was the Diputación Provincial, which had only certain limited administrative and advisory functions but which provided a forum for local expression.[9] Most of its members were elected, but the institution was suppressed several times, even under liberal governments. The Governor managed to control the Diputación for a good part of its checkered existence and made it an instrument of his policies.

During the first three centuries of Spanish rule, side by side with the intricate web of laws, ordinances, and decrees, another order, less concerned with right and wrong, existed. The law restricted commerce to Seville, but smuggling was a main way of life. The Indians, who were supposed to be enlightened by the Spaniards and treated kindly, were promptly extinguished. Slave owners, who included the island's only bishop, ruled Africans with a heavy hand, contrary to standing instructions. The Captain General's discretion, supposedly limited by the imposing façade of the Laws of the Indies, knew no bounds. The population was expected to participate in certain minor elections, but they were held rarely or were manipulated by the Governor. What little representation was permitted to the local people, the *criollos,* was restricted to the wealthy. No political parties were allowed. There was a surfeit of laws, but, except for a very brief period, no *jueces letrados* or judges trained in the law to apply them. In 1509 King Ferdinand prohibited lawyers from going to the Indies without royal permission. The few who had traveled there, the wise king explained in his decree, had already created too much trouble.[10]

To add to this, the population lived in constant fear of foreign attack. The French, the British, and the Dutch all raided this bastion of Spanish military strength several times. Sir Walter Raleigh, Sir Francis Drake, John Hawkins, the Earl of Cumberland, Boudewijn Hendrickzoon, Sir Ralph Abercromby, and many others attempted to invade the island. In 1596 Puerto Rico actually became British for a number of days. The last attack occurred in 1797.

Puerto Ricans were not the only people in the area subject to barbaric rule. Britain, France, and the Netherlands also governed their New World possessions with a heavy hand. Residents of these colonies had a semblance of greater participation in consultative and even deliberative bodies, but the absolute subjection to the imperial will could not be hidden. The thirteen American colonies were the first to rebel. The American revolution led the way in the decolonization process of the New World. The Caribbean would not start to learn about freedom until much later.

In the last quarter of the eighteenth century the population of Puerto Rico tripled. In 1802, of 163,192 inhabitants, 78,281 were white, 55,164 mulattos, 16,414 free blacks, and 13,333 slaves. A great rate of growth was to be maintained through the nineteenth century, as economic conditions improved somewhat and the people acquired a political conscience.

The nineteenth century was a troubled one in Spain. From 1833 to 1892 alone Spain had seventy-five governments, of which sixty-eight were in power for less than two years; the longest lasted four years and seven months. There were several wars and uprisings during this time, and a blizzard of constitutions.[11]

Subservient to France since 1795, Spain was forced by Napoleon in 1800 to cede Louisiana to France. In 1808 Napoleon invaded Spain and installed his brother Joseph as king. The Spaniards, with the aid of the British, fought the French and four years later were able to expel them and restore Ferdinand VII to the monarchy. A weakened Spain then faced the Wars of Independence of the Latin American republics. Within a few years it lost all of its New World empire except for Cuba and Puerto Rico.

The Spaniards also fought other Spaniards. The followers of the old absolute monarchy warred against the believers in a constitutional monarchy, and all fought each other in wars of succession. The political fortunes of Cuba and Puerto Rico suffered through the century the vagaries of Spanish politics.

The first Spanish written constitution, forced upon Ferdinand VII upon his restoration to the throne in 1812, was ahead of its time. No other colonial power in the New World had granted so many rights and privileges to its possessions. The constitution was in effect a last-ditch attempt at keeping the Spanish-American colonies from seceding. The colonies, including Puerto Rico, were granted the status of Spanish provinces, with full voting representation in the Cortes, something that the English colonies never had, and which the French territories would not achieve until 1946, nor the Dutch, under a different kind of structure, until 1954. Puerto Rico has not known either under the United States, although its residents were given citizenship of sorts in 1917. Spanish citizenship, under conditions of full equality with Spaniards, was also extended to free Puerto Ricans. Puerto Rico, together with the other colonies, also obtained the right to male universal suffrage, a right unknown to the French colonies until the Second Republic (1848), to the Netherlands Antilles until 1936, and to the British colonies until first given to Jamaica in 1944. Puerto Rico was also granted for the first time a Diputación Provincial, municipal offices again became elective, and freedom of expression and assembly and other human rights were recognized for the first time. Although formal political parties as such were not established, this was Puerto Rico's first experience with representative institutions.

The 1812 constitution—or the Cádiz Constitution, as it is also known— did not last long. In 1814 the conservatives overthrew it by force and restored absolute power to the king. Puerto Rico went back to its former condition of a colony subject to the unrestricted power of the Spanish monarch.

In 1820, the liberals staged another revolution and forced the king again to proclaim the Cádiz Constitution. Three years later, another insurrection repealed the constitution and Puerto Rico's freedoms were snatched away again.

Shortly after the Spanish lost the final battle for Latin American independence in 1824, Puerto Rico was subjected to as repressive a regime as it had ever known. The Spanish Governor was granted absolute powers (*omnímodas*) to rule, powers "as absolute as those enjoyed by the commander of a besieged city," the decree read.[12] The subtle theory was that Spain had lost its American colonies not by reason of despotic government, but because too much freedom had been granted them. For a long time, Spanish political developments ceased having an effect on Puerto Rico. Liberal and conservative governments all agreed on giving Puerto Ricans as few human rights as possible. The omnímodas lasted until 1869.

When a new constitution was approved in 1834—the Estatuto Real, which was of conservative bent—it was not extended to Puerto Rico. Even when the Cádiz Constitution was restored in 1836 for a third time and a new liberal constitution was adopted a year later, Puerto Rico was still left out. Its deputies were denied access to parliament, and the islanders were stripped of their Spanish citizenship and earlier freedoms. The 1837 constitution simply stated that "the overseas provinces were to be governed by special laws."

In the absence of such laws (which were never enacted), the authoritarian regime continued. The constitutions of 1845 and 1854, again of conservative design, brought about no change. In 1869, after another revolution, the most liberal of nineteenth-century Spanish constitutions was adopted. The constitution's generous bill of rights was not extended to Puerto Rico until 1873, and some of the most despotic governors that Puerto Rico had ever known were sent to the island.

Under the 1869 constitution, political parties were first allowed to organize. The first political party in Puerto Rico, the Liberal Reformist party, was founded in 1870. Many of its principal leaders believed in full self-government for Puerto Rico, but the word *autonomy* was not used, as it was banned at the time. The party program was accordingly couched in guarded terms. It called for powers as extensive as those wielded by the Spanish provinces, a status that Puerto Rico had enjoyed under the 1812 constitution, as well as discretion "to solve such questions as were of the exclusive interest of Puerto Rico and its municipalities."[13]

The Conservative party, later called the Unconditionally Spanish party, was founded a year later, in 1871. Men of property and all sorts of Hispanophiles flocked to its ranks. Its program was simple: believers "in the principle of authority, we have not and will not oppose the will of the Sovereign." The program further warned against Spain's extending too much liberty to the island

and ended by proclaiming its pride in being Spanish subjects, "a condition to which we subordinate everything."[14]

Upon proclamation of the First Republic in Spain in 1873, most of the demands of the Liberal Reformists were met. Freedom of speech and of the press, together with other provisions of the 1869 constitution, were extended to Puerto Rico, and slavery was abolished. In 1874, however, upon restoration of the monarchy, these liberties were again taken away. The newly established political parties were not suppressed, but they languished under the vigilant eye of the Governor, who did not hesitate to persecute their members, particularly the Liberals, on appropriate occasions, which happened to be many.

The 1876 constitution, which lasted until the proclamation of the Second Republic in 1931, represented an attempt to bring internal peace to Spain by steering a middle course between the 1869 liberal constitution and the ultra-conservative one of 1845. Its bill of rights was severely narrowed; universal male suffrage was abolished; the king was given greater power vis-à-vis parliament. The new constitution retained the Diputación Provincial, as well as the elective cabildos, the right to representation in the Cortes (which had been reestablished in 1869), and Spanish citizenship.

The 1876 constitution was formally extended to Puerto Rico in 1881. The gesture did not mean much, as the necessary legislation to extend the human rights provisions to Puerto Rico was not approved until 1897.

In 1887, unsatisfied with the somewhat timorous Liberal Reformist party, many of the old leaders and a new generation of men who would lead Puerto Rico for most of the first three decades of the twentieth century established the Autonomist party. The new party asked, still in coded language, that the Diputación Provincial (this now meant a local parliament) be vested with power, subject to Spanish approval, to attend to all local matters, which were defined specifically to include education, the budget, public works, health, agriculture, banking, the police, immigration, waters and harbors, commerce, duties, and commercial treaties. Assimilation to Spain as a province, as under the 1812 constitution, was no longer a goal. The demand for equality of treatment was reserved to such matters as representation in the Cortes, freedom of the press and of assembly, and anything else having to do with civil rights. The party's platform requested recognition of the human rights provisions in the constitution. The Autonomist party had strong ties to the criollo, as opposed to the peninsular or native Spanish element of the population.[15]

The principal political parties in Spain reacted violently against the estab-

lishment of the Autonomist party. Nothing which "curtails the national sovereignty will ever be acceptable," intoned Práxedes Sagasta, the leader of the party
in power, who favored provincehood or full integration with Spain and abhorred
the word *autonomy,* no longer prohibited but still hateful to the peninsulares'
ears.[16] His words were echoed by the opposition and magnified by the dutiful
Unconditionally Spanish party in Puerto Rico. Action soon followed words, and
the Autonomists were hounded and occasionally jailed thereafter until the
threat of the Spanish-American War loomed. Puerto Ricans reacted with a
number of violent incidents and attempts at rebellion, including the insurrection at Lares, where independence was proclaimed, but contrary to the situation in Cuba, where agitation for freedom continued unabated, Spain was able
to contain the rebels.

Thus more than one hundred years ago public opinion in Puerto Rico was
divided in much the same way as it is now. A group, many of them in exile in
Spanish times, clamored for independence; another wanted full integration or
assimilation to the metropolis; and a third opted for a middle way.

The problems flowing from such a split, which is common in colonial societies, were compounded by Spain's indecision. On one thing Spain was clear: it
did not want Puerto Rico and Cuba to go the way of the other Latin American
countries. On the other hand, it hesitated between admitting them to Spain as
provinces or granting them a significant degree of self-government while keeping close ties with the metropolitan country. Colonial powers frequently remain
undecided as to whether to free their wards, admit them to their house, warts
and all, under equality of conditions, or allow them full powers of self-government in association with the metropolis.

Increasingly concerned with the situation in Cuba, where the rebels were
fighting for freedom, the United States pressured Spain for a prompt solution
to the crisis. American sugar interests in Cuba were pressing for United States
intervention.[17] On September 18, 1897, the American ambassador to Spain formally asked the Spanish Secretary of State to give "before the first of November next, such assurance as would satisfy the United States that early and certain peace can be promptly secured; and that otherwise the United States must
consider itself free to take such steps as its Government should deem necessary
to procure the result, with due regard to its own interests and the general tran-
quillity."[18] At the end of October the Spanish government answered that it
would grant autonomy to Cuba and Puerto Rico by November 23 or 25 at the
latest.

Such was the genesis of the Autonomic Charter and the other decrees of

November 25, 1897. The first steps toward them had been taken in 1892 and their main features had taken shape by August 1897, but the Cuban fighters for independence and the United States deserve the credit for provoking the final result. The new measures did not go through the normal parliamentary process. Indications were that the Spanish government would have been unable at the time to obtain consent from the Cortes. Autonomy was granted by decree, and an indemnity bill was later sought from the parliament, which reluctantly granted absolution for the constitutional infraction.

The Autonomic Charter went further than the demands of the Autonomist party itself. It was the most advanced document of any Caribbean colony until after the Second World War. Although it was flawed in several respects, the degree of self-government which it granted Puerto Rico was much greater in several aspects than what the United States has been willing to concede up to the present. The British dominion concept, well under development by the end of the nineteenth century, was evidently the chief model followed.

The Autonomic Charter granted Puerto Rico a local parliament composed of two chambers: the House of Representatives and the Council of Administration. The entire House was elected by universal suffrage. The council had fifteen members, eight of them elected and seven appointed by the Governor, in the name of the king. The king could, however, disallow any law approved by the Insular Parliament or postpone its consideration. Bills could only be initiated by the Governor through the local minister, which meant that neither had the power to sponsor a bill on his own. Is spite of these limitations, familiar to other Caribbean colonial systems, Puerto Rico was ahead of the British, French, and Dutch colonies, none of which had a legislature with a majority of elected members until after the Second World War.

The powers of the Insular Parliament were extensive, as it could legislate on all matters not reserved to the Cortes or the peninsular government. This basically meant that the Insular Parliament could legislate, among other matters, on education, the treasury, economic development, import and export duties, banking and the monetary system, the public credit, public works, the public health, and municipal administration.[19] The central government took care of foreign affairs, except that Puerto Rico could negotiate commercial treaties (subject to Spanish approval), defense, and general matters of national concern, such as the organization and administration of the judiciary, the Civil Code, and the Commerce Code. The concession of tariff autonomy was one feature that revealed the influence of the British treatment of certain major colonies outside the Caribbean area. Tariff autonomy had been enjoyed by Canada since 1859.

The Governor General wielded great power. In his capacity as representative of the king and his government he still commanded the armed forces (although no longer a Captain General), and he held some of the old attributes,
such as acting as delegate of the Spanish ministries, heading the police, and con
firming ecclesiastical appointments. He could, after consulting the insular
Council of Ministers, suspend freedom of speech, the press, and assembly, ar-
rest people, order searches and seizures, and temporarily shelve other major
civil liberties. He could also suspend the execution of any law or administrative
act of the central government considered to be harmful to the national interests
or those of Puerto Rico, this time with the consent of the Insular ministers.

As chief of the local government, the Governor appointed the Insular ministers, who in their turn were responsible to the Insular Parliament. In this respect, care should be taken to distinguish between the British and the Spanish
ministerial systems. In British terms, "responsible government," which would
not be achieved by any British, French, or Dutch colony in the Caribbean until
after the Second World War, meant that the ministers were appointed by the
Governor, but selected and subject to dismissal by the local legislature alone and
thus solely responsible to it. Within the Spanish constitutional system, appointment by the Governor meant that the ministers were responsible to both
the Governor and Parliament. The Insular ministers had to enjoy the confidence
of both.

The ministers could be members of either chamber of parliament and as a
matter of practice had to be. Except for functions derived from his capacity as
representative of the king and the national government, the Governor could not
take actions without the written consent of the minister involved. The Governor now appointed and dismissed all government employees, but he could not
do either except at the request of the corresponding minister. The whole judiciary, however, continued to be appointed by the Spanish government.

The other autonomic decrees had to do with the extension to Puerto Rico
of the Spanish laws required to make effective the provisions of the 1876 constitution relating to human rights, male universal suffrage, and Puerto Rico's
right to full representation in the Spanish Parliament, a right which it had under the 1812 constitution and regained in 1869. Puerto Ricans also continued,
as under prior constitutions, to be full Spanish citizens.[20]

Perhaps the most significant trait of the charter was, finally, that it was not
subject to amendment except by law enacted at the request of the Insular Parliament. The idea of a relationship based on such a compact has since been basic to autonomist thinking in Puerto Rico. One of the difficulties that the au-

tonomist movement has had with the U.S. Congress in the second half of the twentieth century has been congressional reluctance to recognize in unequivocal fashion such a fundamental part of government by consent, which Puerto Rico enjoyed at the end of the nineteenth century, although largely on paper and with no guarantee, given the past history of rights bestowed and later withdrawn, that it would survive the swings of Spanish politics. In this respect the Autonomic Charter has been unduly romanticized by many, although the achievement of such a high level of self-government at the time should not be minimized, either.

The first elections under the charter were delayed in Puerto Rico because of a dispute which had arisen sometime before within the Autonomist party. A faction led by José C. Barbosa wanted no ties with the monarchist Liberal party, headed by Sagasta, while another splinter group, captained by Luis Muñoz Rivera, had vowed to favor Sagasta, in spite of his earlier views, if he could bring about autonomy. A provisional cabinet was installed on February 10, 1898. Five days later the U.S.S. *Maine* blew up in Havana's harbor.

On March 27 parliamentary elections were held. Muñoz Rivera won in a landslide against both the Barbosa faction and the incondicionales. The Insular Parliament was convened for April 25, 1898—the very day the United States declared war on Spain.

What was Puerto Rico like at the end of the nineteenth century? The island's population had grown by leaps and bounds in the course of the century, to 953,243 in 1899. It was a young population: 31 percent was under ten years old, as compared to 24 percent in the United States. Only 11 percent was over forty-five years old; the comparable figure for the United States was 17.2 percent. Only 2.8 percent of Puerto Rico's residents were Spanish-born. Blacks and mulattos represented 38.2 percent of the population, somewhat higher than the 36.2 percent which inhabited the American Atlantic southern states.

Puerto Rico was still a rural society. In 1899, only 32,048 people lived in the largest city, San Juan, up from 9,000 in 1800. A scant 8.7 percent inhabited towns with more than 8,000 people, as compared to 32.3 percent in the United States.

Spain's neglect of education in Puerto Rico was reflected in the illiteracy rate, which was the highest in the West Indies, at 83.2 percent. "Education lost the Americas," a leading Spanish statesman said in the nineteenth century, regretting even the scant educational facilities that had been allowed there. Spain itself had an illiteracy rate of 75 percent in 1860 and 63 percent in 1900.

Aside from some scattered efforts by religious orders, there were no schools in Puerto Rico. A secondary school system was not established until 1882. There were 529 schools in the island, of which only six were housed in public buildings. There was no university; postsecondary studies had to be undertaken in Spain, although a few students went to France or the United States. There was no department of education until the issuance of the Autonomic Charter in 1897.

The economic situation was precarious. The insular annual budget amounted to a little more than $3 million. Out of that, Puerto Rico had to pay 250,000 *pesos* ($150,000 in 1899) to Spain as compensation for war expenses; another half a million pesos was retained as Puerto Rico's contribution to the expenses of the Spanish Ministry for Overseas Possessions; and 200,000 pesos went to the support of the clergy, a state obligation at the time.

Coffee was the most important crop in 1897 (prior to its devastation by a hurricane the next year), followed by sugar and tobacco. The value of all exports was less than 19 million pesos ($11.4 million). Food amounted to 45 percent of all imports.

Cane workers were the highest paid, earning the equivalent of 35–50 cents a day. Women and children earned 25–30 cents and in other industries 12–18 cents a day, working from sunrise to sunset.

Public services were few. Only San Juan, Ponce, and Mayagüez had home lighting, San Juan by gas and the others by electricity. Water service in San Juan was available in certain public places, but did not reach individual residences. San Juan was the only town with sewer service, and only in a few private houses. Health conditions were deplorable. Outside of a few large towns there were no hospitals or physicians. Tuberculosis, malaria, yellow fever, smallpox, and other diseases were rampant and kept the death rate high. Roads were few. Since 1886 a good road connected San Juan and Ponce, but the cost of transportation (by public carriage, a *diligencia*) was expensive, 30 pesos one way. Few towns were connected by anything more than an unpaved path.

Newspapers were the only windows to the world. There were many newspapers, which were passed from hand to hand, and news traveled quickly. Printing presses were cheap at the time, and it did not take much to start a paper. The political parties had papers which represented their points of view. The parties covered the island, their leaders frequently visiting the towns and many remote villages. Despite the illiteracy rate, political awareness ran very high. During periods of universal male suffrage, men flocked to the polling stations. Puerto Rico has always taken pride in its rate of voter turnout, one of the highest in the world.

Adequate housing was scarce. In rural areas, *bohíos*—small, windowless cabins made of wood, dried palm fronds, or hay—were the typical dwelling. Modest wooden shacks, with a thatched or at most a zinc roof, could also be seen. None had running water, electricity, or sanitary facilities. Houses had few furnishings, except for a few rustic chairs and tables. The inhabitants slept in hammocks. Families were large and normally lived in very crowded conditions, at times with many people in a single room. The flimsy structures were easy prey to hurricanes. In 1899 the San Ciriaco hurricane, with winds over 150 miles per hour, devastated the island.

In the older towns, which were rigorously planned, as required by the Laws of the Indies, the wealthy built beautiful brick houses, although there were many wooden ones with simple zinc roofs. Colonial San Juan was one of the most striking Latin American towns of the period, with impressive public buildings and stately houses from the seventeenth, eighteenth, and nineteenth centuries.

Good or even fair clothing was a luxury. The *jíbaros*, as the people from the rural areas were called, usually went barefoot, and shoes and socks, if they owned them, were reserved for special occasions, like going to church, weddings, baptisms, and dances. Laborers in the field usually wore long pants of coarse cloth tied around the waist with a cloth band or a string, a shirt, and a wide straw or woven palm frond hat to guard against the sun. Women also went barefoot, except on gala occasions, when they wore crude sandals. They sewed their own simple clothes and were busy day after day washing the family laundry, bent over the washboard or squatting by the side of a brook or a river, mending clothes, gathering or buying the little food they could afford on their husbands' salaries, cooking in primitive stoves, bearing baby after baby, assisting the young and the sick, and getting old before their time.

The jíbaros rarely owned land or even their flimsy dwellings. They were mostly *agregados* (sharecroppers), people who were allowed a place to live in exchange for working the land and giving the owner the major share of the crop, or salaried *peones*, employees of a sugar, coffee, or tobacco plantation who were permitted to live on the company property.

The diet was simple: plantains, tubers, fruit planted in their backyards or nearby; milk if the family was able to own a cow or a few goats; pork, chicken, and eggs, if likewise lucky; and rice and beans, which were eaten daily, together with salt and sugar and an occasional piece of meat or dried cod. As employment in the field was seasonal, food (including the staples, rice and beans) had to be bought on credit. Savings were something they dreamed about. Illegal stills provided plenty of raw rum, the national drink, consumed with patriotic fervor at *fiestas* and other communal activities. In each town there was a municipal marketplace, where housewives (or their cooks, if they happened to be relatively affluent), went daily for their supplies. There were no iceboxes or other refrigeration facilities.

Poverty did not prevent the development of a varied cuisine, with Indian, African, Spanish and other European influences. Puerto Rico received massive migratory waves from different parts of Spain, each with their distinctive tastes and culinary traditions, including Andalusia, Asturias, Cataluña, Mallorca, the Basque provinces, Galicia, Valencia, Extremadura, and the Canary Islands. A significant portion of the population also came from Corsica, and large numbers of French farmers, mostly from other Caribbean areas, settled in Puerto Rico during the nineteenth century. By 1859 the first Puerto Rican cookbook, *El Cocinero Puertorriqueño* (The Puerto Rican chef), was published.

Abysmal poverty and adversity did not prevent Puerto Ricans of town and country from enjoying themselves.[21] Dances were held everywhere at the slightest pretext or none at all, in the *bateyes* or backyards of the bohíos, or in the larger houses. The *tiple,* the *cuatro,* and the *bordonúa,* variations of the Spanish guitar, were all locally invented and produced and provided the chief basis of the jíbaro music. In addition to fashionable Spanish dances, Puerto Rico created many other forms, several contributed by the population of African descent. Musicians, mostly unschooled, were plentiful, and for popular gatherings it was easy to get together the necessary string and percussion players in practically no time.

In other areas of the arts during the nineteenth century, Puerto Rico produced a number of poets, essayists, playwrights, and painters, some of continental stature. Two of the prominent political leaders, Luis Muñoz Rivera and José de Diego, were distinguished poets.

Poetry and music were not limited to the literate. Out of the great mass of the unschooled or poorly schooled rose the *décima* writers and singers. The décima was an old Spanish form, a ten-line stanza, eight syllables per line, with a complicated rhyming pattern, sung to a set music normally played with guitars and native instruments. At public events and gatherings it was usual to hold "duels" between two well-known popular poets. The contestants had to end all the décimas with the same line, which was given to them only at the start of the competition.

Oratory was an art form enjoyed by old and young, rich and poor. Political rallies drew great crowds, eager to listen to spell-binding speakers, usually part of the leadership, but some of them quasi illiterate or illiterate political workers.

Election time was an occasion for widespread festivity almost as much as Three Kings' Day.

Besides the love of song, dance, and public speaking, there were many other binding forces in this society, otherwise so divided by levels of education and affluence and afflicted by misfortune.

Language was, of course, the most powerful component. Spanish, enriched with Indian and African contributions as in the case of most other Spanish colonies in the New World, had extraordinary vitality. A great sense of pride in the language also helped establish bonds between Puerto Rico and the rest of the Spanish-speaking world, especially Latin America, whose brand of Spanish resembles Puerto Rico's and does not differ much from the mother tongue. Such pride survives to this day, perhaps with greater force, as the Spanish language had to compete with English for a long time to assure its survival as the primary language of Puerto Rico.

Religion was another factor. The Catholic faith had held sway in Puerto Rico since the start of colonization. Until the end of Spanish rule it was the official religion of the island, and there was no separation of church and state. Pursuant to the Laws of the Indies, each town had to have a central plaza, where the church and the Casa del Rey (city hall, literally, the house of the king), usually the most important buildings in town, were located. Every Sunday, town and country would meet in church. Catholic priests occupied a high social position.

History and geography were, finally, strong levelers. A past of foreign hostility and domestic injustice, deeply impressed in the collective memory, helped forge a sense of common destiny. Living on a small island also tends to bring people together, pressing them against each other, encouraging a common purpose, although, unfortunately, not necessarily agreement on the means to achieve it.

At the end of the nineteenth century Puerto Rico had thus a well-defined national identity, a strong sense of its own culture, part of the Spanish-speaking Latin American and Caribbean communities, with its own singularities and as much right as others to freedom and respect.[22]

Beneath the comings and goings of constitutions, the constant granting and snatching away of rights, the people of Puerto Rico were being ruled by rank injustice, political, social, and economic. Although constituting a distinct society, the people were deeply divided in many ways, especially by the asperities of the life to which most were subjected. The dominant sectors—the peninsulares, the hacendados, the large merchants—lived in a different world from that of the subservient—the agregados, the peones, the mass of the unemployed, the illiterate, the destitute, the disenfranchised. The antinomies were many, between peninsulares and criollos, town and country, coastal towns and mountain regions, white and black, landowners and landless, professionals and unschooled, wealthy and poor.[23]

This was the Puerto Rico that the United States invaded on July 25, 1898—a country that wanted political, economic, and social justice, but not colonial tutelage, however well meant. Although different in so many ways from prior periods, a difficult century was to follow.

2

The Annexation

The annexation of Puerto Rico by the United States must be studied in the light of previous U.S. interest in the Caribbean and the prevalent American ideological climate at the time in order to understand the policies that initially marked the relationship between the United States and Puerto Rico.

American interest in the Caribbean antedates the Declaration of Independence. Benjamin Franklin advised Great Britain to invade Cuba.[1] After the American revolution, acquiring Cuba was actively considered by the five presidents of the United States who followed George Washington. Thomas Jefferson initially favored the addition of Cuba, but decided that this could not be done without serious risk of war with the British.[2] When the Spanish South American territories started their wars of independence, the United States became rightly fearful that England or France would attempt to take over Cuba. From 1809 to 1823 United States policy accordingly favored the continued possession by Spain of Cuba and Puerto Rico. John Quincy Adams, when Secretary of State to President James Monroe, thus instructed the American ambassador in Madrid in 1823:

> Cuba, almost in sight of our shores, from a multitude of considerations,
> has become an object of transcendent importance to the commercial and
> political interests of our Union. . . . [I]t is scarcely possible to resist the
> conviction that an annexation of Cuba to our federal republic will be in-
> dispensable to the continuance of the Union itself. It is obvious, how-
> ever, that for this event we are not yet prepared . . . but there are laws of
> political as well as physical gravitation and if an apple, severed by the
> tempest from its native tree, cannot choose but fall to the ground, Cuba,
> forcibly disjoined from its own unnatural connection with Spain and in-
> capable of self-support can gravitate only towards the North American
> Union, which by the same law cannot cast her off from its bosom.[3]

Preoccupation with Cuba was thus one of the principal considerations which led to the proclamation of the Monroe Doctrine on December 2, 1823, declaring that any European nation's effort to extend its dominions in the hemisphere or act contrary to the independence of the new republics that had been colonies of Spain would be seen as unfriendly and dangerous to the peace and safety of the United States. At the same time, Monroe's declaration made clear, "with the existing colonies or dependencies of any European power we have not interfered and shall not interfere." Cuba and Puerto Rico were thus left to Spanish solicitude. Simón Bolívar had planned to extend the Spanish-American revolution to both, but his plans were scrapped after he was told in very clear terms that the United States was opposed to the independence of Cuba and Puerto Rico from Spain.[4]

The Monroe Doctrine was later expanded in order to discourage any attempt to transfer Cuba to another European power. During his presidency (1845–49), while favoring the annexation of Texas and approving that of California, New Mexico, and Utah, James K. Polk tried on several occasions to purchase Cuba, a move firmly opposed by the Northern states because of the slavery issue.[5] The seeds of what was to be known as Manifest Destiny were planted in Polk's time. In the 1850s, at the suggestion of his Secretary of State, President Franklin Pierce's ambassador to Spain issued, together with the ambassador to Great Britain and that of France, the Ostend Manifesto. The document stated that if the United States was not able to obtain Cuba by peaceful means, then "by every law, human and divine, we shall be justified in wresting it from Spain if we possess the power."

America's interest was not limited, however, to Cuba and, to a lesser degree, Puerto Rico. In 1860 the United States tried to purchase five smaller Caribbean islands to guard the approaches to the Isthmus of Panama.[6] William H. Seward, Secretary of State under Abraham Lincoln and Andrew Johnson, after negotiating the purchase of Alaska and the occupation of Midway Island by the navy in 1867, attempted to acquire the Danish Virgin Islands, as well as Culebra and Culebrita, two islands which are part of Puerto Rico.[7] Congress disapproved of the administration's proposal and passed a resolution condemning the acquisition of additional territory. There were by then, however, Congressmen who favored the acquisition of the whole of the West Indies.[8] Expansionist feelings concerning the Caribbean continued to deepen until conditions became ripe for John Quincy Adams's apple to fall.[9]

Growth of the United States on the continent had occurred rapidly. The United States made the Louisiana Purchase from France in 1803 and Florida from Spain in 1819. Continental expansion was completed upon the acquisition of Texas in 1845, the cession by Britain of the territory of Oregon in 1846, and the acquisition of the Mexican territory through the 1848 Treaty of Guadalupe Hidalgo and the Gadsden Treaty of 1853. The phrase "Manifest Destiny" was coined in 1845.[10] Expansionist feelings receded during the Civil War, but later reacquired vigor, especially in the 1890s, and the Manifest Destiny doctrine took shape. The historian John Fiske wrote: "It is enough to point to the general conclusion that the work which the English race began when it colonized North America is destined to go on until every land on the earth's surface that is not already the seat of an old civilization shall become English in its language, in its religion, in its political habits and traditions, and to a predominant extent in the blood of its people."[11]

This peculiar brand of political Darwinism found many exponents. Josiah Strong, an influential clergyman of the time, stated: "Then this race of unequaled energy, with all the majesty of numbers and the might of wealth behind it—the representative, let us hope, of the largest liberty, the purest Christianity, the highest civilization—having developed peculiarly aggressive traits calculated to impress its institutions upon mankind, will spread itself over the earth. If I read not amiss, this powerful race will move down upon Mexico, down upon Central and South America, out upon the islands of the sea, over upon Africa and beyond. And can any doubt that the result of this competition of races will be the 'survival of the fittest'?"[12]

Captain Alfred T. Mahan, a highly regarded naval theoretician, based his expansionism on other, more sober, considerations. His principle, which profoundly influenced the thinking of Theodore Roosevelt and Senator Henry Cabot Lodge, was that naval power was the key to national greatness. The United States needed a great fleet, and that was not possible without adequate naval stations to support it. According to Mahan's worldview, United States security required a canal across the Isthmus of Panama and full dominion of both the Caribbean Sea and the Pacific Ocean around Hawaii. The Mona Passage, between the Dominican Republic and Puerto Rico, was one of the two ways of reaching the Caribbean Sea from the Atlantic Ocean. The control of Hawaii by a foreign power would seriously hamper the defense of the United States West coast.[13]

During Benjamin Harrison's administration (1889–93), Secretary of State James G. Blaine wrote to the President in 1890: "I think that there are only three places that are of value enough to be taken; one is Hawaii and the others are Cuba and Puerto Rico. Cuba and Puerto Rico are not imminent and will not be for a generation. Hawaii may come for decision at any unexpected hour, and I hope we shall be prepared to decide it in the affirmative."[14]

United States interest in Hawaii had a long history. During the presidency of Franklin Pierce (1853–57), a treaty for the purchase of Hawaii was negotiated, but the Hawaiian government failed to ratify it. A few decades later a revolution was instigated in Hawaii to bring about its annexation to the United States, but the expansionist movement was not strong enough yet and Congress rejected the proposed annexation in 1894.[15]

President Benjamin Harrison's idea of acquiring insular possessions in the Caribbean and the Pacific did not have sufficient support, either, nor did the idea fare well during Grover Cleveland's second administration (1893–97). Cleveland unsuccessfully tried to purchase Cuba at the start of the Cuban revolution as a way of avoiding war with Spain, a move which was gathering force in Congress. The 1896 Republican platform called for the acquisition of Hawaii and the Danish islands (now the United States Virgin Islands), as well as the independence of Cuba and the complete withdrawal of all European powers from the Western Hemisphere.

President William McKinley, fresh from his victory against William Jennings Bryan and the Democratic party, was initially opposed to the annexation of Hawaii, but later relented. The annexation treaty—Hawaiian politics were already under control of American enterprises in Hawaii—was signed on June 16, 1897, but made no headway in Congress until the Spanish-American War broke out. The change in the Congressional climate brought about by the war and the annexation of Hawaii would influence the reaction to the Treaty of Paris.

In his 1897 State of the Union message, McKinley favored staying any action until the effect of the Spanish autonomic decrees was determined. Theodore Roosevelt, then Assistant Secretary of the Navy, together with Senator Lodge, backed armed intervention. On May 9, 1897, Roosevelt wrote to a friend: "It is very difficult for me not to wish for a war with Spain, for such a war would result at once in getting us a proper navy and a good system of coast defense."[16] The sinking of the *Maine* on February 15, 1898, together with the continuing revolution in Cuba, started to change public opinion. In early March a large appropriation for the national defense was approved. On April 11, the President asked Congress for authority "to take measures to secure a full and final termination of hostilities between the Government of Spain and the people of Cuba."[17] Roosevelt and other interventionists, including Joseph B. Foraker, the future architect of the first organic act for Puerto Rico, thought the proposed resolution to be too weak, as it left the decision to intervene in the President's hands and kept silent as to Cuba's political future.

The Democrats, in the meantime, were forging an alliance with the populists and the Republicans who favored the silver standard. The expansionists were able to pass a series of resolutions on April 19 requiring Spain to renounce its sovereignty over Cuba immediately and authorizing in vigorous terms American armed intervention. The Democrats and their Republican allies secured a resolution (the Teller Amendment), however, which stated, "the United States hereby disclaims any disposition or intention to exercise sovereignty, jurisdiction or control over said Island [Cuba] except for the pacification thereof, and asserts its determination, when that is accomplished, to leave the government and control of the Island to its people."[18] Although this was technically in accord with the Republican platform, the resolution represented a personal defeat for McKinley, for the majority leader in the Senate, Orville H. Platt, and for the expansionists. Henry Moore Teller was then head of the dissident silver standard Republicans. Annexation of Cuba was out of the question.

These resolutions amounted, of course, to a virtual declaration of war. The President signed them on April 20, 1898. The next day Spain broke diplomatic relations with the United States. One day later the American navy blockaded Cuba. On April 24 Spain declared war. The next day the United States did likewise, retroactive to four days earlier.

It was, as Secretary of State John Hay put it, a "splendid little war." On May 1 Admiral George Dewey, who had been waiting in Hong Kong since February 28, engaged the Spanish fleet in Manila and completely destroyed it in a matter of hours. Troops were sent from San Francisco to occupy Guam. On July 13, 1898, Manila fell.

General Nelson Appleton Miles, who had gained national fame in campaigns against the Indians, especially the Apaches under Geronimo and Natchez, was put in charge of operations in the Caribbean theater. He favored the invasion of Puerto Rico as the first step. On June 14 the troops left instead for Daiquirí, a few miles from Santiago de Cuba, and started disembarking on June 22. Santiago surrendered on July 17, and four days later General Miles sailed for Puerto Rico.

The operation was so successful that Roosevelt feared that McKinley would agree to peace terms before there was a chance to capture Puerto Rico and the Philippines. On June 12, 1898, Roosevelt had written to Lodge: "You must get Manila and Hawaii, you must prevent any talk of peace until we get

Porto Rico and the Philippines as well as secure the independence of Cuba."[19] Since at least June 3, however, it had been clear that the annexation of Puerto Rico was a prime target. On that date McKinley had written to an intermediary, Britain's Foreign Secretary, Lord Salisbury, that Puerto Rico had to be handed over as part of the compensation for the war.[20]

Miles started disembarking his troops in Puerto Rico on July 25, 1898. They were joyously received. One of his companions called the invasion a "fête des fleurs." Some newspapers referred to it as a "military picnic." There was no resistance to speak of, and the armistice was proclaimed on August 12.

The short war did release strong, pent-up feelings in the Puerto Rican population against the economic and political exploitation to which it had been subjected for so long. From July 1898 to their suppression by the military government in February 1899, armed bands attacked stores, warehouses, and the houses of the well-to-do, especially in the mountain region, taking revenge on the Spanish and other members of the elite. The basis for deep social divisions was being laid.[21]

Peace conversations had started in mid-July. From the beginning McKinley made clear that, in addition to renouncing its sovereignty over Cuba, Spain had to cede Puerto Rico to the United States, as well as an island in the Ladrones (now the Marianas) in the Pacific. For a short time the United States government was willing to accept Spanish sovereignty over the Philippines in exchange for Manila or another suitable port.

Spain for a time resisted handing over Puerto Rico. However, in an official communication dated August 7, 1898, to Secretary of State Hay, Spain agreed to cede Puerto Rico and its neighboring islands, together with an island in the Ladrones, to the United States.[22] A peace protocol along those lines was signed on August 12, bringing an end to hostilities, and commissioners were named to negotiate a treaty of peace. The protocol already contained the language of what was to become article II of the Treaty of Paris. It stated: "Spain will cede to the United States the island of Puerto Rico and other islands now under Spanish sovereignty in the West Indies and also an island in the Ladrones, to be selected by the United States."[23] Contrary to Cuba's case, Puerto Rico had no Teller Amendment to protect it from actual cession.

After a period of prolonged uncertainty as to the extent of American interest in the Philippines, the decision was made to take over the entire archipelago. When questioned later as to why the United States had not bothered to consult the people of the Philippines and Puerto Rico as to their annexation, McKinley blandly replied, in the spirit of the times: "Do we need their consent to perform a great act for humanity? We have it in every aspiration of their minds, in every hope of their hearts."[24] McKinley later explained his tribulations about the Philippines:

> The truth is I didn't want the Philippines, and when they came to us as a gift from the Gods, I did not know what to do with them. . . . I walked the floor of the White House night after night until midnight; and I am not ashamed to tell you, gentlemen, that I went down on my knees and prayed Almighty God for light and guidance more than one night.
>
> And one night it came to me this way—I don't know how it was, but it came; 1) That we could not give them back to Spain—that would be cowardly and dishonorable; 2) that we could not turn them over to France or Germany—our commercial rivals in the Orient—that would be bad business and discreditable; 3) that we could not leave them to themselves—they were unfit for self-government—and they would have anarchy and misrule over there worse than Spain's was; and 4) that there was nothing for us to do but to take them all, and to educate the Filipinos, and uplift and civilize and Christianize them, and by God's grace do the very best we could by them, as our fellow men for whom Christ also died. And then I went to bed and slept soundly.[25]

History does not record any such tribulations concerning taking over Puerto Rico. McKinley's anguish was somewhat assuaged by his conviction, as he once stated, that "We have good money, we have ample revenues, we have unquestioned national credit, but what we need is new markets, and as trade follows the flag, it looks very much as if we are going to have new markets."[26]

The Treaty of Paris was signed on December 10, 1898. In Article II Spain ceded to the United States "the island of Puerto Rico and the other islands now under Spanish sovereignty in the West Indies, and the island of Guam in the Marianas or Ladrones."[27] Article III provided that "Spain cedes to the United States the archipelago known as the Philippine Islands." The last paragraph of article IX read: "The civil rights and political status of the territories hereby ceded to the United States shall be determined by the Congress." That last paragraph represented a substantial departure from the normal language employed by the United States in prior acquisition treaties. Article III of the 1803 treaty with France for the Louisiana Purchase had provided: "That the inhabitants of the ceded territory shall be incorporated in the union of the United States, and admitted as soon as possible according to the principles of the Federal Constitution to the enjoyment of all the rights, advantages and immunities of the citizens of the United States, and in the meantime they shall be maintained and protected in the free enjoyment of their liberty, property, and the religion which they profess."[28]

The difference, of course, consisted in the omission in the Treaty of Paris of any incorporation language and of any kind of promise concerning the immediate or future enjoyment of citizenship rights. The 1819 treaty with Spain for the cession of Florida basically followed the same pattern as that with France.[29] Incorporation and the enjoyment of the privileges, rights, and immunities of citizens was to happen as soon as possible. The 1848 Treaty of Guadalupe Hidalgo for the acquisition of a large part of Mexico also followed established precedent, as did the Treaty of 1867 for the purchase of Alaska. The July 7, 1898, Congressional resolution for the annexation of Hawaii went further.[30] Hawaii was formally incorporated to the Union at that time, and the Hawaiians were made American citizens in 1900.

The meaning of all this is that a new policy was being born, the shape of which was not yet clear. An acrimonious constitutional debate was looming. In an 1850 case, the United States Supreme Court, referring to the American occupation of the port of Tampico in Mexico, had declared: "The country in question had been conquered in war. But the genius and character of our institutions are peaceful, and the power to declare war was not conferred upon Congress for the purposes of aggression or aggrandizement, but to enable the general government to vindicate by arms, if it should become necessary, its own rights and the rights of its citizens."[31]

The ratification of the treaty was debated from January 4 to February 6, 1899. The constitutional debate that was to characterize Congressional consideration of the first American civil government for Puerto Rico started at this time. A number of Senators maintained that the United States lacked power under the Constitution to acquire territory for the purpose of holding them forever as colonies. The expansionists held to the contrary position, adding that the United States was under no obligation to extend self-government rights to conquered peoples until it considered them fit to exercise them. Resolutions to the effect of granting independence to Puerto Rico, Cuba, and the Philippines received scant attention, as did others, presented after ratification of the treaty, proclaiming that there was no intention to annex Puerto Rico and the Philippines. The heady fumes of empire were clearly in the air. A year before the approval of the Foraker Act, which established a civil government for Puerto Rico in 1900, it was evident that the United States was bent on annexing the island for an indefinite period of time. Even so, the treaty was ratified by only one vote over the required majority. The President signed the treaty on February 6, 1899, and, after ratification by Spain, it was proclaimed on April 11, 1899.

Seen in the context of the troubled world of the late nineteenth century, expansionism cannot be singled out as an American malady. England, France, Germany, Italy, Portugal, and other European powers were engaged in a feeding frenzy in Africa and other places, especially in the nineties. After expanding its frontiers west and south, the United States caught the malevolent virus, although Mexico can rightly charge that the disease started much earlier. The imperialist sickness was not upsetting to watch in others who made no claim to virtue, but for the United States—the shining example of democracy and freedom in a cynical world—to catch it was, to say the least, unsettling. Even more worrisome was to be the tenacity of the disease.

3

Military Government

The United States' failure to treat Puerto Rico the same way as Cuba represented a great disappointment to many.[1] Eugenio María de Hostos (1839–1903), the Puerto Rican writer and educator who distinguished himself in Chile, Argentina, Venezuela, and the Dominican Republic, returned to the island from his exile, brought about by his belief in the independence of Puerto Rico. Hostos was one of the few who attacked the approval of the treaty of annexation without first seeking the consent of the Puerto Rican people. His call for a plebiscite on the question went unheeded, although it was clear at the time that the United States was seen by Puerto Ricans as the bearer of freedoms long denied them.

Upon his arrival on the island, General Miles issued a proclamation which is still quoted with bitterness by many Puerto Ricans:

> In the prosecution of the war against the Kingdom of Spain by the people of the United States, in the cause of liberty, justice and humanity, its military forces have come to occupy the island of Porto Rico. They bring you the fostering arm of a nation of free people, whose greater power is in its justice and humanity to all those living within its folds. . . .
>
> The chief object of the American military forces will be to overthrow the armed authority of Spain and to give to the people of your beautiful island the largest measure of liberty consistent with this military occupation. We have not come to make war upon the people of a country that for centuries has been oppressed, but on the contrary, to bring you protection, not only to yourselves but to your property, to promote your prosperity and bestow upon you the immunities and blessings of the liberal institutions of our Government. . . . This is not a war of devastation, but one to give to all within the control of its military and naval forces the advantages and blessings of enlightened civilization.[2]

Many still consider these words the product of General Miles's rhetorical inclinations. They were, however, basically set forth as part of the routine General Orders issued by the Department of War to invading commanders.[3] Essentially the same proclamation was issued in Cuba and in the Philippines.

Miles left Puerto Rico two days after the signing of the peace protocol. On October 18, 1898, the United States took over formal control of the island, and General John R. Brooke became its first military governor. Brooke, contrary to the General Orders, which called for keeping the local institutions and system of laws to the extent possible, started acquainting Puerto Ricans with the blessings of enlightened civilization by suppressing Parliament and the older, less powerful Diputación Provincial and making extensive changes in the judicial system. He retained the Cabinet, however, and on December 9, 1898, left the island to accept the governorship of Cuba.

He was succeeded by General Guy V. Henry, under whose command Puerto Rican hostility to the military governors, which naturally started with Brooke, grew measurably. A few days after his arrival he threatened a major newspaper because it dared state that military government should soon be brought to an end. The paper was owned by Luis Muñoz Rivera (1859–1916), Prime Minister of Puerto Rico at the time of the invasion, who also wrote most of its editorials. Muñoz Rivera, a man of modest beginnings from the small mountain town of Barranquitas, became at a young age one of the top political leaders of his time. Governor Henry admonished the paper and published the following statement: "This General Government does not allow the publication of writings in which reference is made to the Army of the United States or to the Military Government, lest the extreme case of such publicity can be justified with conclusive proof."[4] He later subjected the paper to criminal proceedings and ordered the suspension of another journal. Henry did not think much of his new subjects. In one of his dispatches to Washington he stated: "I am getting in touch with the people and trying to educate them to the idea that they must help themselves, giving them Kindergarten instruction in controlling themselves without allowing them too much liberty, and in this way satisfy their . . . pride that they have some interest in their own government."[5]

The good General did not think that Brooke's practice of keeping untutored natives in positions of power was wise, and he accordingly began to name Americans to the various ministries, although leaving Muñoz Rivera untouched for a while. On February 12, 1899, Henry dissolved the Council of Ministers and added for good measure, after referring to Muñoz Rivera's ouster: "Heads of departments or others objecting to the introduction of American methods of business and progress or to the investigation of the affairs of the departments when properly ordered will be relieved from office or their resignations accepted if tendered."

A month later Muñoz left for the United States. Henry stated that if he ever returned to the island—which Muñoz, of course, was free to do—the harm that Muñoz would inflict on the Puerto Ricans would indeed be serious.[6] The people did not take this prophecy to heart. Muñoz Rivera did return to Puerto Rico in 1904 (he had come back briefly in 1899), again to run for public office, was promptly elected by an overwhelming margin, and thereafter won every election held until his death.

Relieved of Muñoz Rivera's presence, Henry continued to shower the blessings of civilization on the Puerto Ricans. He intervened openly in the administration of the municipalities, firing mayors and councilmen at will and suspending the civil authority. Contrary to the Philippines, however, there was no insurrection or even any sporadic acts of violence against American rule. Just in case, Henry placed an American at the head of the police force, a practice that the American Governors would continue until the 1940s.

The General Orders that governed the military government were specific concerning the role of the ruling Governor:

> Though the powers of the military occupant are absolute and supreme and immediately operate upon the political conditions of the inhabitants, the municipal laws of the conquered territory, such as affect private rights of persons and property and provide for the punishment of crime, are considered as continuing in force, so far as they are compatible with the new order of things, until they are suspended or superseded by the occupying belligerent, and in practice they are not usually abrogated, but are allowed to remain in force and to be administered by the ordinary tribunals, substantially as they were before the occupation. This enlightened practice is, so far as possible, to be adhered to on the present occasion.[7]

Henry and his successors had their own views, however, as to the requirements of the new order of things. Even before Congress acted under the Treaty of Paris, Henry thought it his duty to assimilate the Puerto Rican political and legal system to the American and was the first to meddle with the Civil Code and other laws affecting private rights. Following the hallowed tradition established by the old Captains General, Henry did not hide his annoyance at the Liberal party (headed by Muñoz Rivera before his self-imposed temporary exile), or his pref-

erence for the old incondicionales (who had immediately changed their unconditional support of Spain to unquestioning support of the occupation forces),
as well as for the followers of Dr. José C. Barbosa, who sang the praises of the
new government. Barbosa, born in 1857 in Bayamón, near San Juan, graduated
from the University of Michigan Medical School. He was a distinguished autonomist leader in Spanish times who in July 1899 founded the first statehood
party. By siding with the new government he wisely aligned his party with the
general repudiation of the old regime and the prevalent desire for a new Puerto
Rico as part of the United States.[8] Barbosa easily led his party to victory in the
elections of 1899, 1900, and 1902. Only when disenchantment set in with the
shortcomings of the military and early civil governments would Muñoz Rivera
be able to return to power in 1904.

On May 9, 1899, Henry was relieved of the governorship at his own request
and was succeeded by General George W. Davis, who remained as military governor until the establishment of civil government on May 1, 1900. General
Davis, like his predecessors, did not have a high opinion of the inhabitants of
the island and their institutions and unfortunately influenced future United
States policy toward Puerto Rico to a great degree. He wrote in one of his official reports: "I have found it necessary, as I believed, in the discussion of civil
affairs, past and present, to advert in strong terms to the general unfitness of the
great mass of the people for self-government, and unfortunately the number of
the intelligent, learned and responsible natives bears a small ratio to the illiterate and irresponsible. If the percentage of those who are not able to read and
write were as small as those who can, I would have the greatest pleasure in recommending the immediate endowment of the island with full autonomy."[9]

His views of the local leadership were not flattering, either: "There is no
lack on the part of these people of pretension to all the virtues, and as beautiful
theories of government as were ever propounded by the wisest men are put forth
continuously. There are very few really public-spirited men who appear to have
ideas of government other than self-seeking, but the number is very small."[10]
The nature of the political relationship with Puerto Rico for many years to come
was taking shape. Puerto Rico was to be pushed further back on the road to self-
government. Not only was it considered unfit for the degree of self-government
that it had obtained from Spain, with the decisive help of the Cuban revolution
and pressure from the United States itself; it was thought unworthy even of territorial government as known until then. Davis was quite clear on this point. He
thus advised the War Department and Congress: "I am satisfied that the island
is not ready for full Territorial autonomy. Only a few desire it, and I fear that the

great mass of the people feel no interest in the question of government at all, beyond the notion they had and have that with American sovereignty would come free trade and high prices for labor and produce, bringing general prosperity."[11]

On July 4, 1899, the Republican party was organized, at its core a mélange of the Barbosa faction of the Autonomist party and the old incondicionales, but with a considerable influx of Puerto Rico's poorest people, who understandably placed great hope in the new regime. The date was carefully selected. Their platform called for "sincere and definitive annexation of Puerto Rico to the United States" and institution of a territorial government as a means to eventual admission to the Union as a state. A full article of the platform was dedicated to the American flag. "We pledge allegiance to the American flag and to American ideas," it read, among other politically correct expressions. It also favored the substitution of English for Spanish as the language of education and the establishment of an "American system of justice." As was the case with the incondicionales in Spanish times, the new republicanos claimed that they were the only true, loyal subjects and that their rivals were actually separatists in disguise, believers in hateful independence. The platform ended by proclaiming: "We rejoice in and congratulate the people of Puerto Rico for being under the protection of the glorious American flag, which is the emblem of liberty, and we shall dedicate all our efforts to make sure that American institutions take root in our soil, teaching the people to love and venerate the illustrious names of Washington, Lincoln and McKinley." Even the ultraloyalist republicanos, who rarely questioned decisions by the military governors, called, however, for return of universal male suffrage, which had been abolished by General Davis.

A few months later, on October 1, 1899, Muñoz Rivera and other autonomistas organized the short-lived Federal party. It was ostensibly in favor of territorial government and eventual statehood, but it also daringly demanded full self-government, based on the consent of the governed, the right to elect its own Governor and a legislature able to approve laws not subject to overrule by Congress, and universal suffrage. The party was viewed with deep suspicion by the military government, which openly sided with the republicanos. Although not sanctioned by the military government, unruly mobs repeatedly attacked Federal party backers and their property, as well as sympathizers of the American Federation of Labor.[12]

The military government left a strong imprint on later times. It was a period of great social upheaval which brought about a realignment of political loyalties and aspirations. Cultural clashes between the American military government and sectors of the Puerto Rican people began to lay a groundwork of resentment. The split in the Puerto Rican family grew wider. Blind enmity, if not actual hatred, divided the basically unconditional backers of the new regime from the seekers of freedoms equal to or greater than those obtained under the Autonomic Charter and prompt economic betterment. General Miles's promises began to sound hollow. In the Philippines, a fight for independence from the United States was raging. In Cuba, the leaders of the revolution against Spain were trying to fend off attempts by the United States to annex Cuba. The military government lasted longer there than in Puerto Rico, until 1902. Cubans had to withstand military intervention again from 1906 to 1909, not without anger and agitation, then living for decades under the indignity of the Platt Amendment, enacted by Congress without consultation with Cuba, which allowed the United States for decades to intervene in its internal affairs at any time that it considered it necessary. Puerto Rico kept quiet, although sullen. Puerto Rican groups did not start taking occasional violent action against the regime until the thirties. Their actions were not condoned by the majority of the population, but a residue of unhappiness was to remain in most.

The period of military government also strengthened the conviction of influential United States officials that Puerto Ricans were generally unfit for the high level of self-government that had finally been granted them at the end of Spanish rule. The local people were not considered ready even for traditional territorial government. In the eyes of the Americans, they first needed to be taught the rudiments of democracy and become acquainted with American institutions, while keeping them firmly subject to United States sovereignty and close supervision. Political considerations with a very long history had dictated the annexation of the island, but during the period of military government that American policy toward its new possession started to take shape, later to be fleshed out in debates over the Foraker Act and in the so-called Insular Cases by the United States Supreme Court.

The serious mistakes of that period, which were compounded during the first half of the twentieth century, should, however, be seen in perspective. The well-intentioned, but woefully unprepared men sent to govern a proud people with a culture so different from their own did not always mean to be harsh. A serious and to a degree successful attempt was made to better the health, educational levels, and living conditions in the island, although the initial zeal lagged and results did not become encouraging until the late 1940s. The misunderstandings bred during these early times would influence policy for years to come.

4

The Shaping of a Colonial Policy

Many sources influenced the shaping of a colonial policy and the establishment of civil government for Puerto Rico. In this chapter I will look at the welter of opinions concerning what should have been done at the time and how the executive branch and later Congress finally approved the Foraker Act of 1900, followed by the reaction of the United States Supreme Court.

In 1898, President McKinley sent Reverend Henry K. Carroll, a distinguished leader of the Methodist Episcopal Church, to Puerto Rico to report on island conditions. Carroll held hearings and advised McKinley of the importance of granting Puerto Ricans a high degree of self-government. He stated in his report: "They expect under American sovereignty that the wrongs of centuries will be righted. . . . They may be poor, but they are proud and sensitive, and would be bitterly disappointed if they found that they had been delivered from an oppressive yoke to be put under a tutelage which proclaimed their inferiority. . . . They will learn the art of governing the only possible way—by having its responsibilities laid upon them."[1]

Carroll recommended a legislature composed of two chambers, both fully elected by universal male suffrage, the grant of American citizenship, the extension of the U.S. Constitution, elective mayors, free trade, and the right to elect a Delegate to Congress. Few of his recommendations would find their way into the first organic act for Puerto Rico.

The Secretary of War, the official in charge of Puerto Rican affairs for many decades, sent his own Insular Commission to Puerto Rico early in 1899. Its report, issued in May, advised that the people of Puerto Rico wanted nothing but American laws, leaving no trace of Spanish legislation. "The only exception to this view," the commission added sarcastically, "comes only from those few who believe they have an inherent right to hold the offices and dictate the laws and policy of the Island, which they call self-government."[2]

The Insular Commission did not favor a local legislature of any kind, even one composed of appointed members only. In testifying before Congress on the report, Judge H. G. Curtis, a member of the commission, stated that the President himself should legislate for Puerto Rico, at the recommendation of the Governor to be appointed by him.[3] The commission also opposed the extension of American citizenship. The commission recommended not one, but three federal courts, one each in San Juan, Ponce, and Mayagüez. Their decisions would not be appealable to any mainland American court, but to the President himself.[4]

General Davis also disagreed with Carroll. In his view, Puerto Rico should be a "Dependency" of the United States under the control of the President, exercised through the Secretary of State. There should be an Executive Council, composed of seven department heads to be appointed by the President, and four persons selected by the Governor from among the members of the legislature. Contrary to the Insular Commission, Davis favored an elected legislature composed of a single chamber. Suffrage should be limited to those men who could read and write or pay taxes.[5] Davis recommended that the justices of the Supreme Court be appointed by the President. There should be a federal court and free trade, but Puerto Ricans should not have American citizenship or representation of any kind in Congress, not even through a delegate.

By that time, the commission that had been set up to recommend a government for Hawaii advised that the Hawaiians should enjoy American citizenship, an elected legislature, a cabinet appointed by the Governor, a Delegate to Congress, and other attributes of full territorial government—all of which Congress soon provided.[6] Davis warned that Puerto Rico should not have such a degree of self-government. According to him, the British Crown colony type of government provided a better model.

Elihu Root, a distinguished New York attorney who served as Secretary of War from 1899 to 1904 and as Secretary of State from 1905 to 1909, awarded the Nobel Prize for Peace in 1912, who much later would come to favor the status of an American protectorate for a free Puerto Rico, did not believe at the time that Puerto Ricans were ready for much self-government. After studying the views described so far, he reported to Congress: "The people have not yet been educated in the art of self-government, or any really honest government. . . . A form of government should be provided for Porto Rico which will assure the kind of administration to which we are accustomed with just as much participation on the part of Porto Ricans as is possible without enabling their inexperience to make it ineffective, and with opportunity for them to demonstrate their increasing capacity to govern themselves with less and less assistance."[7]

Root therefore recommended that the Governor and his cabinet be appointed by the President, with the advice and consent of the Senate. The idea of an Executive Council to assist the Governor, as recommended by Davis, was unacceptable to him. He did not favor the establishment of a legislature, as suggested by Carroll and Davis, either. He recommended instead a Legislative Council, in the English colonial fashion, composed of the department heads and a minority of members appointed by the President. Laws were to be subject to veto by the President and also by Congress.

Root opposed universal male suffrage for Puerto Rico, as well as the grant of American citizenship. He also believed that United States laws should not apply in Puerto Rico, except in matters specifically to be enumerated by Congress.

The administration's theory as to the power to govern the new possessions was devised chiefly by Root. He thought that the Constitution did not apply automatically, *ex proprio vigore*, to the new dependencies and that they were accordingly subject "to the complete sovereignty of [Congress], controlled by no legal limitations except those which may be found in the treaty of cession."[8] Root did add that government officials could hardly be delegated power to act, for example, without due process of law, but he put this forward as a moral, rather than a legal limitation. In his message to Congress prior to presentation of the Foraker bill, McKinley basically adopted the position developed by his Secretary of War.

Prior to the Spanish-American War, since the Northwest Ordinance of 1787, a different view held. Territories were acquired with a view to eventual admission to the Union. They were part of the United States in both the domestic and the international sense. The Constitution followed the flag and accordingly applied in all of them, only they were governed under the plenary powers granted Congress by the so-called territorial clause of the Constitution. The inhabitants were made citizens of the United States.

The acquisition of the new colonies—the start of an empire—led the administration to devise a policy different from the established territorial one from the mass of theories within it, some of them conflicting. Its fundamental tenets would be that the people of Puerto Rico were not ready for self-government; a learning period, of unspecified duration, was necessary before self-government could be extended; the eventual status should be neither statehood nor independence, but a self-governing dependency, subject to the plenary power of Congress; the learning process required a policy of political and cultural assimilation, which necessarily involved the extension of United States laws, institutions, and language to the island; and living conditions should be improved to the extent possible. This colonial policy, still incipient at that moment, would prove to be a hardy one once it jelled. Parts of it still plague the relationship between the United States and Puerto Rico.

There were both sharp criticism and unstinting praise of the emerging policy on the part of distinguished academicians. William Graham Sumner, professor of political and social sciences at Yale University, wrote in a biting article entitled "The Conquest of the United States by Spain":

> There are plenty of people in the United States today who regard Negroes as human beings, perhaps, but of a different order from white men, so that the ideas and social arrangements of white men cannot be applied to them with propriety. Others feel the same way about Indians. . . . The doctrine that all men are equal has come to stand as one of the cornerstones of the temple of justice and truth. It was set up as a bar to just this notion that we are so much better than others that it is liberty for them to be governed by us. . . .
>
> The Americans have been committed from the outset to the doctrine that all men are created equal. . . . It is an astonishing event that we have lived to see American arms carry this domestic dogma out where it must be tested in its application to uncivilized and half-civilized peoples. At the first touch of the test we throw the doctrine away and adopt the Spanish doctrine. We are told by the imperialists that these people are not fit for liberty and self-government; that it is rebellion for them to resist our beneficence; that we must send fleets and armies to kill them if they do it; that we must devise a government for them and administer it ourselves; that we may buy them or sell them as we please, and dispose of their "trade" for our own advantage. What is that but the policy of Spain to her dependencies?[9]

Sumner's views would be echoed by many Democratic Congressmen and Senators in the course of the debates on the Foraker bill. Sumner and those members of Congress, if alive today, would be surprised to hear that administration officials and many in Congress still cling to the notion that the United States has plenary power to govern Puerto Rico as it pleases and that the limited self-governing powers of Puerto Rico are subject to sufferance by the Congress under the territorial clause of the United States Constitution.

Other distinguished professors backed the administration. James Bradley Thayer, of Harvard Law School, criticized Sumner's position and wrote, in impeccable colonialese, about "the childish literalness which has crept into our no-

tions of these principles, as if all men, however savage and however unfit to govern themselves, were oppressed when other people governed them; as if self-
government were not often a curse; and as if the great nation does not often owe
its people, or some part of them, as its chief duty, that of governing them from
the outside, instead of giving them immediate control of themselves."[10] In another article, Simeon E. Baldwin, of Yale Law School, wrote: "Our Constitution was made by a civilized and educated people. It provides guaranties of personal security which seem ill-adapted to the conditions of society that prevail in
many parts of our new possessions. To give the half-civilized Moros of the
Philippines, or the ignorant and lawless brigands that infest Puerto Rico . . . the
benefit of such immunities from the sharp and sudden justice—or injustice—
which they have been hitherto accustomed to expect, would, of course, be a serious obstacle to the maintenance there of an efficient government."[11] The
strong brew of imperialism, with its deadly ingredients of Manifest Destiny, the
white man's burden, and other powerful additives, also affected the judgment
of the good professors.

Senator Joseph Benson Foraker presented his first bill to provide a civil government for Puerto Rico in January 1900.[12] Foraker, born in 1846, had been a
judge in Cincinnati, twice Governor of Ohio, and Republican Senator for Ohio
since 1897. His bill was much less restrictive than the one recommended by the
President and the Secretary of War. The bill granted American citizenship to all
the inhabitants of Puerto Rico who chose to accept it and extended the United
States Constitution to Puerto Rico. It provided for an elected House of Delegates as recommended by Davis. A bill would also be presented in the House.[13]

Puerto Rico's leaders did not attend the Congressional hearings. The sole
voice from Puerto Rico critical of what had happened so far was that of Dr. Julio
Henna, a fighter for independence in Spanish times, who stated at the end of his
testimony, which had been fairly conciliatory in tone: "The occupation has been
a perfect failure. We have suffered everything. No liberty, no rights, absolutely
no protection. . . . We are Mr. Nobody from Nowhere. We have no political status, no civil rights."[14]

General Davis testified twice. The second time around he changed his mind
about the readiness of Puerto Ricans to have a legislature.

The Senate Committee report reflected the views of the administration
concerning the constitutionality of holding colonies, a topic on which a debate
was then raging in Congress, newspapers, and academic journals. The Constitution did not follow the flag, the committee held. Colonies could be acquired

and governed by the United States without regard to the strictures of the Constitution. As the report put it, without mincing words:

> If we should acquire territory populated by an intelligent, capable and law-abiding people, to whom the right of self-government could be safely conceded, we might at once, with propriety and certainly within the scope of our constitutional power, incorporate that territory and people into the Union as an integral part of the United States, and . . . extend to them at once the Constitution of the United States; but if the territory should be inhabited by a people of wholly different character, illiterate, and unacquainted with our institutions, and incapable of exercising the rights and privileges guaranteed by the Constitution to the States of the Union, it would be competent for Congress to withhold from such people the operation of the Constitution and the laws of the United States, and, continuing to hold the territory as a mere possession of the United States to govern the people thereof as their situation and the necessities of the case may require.[15]

Behind the abstruse debate as to whether the Constitution applied in full to the new possessions there were, of course, realities of a different order. The doctrine of the selective, nonautomatic applicability of the Constitution and the consequent plenary powers of Congress to govern the new possessions was essential to two types of protectionists: the opponents of free trade, who feared the influx of Puerto Rican and Philippine products to the United States market; and the noneconomic protectionists, who wanted to prevent the extension of American citizenship to peoples of a different race and, with even greater intensity, forestall any move toward eventual statehood. The proponents of free trade, who comprised the sugar refiners, the wheat producers, and the manufacturers interested in new markets for their products, favored the automatic application of the whole Constitution. In 1900, destitute Puerto Rico was the fifth largest market for American products in Latin America and twenty-seventh in the world. By 1910 it was fourth in Latin America and eleventh in the world.

The committee did favor the extension of American citizenship, the establishment of a legislature as recommended in the Foraker bill, the election of a Delegate to Congress, limited suffrage, and the imposition of a 25 percent tariff on products imported to the United States from Puerto Rico.

Senator Orville H. Platt, from Connecticut—then an important tobacco state—proposed a tariff of 80 percent on all products. Senator McEnery, from Louisiana, was happy with just 50 percent. Senator Fairbanks, from Indiana, proposed another type of amendment to the bill: the application of the immigration laws to Puerto Rico. Some Republicans, bothered by the accusations of imperialism hurled at them by the Democrats, favored a resolution to the effect that the United States would not govern a people without their consent. The Democratic opposition largely contended that the United States had no power to acquire territories for the purpose of governing them as colonies.

The debate on the tariff imperiled passage of the bill. A compromise was reached which allowed two amendments suggested by McKinley to go through in the House by the narrow margin of eleven votes: a tariff of 15 percent would be imposed on Puerto Rican products, but the provision would last only for two years, unless extended by Congress. The amendments, of course, constituted an assertion of Congressional power to tax commerce with the new possessions, a statement sought by those whose main preoccupation was the Philippines, rather than Puerto Rico.

Opposition to the grant of American citizenship was so powerful that Foraker was forced to give up this provision, though it was backed by the administration. The measure granting Puerto Rico a nonvoting delegate in Congress also had to be discarded. Instead, Puerto Rico would have a Resident Commissioner in Washington, with no legal right as such to sit in Congress. In 1902 an amendment to the House rules allowed the Resident Commissioner to participate in Congressional deliberations, but without power to vote on any matter. The extension of the Constitution likewise fell by the wayside. Efforts failed to give Puerto Rico a wholly elected legislature and the rights to adopt its own constitution and to be consulted as to whether they favored the annexation. The bill passed the Senate, 40–31, and the House, 161–153. President McKinley signed the Foraker Act into law on April 12, 1900.[16]

The Foraker Act, or first organic act, called for a Governor appointed by the President of the United States, with the advice and consent of the Senate, for a four-year term, but removable by the President at will. There were to be six departments, the heads of which were also to be appointed by the President, with the advice of the Senate. Together with five citizens, who had to be born in Puerto Rico, they composed the Executive Council, which functioned as a second legislative chamber. The other chamber of the Legislative Assembly was a House of Delegates, constituted by thirty-five elected members for a term of two years. The members had to be able to read and write either English or Spanish and had to own property subject to taxation. Universal male suffrage would not apply unless the legislature so decided, which meant that such a move could be prevented by the Executive Council and the Governor. As a further precautionary measure, the Congress retained the capacity to annul at any time any law approved by the Puerto Rican legislature. A Resident Commissioner would be elected every two years to represent Puerto Rico before the executive departments. No provision was made for representation in Congress.

The judicial power was vested in a Supreme Court of Puerto Rico, whose members were to be appointed by the President, with the advice and consent of the Senate, and in the courts created during the time of military government. The Governor would appoint the lower court judges, with the advice and consent of the Executive Council. Decisions by the Supreme Court of Puerto Rico could be appealed to the United States Supreme Court. A federal court was also established, as under the occupation, and all proceedings therein had to be conducted in English.

Senator Foraker's initial proposal to extend American citizenship to Puerto Ricans was rejected. The inhabitants of the island were declared to be "citizens of Puerto Rico." The act was silent as to their right to travel to the United States, a matter which later would be decided in the affirmative by the courts. There was no Bill of Rights.

There would be a customs union between the United States and Puerto Rico, but Puerto Rico would not participate in the process of approving the tariffs, as in Spanish times. The coastwise shipping laws, prohibiting less expensive foreign carriers from carrying cargo between Puerto Rico and the United States, were specifically made applicable to the island, with severe economic consequences through the years. All United States laws were extended to Puerto Rico, unless found to be locally inapplicable; no federal law has ever been found to be locally inapplicable to Puerto Rico.

The Foraker Act did away with most of the liberties that Puerto Rico was able to achieve with such difficulty in the course of four hundred years of Spanish rule. Puerto Ricans lost equality of citizenship with the metropolitan country; full representation in the metropolitan legislature; the right to universal male suffrage; a parliament of its own, composed of a fully elected lower house and a majority of elected members in the upper chamber and with far greater powers of legislation; the right to impose its own tariffs and to enter into commercial treaties; and several other rights described in chapter 1. Above all, Puerto Rico lost the right to government by consent of the governed: the Autonomic Charter was not amendable except at the request of the insular parliament, while the Foraker Act was subject to the unilateral will of Congress.

The Foraker Act was supposed to be a temporary measure to provide a civil government for Puerto Rico, which fact was expressed in its title, but it has never been repealed. Although parts of it have been replaced, some of its sections live to this day as part of the Federal Relations Act.

The controversy about the right of the United States to acquire territory for purposes of empire and to govern it without being subject to the full limitations of the Constitution soon reached the courts. Between 1901 and 1905 the Supreme Court decided a number of controversies concerning the status of the new possessions which came to be known as the Insular Cases.

After the approval of the Foraker Act, the matter of self-governance continued to be the subject of intense public and academic debate. The Democratic party platform in 1900 endorsed the principle of government by consent of the governed and stated that the Constitution applied wherever the American flag flew.[17] Many other voices condemned the holding of colonies and the plenary powers theory, including Republican leaders like John Sherman, former Secretary of State under McKinley, Senator George F. Hoar and Thomas B. Reed, the former Speaker, as well as former President Cleveland, Charles Eliot (president of Harvard), William James, Jane Addams, Samuel Gompers, Mark Twain, and Andrew Carnegie.[18]

The constitutional controversy naturally engaged the interest of many academicians. All shades of opinion were represented, foreshadowing the basic views set forth by various justices in the Insular Cases. Dean Langdell of Harvard Law School was a fervent advocate of the plenary powers doctrine, while opposing the possibility of statehood for the islands.[19]

A second group, part of the so-called Anti-Imperialists, upheld the *ex proprio vigore* doctrine—the theory that the Constitution followed the flag, that new territories could be acquired by conquest or cession, but only to be governed subject to the full limitations of the Constitution and solely with the purpose of eventually admitting them to the Union in equality with other states. Many of the Anti-Imperialists were, however, against the admission to the American Union of societies with a different racial and cultural background and therefore opposed the annexation of the islands.[20]

Professor Abbott Lawrence Lowell of Harvard, later its president, was the principal exponent of a third view, the one espoused by the administration, with somewhat less precision, and eventually adopted by the Supreme Court. Lowell thought that the Constitution allowed for two kinds of territories: those that were part of the United States and those that were not part of but were instead possessions of the United States. The Constitution did not extend completely to the latter, but there were certain provisions embodying certain rights that limited the otherwise plenary powers of Congress.[21]

Downes v. Bidwell, decided in 1901, was the most important of the Insular Cases.[22] *Downes* is essential to the proper understanding of the political status to which Puerto Rico was to be relegated. The case was brought by an importer of oranges sent from San Juan to New York, who complained about the 15 percent duty levied on the product. He claimed that the imposition violated the clause of the United States Constitution that commands that "all duties, imposts and excises shall be uniform throughout the United States." This claim effectively put into question the right of the United States to establish a colonial empire, to own territory to which the Constitution would not extend. Five opinions were issued by the Court, none commanding a majority, but three of them upholding the administration's power to govern territory acquired by conquest or treaty without the restraints imposed by the Constitution.

The Fuller Court, as it was known, was not a distinguished court. This was the court that sanctioned racial discrimination in the United States in the notorious *Plessy v. Ferguson* case of 1896; justified the use of injunctions against labor unions and upheld the imprisonment of its leaders for conduct later considered to be protected by the Constitution; frequently employed the due process clause to annul progressive social legislation, such as that limiting daily working hours; considerably reduced state power to regulate the tariffs charged by public service companies; and exempted the American Sugar Refining Company, which controlled 98 percent of the sugar sold and refined in the United States, from the strictures of antitrust legislation.

Six of the justices had been appointed by Republican Presidents: John M. Harlan, Horace Gray, David J. Brewer, Henry B. Brown, George Shiras, and Joseph McKenna. The three Democrats were Chief Justice Melville W. Fuller, Edward D. White, and Rufus W. Peckham. The majority in *Downes* was composed of four Republicans (Brown, McKenna, Shiras, and Gray) and a Southern Democrat (White). Two Republicans (Harlan and Brewer) joined two Democratic appointees (Fuller and Peckham) to form the minority. The three opinions that favored the position of the administration were written by Brown, White, and Gray. White's theory eventually would prevail in the Insular Cases and beyond. Fuller and Harlan wrote the dissenting opinions. Let us take a closer look at the dramatis personae, beginning with the writers of the opinions that made the majority.

Brown served with little distinction in the Court from 1891 to 1903. He was notoriously insensitive to questions of racial equality. His best-known opinion was the majority opinion in *Plessy v. Ferguson,* where he stated: "We consider the underlying fallacy of the plaintiff's argument to consist in the assumption that the enforced separation of the two races stamps the colored race with a badge of inferiority. If this be so, it is not by reason of anything found in the act, but solely because the colored race chooses to put that construction upon it. . . . If one race be inferior to the other socially, the Constitution of the United States cannot put them upon the same plane."[23] Brown's opinion in *Downes* reveals his deep preoccupation with the supposedly grave consequences of making Puerto Ricans and Filipinos citizens of the United States and extending the United States Constitution to strange peoples and lands.

White was an ardent protectionist from Louisiana, where he served briefly on the state supreme court and later became a Senator. Oliver Wendell Holmes, who served with him on the United States Supreme Court for nineteen years, said that White was "built rather for a politician than a judge."[24] A subsequent critic wrote: "What impresses later generations in White's opinions is less their substance than their extraordinary form. He moved portentously across the thinnest of ice, confident that a lifeline of adverbs—'inevitably,' 'irresistibly,' 'clearly,' and 'necessarily'—was supporting him in his progress."[25]

Gray, the author of the third majority opinion, had perhaps the best professional credentials prior to his appointment. A reputable Boston lawyer, he had served for a creditable number of years in the Massachusetts Supreme Court. Although deriving from the same cultural and social milieu as Holmes, his record in civil rights cases was dismal. He voted with the majority in the Civil Rights Cases, in which the Court annulled the federal 1875 Civil Rights Act, which required equal treatment for every American citizen, regardless of color, in any place under the jurisdiction of the federal government. He also authored the opinions that denied United States citizenship to American Indians and severely limited the human rights of foreigners residing in the United States.

The fourth member of the majority, Shiras, was a railroad lawyer from Pittsburgh, ultraconservative in matters of social legislation but with a liberal bent in civil rights issues.

The fifth member, McKenna, was the sole McKinley appointee to the Court. He was a former Congressman from California, identified with the political machine of the railroad magnate Leland Stanford. His lack of professional preparation has often been commented upon: "His mind uncluttered by the complex dicta of legal scholarship, McKenna tended to decide each case individually as it came before the Court, mostly on the basis of the application of 'common sense.' The net result of his erratic empiricism is a series of frequently conflicting opinions and votes. . . . The quilted pattern of McKenna's legal decisions largely defies logical analysis."[26]

Among the dissenters, Fuller was a Grover Cleveland appointee and a vigorous critic of the extension of the national powers, contrary to the nationalist inclination of the majority of his court. Although his civil rights record was not good, he had written several dissents defending minorities from the use of arbitrary power.

Harlan, the author of the second dissenting opinion in *Downes*, had and still deservedly has a considerable reputation. Defeated in his bid to be Governor of Kentucky, he was later considered as a vice presidential candidate. He dissented in *Plessy v. Ferguson*, the Civil Rights Cases, *Lochner* (the maximum hours case), and many others.

Finally, Brewer was the most conservative judge of the Court in 1901. His strong disapproval of government intervention in individual economic activities did make him at times, however, a defender of personal liberty in other fields. He was also fundamentally at odds with the expansionism that characterized the age.

Brown's position was, in brief, that the Constitution applies only to the states and to territories where Congress decided to extend the Constitution. There could be territories subject to the jurisdiction of the United States, but to which the Constitution did not apply, except to the extent that certain of its provisions restricted the powers of Congress. Evidencing his concern about different races, the author of the majority opinion in *Plessy* wrote in *Downes:*

> We are . . . of the opinion that the power to acquire territory by treaty
> implies, not only the power to govern such territory, but to prescribe
> upon what terms the United States shall receive its inhabitants, and what
> their status shall be in what Chief Justice Marshall termed the "American empire." There seems to be no middle ground between this position
> and the doctrine that if their inhabitants do not become, immediately
> upon annexation, citizens of the United States, their children thereafter
> born, whether savages or civilized, are such, and entitled to all the rights,
> privileges, and immunities of citizens. If such be their status, the consequences will be extremely serious. Indeed, it is doubtful if Congress
> would ever assent to the annexation of territory upon the condition that
> its inhabitants, however foreign they may be to our habits, traditions,
> and modes of life, shall become at once citizens of the United States.[27]

Brown's theories fit nicely with the position backed by the administration.

White, whose opinion would eventually triumph, reached the same result as Brown through different semantics. He held that there were two types of territories, both subject to the jurisdiction of the United States: those incorporated to the nation and those that were not. The Constitution extended to the first group, but not to the second, except those parts of the Constitution that referred to principles that could be termed fundamental. White firmly rejected the view that the United States could not constitutionally acquire colonies: "While no particular provision of the Constitution is referred to, to sustain the argument that it is impossible to acquire territory by treaty without immediate and absolute incorporation, it is said that the spirit of the Constitution excludes the conception of property or dependencies possessed by the United States and which are not so completely incorporated as to be in all respects a part of the United States. . . . But this reasoning is based on political, and not judicial, considerations."[28]

White considered that the acquiring country had unrestricted power to determine what rights to concede to the acquired territory. To say otherwise, he ruled, would be "to say that the United States is helpless in the family of nations, and does not possess the authority which has at all times been treated as an incident of the right to acquire."[29] Puerto Rico's constitutional status was therefore thus defined: "While in an international sense Porto Rico was not a foreign country, since it was subject to the sovereignty of and was owned by the United States, it was foreign to the United States in a domestic sense, because the island has not been incorporated into the United States, but was merely appurtenant thereto as a possession."[30]

The nature of this holding is not generally known in either the United States or Puerto Rico. The typical American or Puerto Rican is shocked to learn that Puerto Rico has never been part of the United States in the domestic sense. It should also be unsettling to know that it is the prevalent position of the United States government, even at present, that Congress still has plenary powers over Puerto Rico, to the full extent declared in *Downes*, and that, accordingly, Puerto Rico is still a territory, possession, or chattel of the United States.

Gray's position was that, until it was ready to establish a complete government for Puerto Rico, Congress could provide a temporary government. Gray did not reach the issue of whether the United States could under the Constitution possess permanent colonies, but in practice Gray went further than Brown or White in defining the extent of United States power over Puerto Rico. He thought that the temporary civil government established by Congress could exercise powers as great as those wielded by the military government, and he was the only justice to abstain from holding that Congressional power over the new territories was limited by certain fundamental or natural rights.

Fuller held in his dissenting opinion that the United States could be composed only of states and territories, to all of which the Constitution applied. To his mind, the Constitution did not allow political entities to be subject to the absolute will of the Congress. He thus summarized the contrary contention:

> The contention seems to be that, if an organized and settled province of another sovereignty is acquired by the United States, Congress has the power to keep it, like a disembodied shade, in an intermediate state of ambiguous existence for an indefinite period; and, more than that, that after it has been called from that limbo, commerce with it is absolutely subject to the will of Congress, irrespective of constitutional provisions. . . .
>
> That theory assumes that the Constitution created a government empowered to acquire countries throughout the world, to be governed by different rules than those obtaining in the original states and territories, and substitutes for the present system of republican government a system of domination over distant provinces in the exercise of unrestricted power.[31]

Fuller accordingly held that the Constitution applied *ex proprio vigore* to Puerto Rico, dismissing as political the argument about the dire consequences of extending the totality of the Constitution to the new territories. The Chief Justice, however, did not believe that extension of the Constitution to the new territories entailed immediate acquisition of American citizenship. While indicating that the issue was not before the Court, he stated: "Doubtless the subjects of the former sovereign are brought by the transfer under the protection of the acquiring power, and are so far impressed with its nationality, but it does not follow that they necessarily acquire the full status of citizens."[32]

Harlan's dissent was a vigorous indictment of the theory that the United States could establish a colonial system. He wrote:

> In my opinion, Congress has no existence and can exercise no authority outside the Constitution. Still less is it true that Congress can deal with new territories just as other nations have done or may do with their new territories. This nation is under the control of a written constitution, the supreme law of the land and the only source of the powers which our government, or any branch or officer of it, may exert at any time or at any

place. Monarchical and despotic governments, unrestrained by written constitutions, may do with newly acquired territories what this government may not do consistently with our fundamental law. To say otherwise is to concede that Congress may, by action taken outside of the Constitution, engraft upon our republican institutions a colonial system such as it exists under monarchical governments. Surely such a result was never contemplated by the fathers of the Constitution. . . . The idea that this country may acquire territories anywhere upon the earth, by conquest or treaty, and hold them as mere colonies or provinces,—the people inhabiting them to enjoy only such rights as Congress chooses to accord them—is wholly inconsistent with the spirit and genius, as well as with the words, of the Constitution.[33]

Thus, by a one-vote margin, the Supreme Court, reflecting the deep division at the time in the body politic itself, confirmed Puerto Rico's status as a colony of the United States.

Yet *Downes* actually opened up the possibility of a different treatment of Puerto Rico under a regime of special laws. After federal taxation started in 1913, Puerto Rico could safely be left outside its scope, although Congress remained free to change its mind. On the other hand, many critics of the present condition of Puerto Rico point to *Downes* and the rest of the Insular Cases as allowing unequal treatment of Puerto Rico in many ways, such as its exclusion from the right to vote for President, full or meaningful representation in Congress, and equal participation in federal aid programs.

The treatment of Hawaii at the same time was quite different. After its annexation in 1898 through the Newlands Resolution, Hawaii's organic act, passed shortly after the Foraker Act in 1900, made Hawaii part of the United States and started it on the path to statehood. That incorporation of Hawaii by Congress had taken place, contrary to what happened to Puerto Rico, was confirmed in 1903 in the *Mankichi* case (another of the Insular Cases).[34] By 1905, in the *Rasmussen* case, the Supreme Court decided that Alaska was also an incorporated territory where the Constitution applied.[35] White's incorporation doctrine commanded a majority of the Court, although it was not until 1922 in the *Balzac* case, where the Court unanimously ruled that the extension of American citizenship to Puerto Ricans did not make Puerto Rico part of the United States.[36]

The Insular Cases, in sum, left the government of the United States free to pursue the policies that had started taking shape during the military government. The main legal assumptions of the imperialists were confirmed: formation of a colonial empire was possible; Puerto Rico was not part of the United States as other territories had been, but instead was a dependency or possession; and Puerto Rico could accordingly be held and governed indefinitely, without the restrictions of the Constitution, except those relating to certain undefined human rights of a fundamental nature. The other elements of the United States' new colonial policy were consequently left undisturbed, and it could hardly be otherwise, given the limitations of judicial power: the cautious extension of limited self-governing powers, as conditions would dictate, but without any promise, explicit or implicit, of eventual independence or statehood; cultural assimilation, considered a necessary part of the Puerto Rican people's education in the art of self-government; and enlightened economic treatment of the island, as the term was understood in those laissez-faire days, long before vast governmental aid programs were launched.

5

Life Under the Foraker Act

Both the Republican and the Federal parties in Puerto Rico initially criticized the Foraker Act. Even before approval of the act, the official organ of the Republican party resented that "this Island be treated as a mere chattel of the United States." Soon, however, the republicanos reverted to their traditional praise and, on occasion, muted criticism of United States actions and condemnation of the Federalists as anti-American. José C. Barbosa thought that the law was imperfect but accepted it as a transitory measure. "We applauded the Foraker Act," he would later explain, "and were grateful to its author. . . . Far from cursing the law, we have maintained that as a transitory measure it was good."[1]

The Federalists were far less diplomatic. Luis Muñoz Rivera termed the law "a ridiculous imitation of the autonomic reforms attempted by [minister of Spain] Cánovas del Castillo."[2] The reforms instituted by Cánovas some years before the Autonomic Charter had been the subject of special derision in Spanish times by both Barbosa and Muñoz Rivera. On July 24, 1900, the day before the celebration of the invasion of Puerto Rico by the American troops, an event declared to be a holiday by the military government, Muñoz wrote:

> The North American Government found in Puerto Rico a degree of autonomy larger than that of Canada. It should have respected and enlarged it, but only wanted to and did destroy it. . . .
>
> Because of that, and other things about which we shall remain silent, we shall not celebrate the 25th of July.
>
> Because we thought that an era of liberty was dawning and instead are witnessing a spectacle of terrible assimilation. . . .
>
> Because none of the promises made were kept and because our present condition is that of serfs attached to conquered territory.[3]

A year later he wrote to the President as follows: "The Foraker Act, Mr. President, though good on economic matters, should never have come out of Congress. Such a law is unworthy of the United States, which imposes it, and of Puerto Rico, which tolerates it. Not even a sliver of democratic thought can be found in it."[4]

Charles Herbert Allen, Assistant Secretary of the Navy, was sworn in on May 1, 1900, as Puerto Rico's first civil Governor under the Foraker Act. He lost no time in openly siding, like Davis and Henry, with the local Republican party and displaying animosity toward Muñoz Rivera. He wrote in his first annual report to Washington:

> There can be no denying the fact that while the Republican party accepts
> the American control of the island in good faith, and gives hearty sup-
> port to the Administration, the same cannot be said of their political op-
> ponents. . . .
>
> The Americans residing in the island regret the course pursued by
> the Federals, because it showed a subserviency to individual political
> control incompatible with true American government. . . .
>
> The Federal party is so subservient to a leader who is malcontent
> that it has followed him to a large extent in his policy of obstruction, and,
> as a natural sequence, has persistently opposed the American policy to-
> ward the island. On the other hand, it should be said that there are a
> good many educated, intelligent, professional and business men in the
> Federal party who would naturally be found upon the side of good order
> and regular development, who, when relieved of bad leadership, can
> confidently be relied upon, it is thought, to be upon the side of such ad-
> ministration of affairs in the island as tend to its permanent advance-
> ment.[5]

In June the President appointed the six department heads and the five other members of the Executive Council. All the department heads were American. Two of the five remaining members were republicanos, two federalistas, and one supposedly independent. The first job tackled by the Council was redistricting the island for electoral purposes. It soon became known that the plan suggested by the "independent" member and approved by the Executive Council was a classic example of gerrymandering at its worst (some of the districts were not even contiguous, as ordered by the Foraker Act) and actually had been drafted by the president of the republicanos. The two Council members from the Federal party, having served a little over two months, immediately resigned. Two Republican party members were appointed in their place.

The Puerto Rican members of the Council were so complaisant—they approved the budget immediately upon presentation by the Governor, without discussion—and played so insignificant a role in its deliberations that one of its most distinguished members, Rosendo Matienzo Cintrón, later resigned and joined Muñoz Rivera in criticizing American rule.

The Executive Council set November 6, 1900, as the date for the first general elections under the Foraker Act. The right to vote was still limited to those men who could read and write or were taxpayers. The Federal party, alleging that the Governor had discriminated against it in determining the composition of the registration boards, abstained from the election. The first House of Delegates was accordingly composed of republicanos only. A Republican Resident Commissioner, Federico Degetau, was likewise elected at this time.

The organization of the courts remained much the same, but Governor Allen discharged all judges who did not belong to the Republican party. The Attorney General was also entrusted, to an even greater degree than under the military government, with enormous power over the courts. He prepared their budget, recommended the appointment or discharge of all judicial personnel, and supervised the entire system. Such a concentration of power in the Attorney General would continue until 1952, when Commonwealth status was established and the people of Puerto Rico obtained the right to draft their own constitution, subject to approval by Congress.

As respects the municipalities, the government wielded great power over them in practice. The Governor could suspend or, after a hearing, fire the mayors, his decision being final, and the Secretary of Puerto Rico, one of the six department heads, could fire the municipal councilors. Vacancies in such municipal offices were filled by the Governor, with the advice and consent of the Executive Council.

The department heads—the Secretary, the Attorney General, the Treasurer, the Auditor, the Commissioner of the Interior, and the Commissioner of Education—as presidential appointees with their own Washington contacts, could make life miserable for the Governor. The distribution of power depended on the personalities involved and their mainland contacts. There were famous cases of Auditors and Attorneys General who tied up the Governor in knots. Although appointed, like the Governor, for a four-year term, the department heads, all with little knowledge of the island, tended to serve for a short time and move on to greener pastures. Resident Commissioner Degetau once spoke thus in Congress: "When you consider, Mr. Speaker, that these gentlemen are sent there to make laws for a country they do not know, for a people whose laws, customs, and language they do not know, and this for an average of seventeen months, you may imagine, Mr. Speaker, the probability of their doing well."[6]

Although the Foraker Act had described the functions of each department head in rather general terms, through the years the job descriptions took on a life of their own, which served to carve special fiefdoms for several departments, strengthened by the commissioners' double capacity as ministers and as members of the upper chamber of the legislature. The Auditor, for example, grabbed both pre-audit and post-audit functions and, to make matters worse, took it upon himself to determine the legality—never mind the Attorney General's opinion—and even the wisdom of legislative appropriations. The Attorney General, for his part, became a stern guardian of the sacred scriptures of the Foraker and later Jones acts and often invalidated proposals for legislation and executive actions. During the first half of this century the organic acts became, well beyond the scope of the letter, severe obstacles to government initiatives. Enterprising Governors like Rexford G. Tugwell would spend a good deal of energy trying to jump over the variety of bureaucratic hurdles set up by their supposedly subordinate executive colleagues.

The department heads were the subject of frequent criticism by the Federal party and its successors. The policy of Americanizing Puerto Rico as fast as possible, one of the major matters on which there was enthusiastic consensus among the Governor and the department heads, was singled out for special attack. The Commissioners of Education ordered all schoolchildren to start the school day by saluting the American flag, declaiming the Pledge of Allegiance, and singing the national anthem and other patriotic songs. The teachers, often in broken English, would lead the exercise while the children mouthed words that most did not understand. The teaching in English of the whole public school curriculum started as soon as teachers became available. The situation was deeply resented by most segments of the population. It was not until the end of the forties, when Puerto Ricans took firm control of the education department and most public offices, that these practices were repealed and Spanish became again the language of instruction, while English was taught intensively as a second language.[7]

The stronger the criticism, the more convinced the American Governors became that Congress had gone as far as prudence allowed in drafting the Foraker Act. Just before resigning as Governor in September 1901, Allen wrote in his official report:

American occupation . . . found the island inhabited by a race of people of different language, religion, customs and habits, with no acquaintance practically with American methods. . . . The accepted form of territorial government would not, I fancy, serve the best purpose here, nor do I think it should be introduced here purely as administered in the United States until the people have been trained to a fuller appreciation of the duties and responsibilities of civil government. I feel, as the result of one year's close study, on the spot, of all the conditions surrounding the problem, that Congress went as far as it could safely venture in the form of government already existing in the island. . . . And I therefore feel that a departure from the present general form, except such minor modifications as experience will show from time to time to be wise and necessary, would be a grave mistake, and likely to be attended with considerable annoyance and anxiety.[8]

Allen's successor, William H. Hunt, a politician and later judge from Montana, echoed his feelings. "The organic act has furnished an admirable form of government for the island," he wrote. "Through its provisions the United States has brought liberty, self-government, and prosperity to a million people."[9] Finding that the Puerto Ricans disagreed, as even the republicanos clamored for at least the traditional territorial form of government, he later wrote to Washington: "It is probable that a majority of the people want Territorial government. But those of us who have participated in affairs for several years unanimously believe that the present form of government should not be changed now. It is liberal in its extension of political autonomy and most generous in its financial benefits. . . . It would be a serious error to move faster than experience warrants, and to yield to their immediate political aspirations would be to imperil their ultimate progress."[10]

The various elements of what had emerged as the United States policy toward Puerto Rico were thus strengthened during this period: the conviction that the few self-governing powers that had been temporarily extended through the Foraker Act were enough for the time being; that greater self-governing powers should be extended very gradually, if at all, as Puerto Rico's education in the democratic way of life should warrant; and that Americanization was essential to such an educational process.

The legislature was controlled by the Governor and the American majority in the Executive Council. The bills presented in the lower house or by the Puerto Rican minority in the Council had little chance of success, as a rule, unless limited to matters of relatively small consequence. The bulk of the legislation originated in the departments and the Governor's office. After a few years as leader of the House, Muñoz Rivera said, "the House of Delegates, the sole body that legitimately represents the country, performs useless work, its initiatives crashing against the perpetual wall of an Executive Council composed of six Continental Americans and five Americanized Puerto Ricans appointed by the President of the United States."[11]

Republican control of the House from 1900 to 1904 allowed the government the means to substitute American laws for civil law institutions in many fields. Whole new codes were imported in haste from California, Montana, and Idaho, the members of the commission which advised such action hailing from such states or being particularly familiar with their laws. In little time Puerto Rico became, like Louisiana and Quebec, a mixed-law jurisdiction.[12] It was during this time that the basic laws governing the school system, the University of Puerto Rico, the municipalities, the police, the tax system and other cornerstones of government were enacted. Once approved, control of the governorship and the Executive Council made it impossible for Muñoz Rivera and his party, which would soon come to power, to alter what had already been done. Self-government did not go that far.

The President wisely left in place the Supreme Court basically as constituted during the military regime, appointing only one American to one of the posts and a little later another, while keeping a majority of right-thinking Puerto Ricans. However, the American judges soon took the lead. As they were most familiar with American law, such matters were normally left to them, and questions of civil law soon came under their control, too—cases which they interpreted in the light of Anglo-American doctrine and practice. Law was the area of Puerto Rican life first Americanized to the fullest degree, as happened at the same time in the Philippines.

The United States District Court provided by the Foraker Act soon became again a privileged forum for Americans, as even resident Americans, contrary to the situation in the states, had access to it for diversity of citizenship reasons. Like his American colleagues on the Supreme Court of Puerto Rico, Judge William H. Holt tended to interpret civil law texts in the light of the common law. He and several of his successors also thought it proper to declare certain local statutes inapplicable in federal court and to rule that some were even contrary to the public interest. The federal court became for many years a powerful force in the drive toward cultural assimilation.

The municipalities as conceived by the Foraker Act were not strong, and were further weakened by a 1902 law that allowed a great degree of intervention in municipal affairs by the central government.

The Resident Commissioner did not have access to the U.S. House of Representatives initially. On June 28, 1902, an amendment to the House rules finally allowed him to appear on the floor and address the body. Two years later an amendment to the rules permitted him to serve as a committee member, with no vote. The Resident Commissioner cut a sorry figure during those early years. None of Federico Degetau's bills were ever approved, as also happened to his successors, Tulio Larrínaga and Luis Muñoz Rivera; most were not even reported out of committee.

The Puerto Rican and Philippine question—the possibility of establishing an American empire—which occupied center stage briefly in 1900, soon ceased being of popular or even party interest. In their 1904 platform the Democrats favored independence for the Philippines and territorial government for Puerto Rico, coming out routinely against "colonial exploitation." The Republicans simply stated in their platform: "We have organized the government of Porto Rico and its people now enjoy peace, freedom, order and prosperity." In his 1902 and 1903 annual messages to Congress, President Theodore Roosevelt spoke briefly of the Philippines—"We have not gone too far in granting these rights of liberty and self-government, but we have certainly gone to the limit that in the interests of the Philippine people themselves it was wise or just to go"—but had no words for Puerto Rico.[13]

Attention to Puerto Rican affairs were thus left in the hands of an obscure bureau in the Department of War, the Bureau of Insular Affairs, which came to amass considerable power over the Governor and other federal officials in Puerto Rico. Puerto Rico lingered for years in the bureaucratic depths of the War Department and, from 1933 to 1952, the Department of the Interior.

In February 1901 Luis Muñoz Rivera resigned as president of the Federal party and again sailed for New York, where he stayed for three years. Working in journalism, he kept in close touch with his political allies in Puerto Rico, having always meant to return when he thought that conditions for challenging Barbosa again were better. In 1902 the Federal party did participate in the elections, after having changed its name to the Federal American party in an apparent effort to shed its reputation as an anti-American organization. It was badly beaten by the statehooders, who garnered 68 percent of the vote and elected twenty-five of the thirty-five members of the House of Delegates.

In January 1904 Muñoz Rivera returned to Puerto Rico. Together with José de Diego (1866–1918), a noted poet, orator, attorney, and fierce fighter for in-

dependence, and others of various persuasions, he was working toward the creation of a new party. He was using as strong a language as ever. In a manifesto to
the country he stated: "You are nothing but slaves. You are ruled by a President
that is elected without your vote. A Council appointed at the whim of the President legislates for you. You do not even effectively intervene in the approval of
the taxes that weigh upon you. Such a shame would not be tolerated by . . . even
the Patagonian tribes; such slavery would be undeserved if you manfully attempt to reject it, but it shall degrade you if you sheepishly accept it."[14]

In February 1904 the old Federal party was abolished and the new party,
named the Union party to signal its openness to all shades of opinion on the status issue, was established. The platform was not well received by American officialdom. It demanded full self-government for Puerto Rico and in its famous
fifth plank stated that such self-government could be achieved by either admitting Puerto Rico to the American Union as a state, equal with others, or by declaring Puerto Rico to be an independent nation under a United States protectorate.

This was the first time that independence was officially mentioned by a
Puerto Rican political party. Governor Hunt hastened to explain to hurt and
puzzled officials in Washington:

> I think there is some notion in the minds of a very few prominent Feder-
> als [he stuck to the old name] that Porto Rico may obtain a form of inde-
> pendence analogous to that achieved by Cuba. But this notion is clearly
> confined to a few older men [Muñoz Rivera was all of forty-four and De
> Diego thirty-eight at the time] who were in active politics under the
> Spanish dominion, and who have little or no acquaintance with the new
> National power, and who cannot realize that in the full development of
> the future every important consideration of political and material good
> for the future demands that the common interest of the people shall best
> be promoted by the encouragement of a patriotic spirit of national pride
> in the United States.[15]

The "few older men" dismissed by Hunt won the 1904 elections decisively
and obtained control of the House by a margin of 25–10. From then on the
Unionists and their successors would win every election held in Puerto Rico for
nearly three decades. From 1907 to 1915 the republicanos failed to elect a single member to the House. The leader of the statehood movement, Barbosa, was
given refuge in the Executive Council.

It is important to understand the alignment of forces and the complex political language and apparently mystifying postures common to most of the Unionist leaders, aimed at satisfying widely different sectors of their electorate. The failure to understand those facts has frequently been responsible for misreadings of some of the key events of the period that led to approval of the Jones Act.

Barbosa and other Republican leaders seemed more forthright than their opponents. Their clearly stated goal was, eventually, statehood. Anything that in their minds facilitated that goal had their backing: the attainment of American citizenship, the acquisition of a delegate in Congress, the achievement of the traditional form of territorial government. The Americanization policy was seen as a necessary process that would bring Puerto Ricans closer to statehood. The step-by-step process toward self-government was part of the ordained ceremony of education in the ways of democracy. This set of Republican beliefs carried a good dividend: official favor. Their talk was music to official ears. The promise of statehood was, of course, sheer nonsense at the time and was never made, but letting the republicanos dream about it did no harm and these were indeed loyal, grateful, supportive, right-thinking subjects, eager to learn and deserving of encouragement in their uphill struggles against their churlish opponents. Even out of power their influence in government circles, in both San Juan and Washington, was normally much greater than that of the unionistas.

The fervent backing of the American government officials had its downside. The republicanos initially commanded the allegiance of the vast majority which expected much from the fact of annexation. After garnering up to 68 percent of the popular vote, the republicanos, however, were repeatedly rebuffed, election after election, after the glow of General Miles's promises had worn off. They failed to represent the growing feeling of discontent.[16] They criticized on occasion the Foraker regime, which was generally resented, but in a low, almost inaudible tone. They appeared to sound too much like the incondicionales of a few years before, supporters of an unpopular regime, no matter what. The unionistas were not so deserving themselves, as they were quite close to the criollo sugar interests and, with their obsession with status matters, failed to represent many of the dispossessed. Instead they supported the established social and economic order and reaped the benefits of the republicanos' fall from power.

If the republicanos perfected at the time the uses of mellowspeak, the unionistas spoke in riddles, if not double-talk. It is a serious historical mistake always to take unionist official documents and speeches at face value. Their speech had on occasion several levels of meaning. As we have seen, the unionistas came out for statehood as one possible status option, which allowed them to broaden their base somewhat and at very little cost, for they knew full well that statehood, at least for a very long time, was then out of the question. The evidence is abundant that to some, like De Diego, Muñoz Rivera, and the bulk of the unionista leadership, statehood was not really acceptable in any shape or form, then or at any time. American citizenship is another example where the unionistas appeared to blow hot and cold on an issue. Even De Diego was for it at one time, although he was the recognized leader of the powerful pro-independence faction of the Unionist party. Muñoz Rivera swung back and forth on the question, although privately, and on many public occasions, he was strongly against the grant of American citizenship.

There was good reason for this apparent ambivalence. In the first place, sharing the citizenship of the metropolitan country was not seen as an obstacle to full autonomy or independence, but as a badge of equality. After all, Puerto Ricans had been Spanish citizens for a long time. The failure of the Foraker Act to extend American citizenship to the island or at least to recognize the existence of a Puerto Rican citizenship with a fuller dimension was considered a slight. Second, the granting of American citizenship meant to the bulk of the people, besides a sign of respect, a promise of larger freedoms. The issue really cut through traditional party lines. It did not make much political sense to leave all of the credit to the republicanos. Third, and here enters the ingredient of calculated ambivalence, most of the unionista leaders deeply feared that Puerto Ricans' receiving American citizenship would facilitate cultural assimilation. While at times requesting such a grant, the unionistas diligently fought it at key moments. At no time did Muñoz Rivera endorse the idea in Congress. His bills on a new organic act for Puerto Rico never included American citizenship as a request of the majority party.

In this respect it is important to understand the Muñoz Rivera public persona, a mixture of dreamer and pragmatist. He was a firm believer in independence for Puerto Rico and as such had De Diego's and the people's respect, but he was also convinced that the United States would not grant independence to Puerto Rico in his lifetime. He saw himself as condemned to try, at the most, to obtain more self-government for his people. He was also acutely conscious of his position as head of the Unionist party. The party had a powerful independence faction, but also a very vocal autonomist wing and a sprinkling of conservatives. Muñoz Rivera saw it as his duty to keep the different strains together for as long as possible. Occasional measured ambiguity and oscillation between differing stands, as well as the employment of aesopic language, were nothing new to him.

In early 1905 the Unionist party requested from Congress a plebiscite for Puerto Rico to express its status choice. Until the United States acknowledged Puerto Rico's right to determine its preferred status, the party asked for greater participation of the island in its government; an elected Executive Council or upper chamber; the appointment of the heads of departments by the Governor, with the advice and consent of the Council; the repeal of the provision granting Congress the right to annul Puerto Rican laws; and the limitation of the jurisdiction of the federal court. Discreet silence was kept as to the possible grant of American citizenship, as had been the case with the 1904 party platform. In his 1905 message to Congress, President Roosevelt came out, however, against any basic changes to the Foraker Act, except for the extension of American citizenship to Puerto Ricans. He said: "The present form of government in Porto Rico, which provides for the appointment by the President of the members of the Executive Council or upper house of the legislature, has proved satisfactory and has inspired confidence in property owners and investors. I do not deem it advisable at the present time to change this form in any material feature. The problems of the island are industrial and commercial rather than political."[17]

The grant of American citizenship to Puerto Ricans was by no means popular in Congress at that time, as the story of the Foraker Act indicates, but the idea had several things going for it. It meant, first, that the United States had no intention to divest itself of Puerto Rico at any time, a declaration that would greatly embarrass the Democrats and their stand against the idea of an American empire; second, it was a sharp rebuff to the Unionist talk about possible independence; third, it was a natural complement to the policy of Americanizing the island; and, finally, it fit well the honorable egalitarian tradition of the country.

Muñoz Rivera strongly criticized the President's refusal to consider any of the political reform proposals presented to him by the Unionist party, as well as the grant of American citizenship as a substitute to needed reforms.[18] The central committee of the Unión did not endorse Muñoz's position on citizenship, but echoed his criticism of the President on the matter of the requested changes.

In 1906 Foraker and others filed bills to grant American citizenship to Puerto Ricans in accord with the President's recommendation. So did the Resident Commissioner elected on the Unionist ticket. Some were reported out favorably, but Congress did not act on them.

In 1907 and 1908 Roosevelt reiterated his endorsement of American citizenship for Puerto Rico. Congress did not act on any of the President's recommendations concerning citizenship nor on the reforms requested by the majority party in Puerto Rico.

The relations of the majority party with the Governor, the Executive Council, and official Washington deteriorated further in 1909 until an impasse was reached. In March of that year a number of Unionist young Turks, unhappy with Muñoz Rivera's ambivalence, were elected to the House of Delegates. They lost no time in proposing that the House express its disapproval of the Foraker Act by refusing to legislate until Congress recognized Puerto Rico's right to self-government. Muñoz Rivera successfully opposed the motion, but the impasse was soon to occur for less respectable reasons.

Petty disputes over patronage were even more common then than today. The unionistas were irked at the fact that the Governor did not always appoint their first choice for municipal judgeships. A bill to deprive the Governor of his power of appointment and vest it instead in the municipal councils was approved by the House and understandably held in abeyance by the Executive Council. To exert pressure upon the Council the House then ill-advisedly passed a budget drastically cutting the salaries of key officials, in some cases by as much as 90 percent, and eliminating certain posts. The Executive Council naturally refused to adopt such a budget, and the House then resolved to recess in March 1909, leaving the island without a budget for the next fiscal year.

President William Howard Taft, who had served as High Commissioner to the Philippines and knew a lot about colonial problems, granted an interview to Muñoz Rivera and other House envoys on the issue, promised to send a representative to investigate the House's complaint, and urged them, to no avail, to approve the budget.

By May, his patience exhausted, Taft sent a message to Congress proposing that should the appropriations necessary for the support of the government not be made in a given year, the sums appropriated in the last appropriation bill would be deemed to be enacted. (Provisions to that effect were part of the organic laws of Hawaii and the Philippines.) In his message the President severely chided the House leadership and stated that what had happened was simply an indication that the United States had gone too far in granting self-governing powers to Puerto Rico.[19] Shortly thereafter the Foraker Act was amended as proposed by the President.[20] The memory of the 1909 impasse widened the breach between the unionistas and Washington and was to color the nature of the reforms soon to be considered.

In the 1910 elections the unionistas again won by a landslide. Muñoz

Rivera, although he still had not learned English, was elected Resident Commissioner. In his first speech to Congress he restated his old policy as to citizenship, saying that Puerto Ricans "would not feel satisfied with American citizenship if American justice is not done them. . . . Puerto Ricans will feel humiliated until you have abolished in the island a colonial system under which the government is not founded upon the will of the governed." He added:

> We never were, or are now, radical in our demands of reform. The Filipinos are struggling for absolute independence; the Puerto Ricans are contending for self-government. . . .
>
> The Puerto Ricans, as all men on earth, love national independence. To all solutions they prefer that which would make them an independent and sovereign nation. But they are an intelligent people; they are thoroughly acquainted with the obstacles that would bar the success of their paramount ideal. Actuated by their patriotism, they are at present moved to fight for practical reforms that may allow them to insure their predominance in the affairs of their country. Besides, we have faith in the American people solving our insular problems promptly and generously. But do not let this faith be lost lest all Puerto Ricans would ask you to do by them as you did by the Cubans, under identical conditions, that the island be delivered to her sons.[21]

In his 1912 message to Congress, his last, President Taft made clear, contrary to assertions by the local republicanos, that the grant of American citizenship, as proposed by the administration, should be entirely divorced from any thought of statehood and expressed his views as to what he thought the ultimate relationship between the United States and Puerto Rico should be:

> I believe that the demand for citizenship is just, and that it is amply earned by sustained loyalty on the part of the inhabitants of the island. But it should be remembered that the demand must be, in the minds of most Porto Ricans is, entirely dissociated from any thought of statehood. I believe that no substantial public opinion in the United States or in Puerto Rico contemplates statehood for the island as the ultimate form of relation between us. I believe that the aim to be striven for is the fullest possible allowance of legal and fiscal self-government, with American citizenship as the bond between us; in other words, a relationship analogous to the present relationship between Great Britain and such self-governing colonies as Canada and Australia. This would conduce to

the fullest and most self-sustaining development of Porto Rico, while at the same time it would grant her the economic and political benefits of being under the American flag.[22]

President Taft's vision of the future became part of the autonomista creed. Opposition to independence was also expressed by Washington officials. In the House report on the Jones citizenship bill, approved on March 12, 1912, it was stated that the bill served the purpose of reaffirming the fact that Puerto Rico "has become permanent territory of the United States," thus discouraging any desire for independence.[23] The Secretary of War commented: "The political situation in Porto Rico has been further complicated by the development in the last few years of a demand for independence of the island under some sort of protection or tutelage of the United States. This demand represents the idea of but a few people. I believe it is idle to consider or to discuss any future for the people of Porto Rico as separated from the United States."[24]

Official discouragement of independence and the link being made between American citizenship and the exclusion of independence as a political possibility for Puerto Rico increased local agitation, and the first parties for the attainment of independence were formed, attracting several prominent unionistas like Matienzo Cintrón, Luis Lloréns Torres, and Manuel Zeno Gandía. The head of the independence faction within the Unión, José de Diego, did not bolt, but in 1913 eliminated statehood in the party platform as one of the acceptable possibilities for attaining self-government, leaving independence as the sole ultimate aim.

In 1913 the Unión's platform called for much wider reforms, until independence could be achieved. It asked for a wholly elected legislature; the appointment by the Governor of all department heads, with the advice and consent of the insular senate; the elimination of the federal court; the grant of its jurisdiction to the Supreme Court of Puerto Rico; the appointment of at least three Puerto Ricans to that Supreme Court; the limitation of the jurisdiction of the United States Supreme Court to the review of federal issues decided by the Supreme Court of Puerto Rico; the right to enter into commercial treaties; and the limitation of the power of Congress to legislate for Puerto Rico on internal matters. American citizenship for Puerto Ricans, then or at any time in the future, was rejected, and the recognition of Puerto Rican citizenship was instead demanded.[25] A year later the Unión would mute its call for independence and revert to its traditional autonomista stance.[26]

The events described in this chapter, especially the pugnacity of the majority party, the confrontational style of its leaders, and the growth of support for independence, hardened the main features of the colonial policy that had taken shape in earlier years. Americans' resolve to hold on to Puerto Rico for an indefinite time was strengthened. Efforts at Americanization increased in the belief that, as acquaintance with American institutions and mores grew, tensions would recede. Bipartisan support in Washington for American citizenship gained momentum as a way to emphasize the permanency of the United States presence in Puerto Rico and to discourage sentiment for independence. The ruling unionistas' continuous criticism of United States policy and their stance during the 1909 impasse also contributed to convincing Washington that it should not go too far at the time in granting Puerto Rico greater powers of self-government.

The din of the status debate of these years did not drown the beat of other drums, which grew louder with time. Largely allied with the propertied classes, the traditional political parties were not adequately representing large sectors of the population. The struggling workers, for example, were powerless before the mighty American sugar companies that were gobbling up the land. Their leader, Iglesias, had been long persecuted by both the Spanish and the American governments in Puerto Rico. In October 1899 he had founded a workers' party, the Partido Obrero, but official resistance had kept the party from participating in the elections held in 1899, 1900, and 1902. In 1904 Iglesias had campaigned for the unionistas. By 1915, under the leadership of Iglesias and others, the workers founded their own party, the Partido Socialista, which would gather considerable force over time.[27] Believers in independence also came to feel uncomfortable within the Unión, laying the basis for the founding in 1922 of the Nationalist party. Shortly after the deaths of Muñoz Rivera, De Diego, and Barbosa, the traditional parties would break down completely in the early twenties.

In all, life under the Foraker Act bred great unhappiness, both as to the internal social and economic conditions of the island and its relationship to the United States. The wall of incomprehension between the United States and Puerto Rico thickened during the Foraker years. Puerto Ricans could not understand why a country with such a glorious tradition in the defense of liberty would insist on treating Puerto Rico as a colony for an indefinite period of time. Official Washington could not comprehend what was seen as the ingratitude of a good part of the Puerto Rican people at being schooled in the ways of democracy while being benignly governed. Underneath there were large reserves of good will on both sides, but many years would elapse before those deposits could be tapped.

6

The Jones Act

In addition to the events described in the past four chapters and the overriding policy which emerged from them, several institutions and personalities influenced the nature of the second organic act for Puerto Rico, the Jones Act.

After 1900, when the legality and morality of establishing an American empire ceased to occupy center stage, the Democratic party began losing interest in the colonies. For a time it routinely accused the Republican party of pursuing imperialist ends, but soon the Republicans' positions became national policy. In its platforms from 1904 to 1912, the Democratic party favored independence for the Philippines. As regards Puerto Rico, in 1904 and 1908 the Democrats favored territorial government without further definition, but in the critical year of 1912, when victory seemed to be in the air, the party refrained from mentioning Puerto Rico at all. At no time did the Democrats refer to the possibility of extending American citizenship to the island's residents.

When Woodrow Wilson became President in 1913, the Democratic party had accordingly no set policy concerning the eventual fate of the island, except that by then the decision to hold on to Puerto Rico was generally accepted. President Wilson had long held that Puerto Rico and the Philippines should be kept as possessions of the United States until they became ready for independence or autonomy. He did not believe that territorial government, leading to eventual statehood, was suited to either of them.[1] Wilson, who since the Spanish-American War had not favored acquisition of the Philippines, believed in training the islands' inhabitants for independence. According to Wilson's statement, Puerto Rico should eventually become an autonomous body politic. The relation of the United States to both should in the meantime resemble a trusteeship.[2] Although through the Jones years Wilson was honing his self-determination rhetoric, at no time did he extend his policies in that respect to Puerto Rico.

As concerns the Philippines, the liberal element in Congress and the ad-

ministration believed that a specific term should be set for Philippine independence, while the moderates supported an indefinite term. Wilson sided with the
moderates, and the second organic act for the Philippines, passed in 1916 (a year
before the approval of the Jones Act for Puerto Rico), contained a promise for
independence sometime in the unspecified future. As respects Puerto Rico, Wilson believed in the need for reforming its regime, but not to the extent sought
by the Unión, the majority party on the island. He thought that American citizenship should be extended to Puerto Ricans, but that the process of increasing
their participation in insular affairs should be gradual and cautious. In that sense
Wilson's view did not differ substantially from those held by Roosevelt and Taft.

Wilson did push from the start, however, for a prudent increase of Puerto
Rican participation in their government. During the first year of his presidency
he decided to grant Puerto Ricans a majority in the Executive Council, a largely
symbolic step, as the Presidential appointees to the Council were carefully chosen with an eye to their support of official policy, but still an advance. Wilson
also involved himself to a greater degree than his predecessors in lobbying for
approval of the Jones Act. In the view of General McIntyre, director of the Bureau of Insular Affairs and a former advisor to one of the military governors, the
Jones Act would not have been passed without active intervention by the President.[3]

As chairman of the House Insular Affairs Committee, Democrat William
Atkinson Jones, born in 1849 in Virginia, played a crucial role in shaping the second organic acts for Puerto Rico and the Philippines. He had been, while in the
minority, quite unhappy with earlier efforts at reform. He favored the grant of
American citizenship to Puerto Ricans, but by a process of collective naturalization, and he did not share the official view that there was little wrong with the
Foraker Act.

In 1912 Jones filed a bill, reintroduced in 1914, to provide a civil government for Puerto Rico on which no hearings were held, but which is of great value
for the history of the second organic act.[4] It anticipated key features of later bills.
Several organizations, notably the Bureau of Insular Affairs, and individuals including Arthur Yager, Luis Muñoz Rivera, and Santiago Iglesias also played key
roles in the events leading up to the passage of the Jones Act.

The Bureau of Insular Affairs at the Department of War traditionally influenced the views of the President and the Secretary of War on Puerto Rican
and Philippine matters and played an important role in preparing the ground
for the Jones Act. Both Roosevelt and Taft relied heavily on the bureau's supposed expertise in the field. The bureau, a truer expert in bureaucratic maneu-

vering, was able to peddle effectively its ideas on insular policy, which were of
an essentially conservative cast. The discrete power of the bureau explains in
large measure why in the process of drafting the organic acts for Puerto Rico the
executive branch of the government, even under Wilson, normally took a more
restrictive view than Congress as to the measure of self-government that should
be granted.

Puerto Rico had by then been enjoying universal male suffrage since 1904.
The bureau thought that the results had been dismal, given the support received
by the unionistas, and favored the return to limiting voting rights to men of
property or at least men who could read and write. The two branches of the legislature could be made elective, but only if the Governor was given absolute veto
power and membership in the legislature was restricted to propertied men. The
powers of the legislature would also be reduced by the establishment of a public service commission, which would control the issuance of licenses and fran-
chises to public service companies, and the creation of more executive departments. As an additional precaution, Congress should retain its power to annul
any insular law at any time.

The bureau agreed with the local suggestion that the department heads be
appointed by the Governor, with the advice and consent of the Senate, but
wanted to keep two appointments in the hands of the President and the Secretary of War, which in practice meant the bureau itself. The bureau also favored
the abolishment of the federal court, the presence of which in Puerto Rico was
sorely resented, and it advocated the grant of its jurisdiction to the insular
Supreme Court, as was done in the case of the Philippines. It believed, however,
that its decisions should be reviewed initially by a circuit court, instead of directly by the United States Supreme Court.

The measure most heartily endorsed by the bureau was the extension of
American citizenship, principally as a form of discouraging any thought of eventual independence. Since Governor Colton's time, during the Taft presidency,
the grant of American citizenship was also seen as indispensable to the survival
of the pro-statehood republicanos as a party.[5] The bureau, however, was most
clear in stressing that no promise of eventual statehood should thereby be im-
plied. The bureau's positions dictated the language of several provisions of the
Jones Act.

Another important figure during this time was Arthur Yager, Wilson's
classmate at Princeton and professor of history and economics in Kentucky,
where he was born. Yager was Governor of Puerto Rico from late 1913 until the
end of Democratic rule in 1921. To Yager, the concession of American citizen-

ship was indispensable to stopping the independence movement. He did not agree, however, with the punitive views of Jones and the War Department that those who did not choose to become American citizens should be ineligible to hold public office. The Governor also favored a wholly elected Senate, but subject to several conditions: the Governor being empowered to veto without recourse any insular law; the appointment by the Governor of four of the six government secretaries; the establishment of a Public Service Commission; the continuation of the federal court; and, as in the Philippines, the election of two Resident Commissioners (a measure proposed by Muñoz Rivera). Yager agreed with the Bureau of Insular Affairs that the right to suffrage should be limited, which in his estimate would cut the electorate by 70 percent.[6]

From 1912 until his death on November 15, 1916, Muñoz Rivera tried to liberalize the Jones bills and the measures backed by the Bureau of Insular Affairs. It was not until 1916 that he became convinced that the chances of improving the proposed legislation were few. In a letter to Yager, bureau director General McIntyre stated: "I think he [Muñoz Rivera] is convinced that it is necessary that the bill pass and believes that we will not be able to get so good a bill from his point of view hereafter."[7]

Muñoz Rivera had filed his own bill on February 27, 1914.[8] His demands were much more modest than those endorsed by his party in the 1913 platform. American citizenship would not be extended to the island. Further, the Senate would be a wholly elected body, composed of nineteen members, two from each of the seven electoral districts and five elected at-large, all serving for a term of four years (proposals which became part of the Jones Act). As a conciliatory gesture in his discussions with the bureau and other officials, Muñoz Rivera accepted the proposed limitations to the right to suffrage, although later he favored universal suffrage. The legislature would be able to approve legislation over the Governor's veto, but Congress would retain its power to annul any insular law.

According to Muñoz Rivera's bill, the Governor would appoint, with the advice and consent of the insular Senate, all government secretaries. All had to be residents of Puerto Rico for at least two years. All judges, including the members of the Supreme Court of Puerto Rico, would be appointed by the Governor with the advice and consent of the Senate. Appeals from the decisions of the Supreme Court would continue to go to the United States Supreme Court. The federal court would be abolished. Puerto Rican affairs would be in the charge of the State Department. Puerto Rico would elect two Resident Commissioners.

As can be seen, the leader of the unionistas had considerably toned down his demands. Muñoz Rivera privately admitted that the granting of American citizenship was by then inevitable.[9] From 1913 to 1915 Muñoz Rivera also labored mightily to prevent his party from choosing independence as its immediate goal. In a 1913 letter he wrote to a friend: "I believe that should we declare for independence we shall lose strength in our battle for home rule and would seriously harm our country." In the same letter he expressed his conviction that the United States would not grant Puerto Rico independence.[10] Luis Muñoz Rivera died on November 15, 1916, before the final chapter on the Jones Act was written.

In the 1914 general elections in Puerto Rico the Republican party finally made a strong showing, after being the majority party from 1900 to 1904, electing sixteen delegates to the Unión's nineteen, and polling a little over 40 percent of the vote. In March 1915, the two parties agreed jointly to petition Congress for a series of reforms, to be included in the legislation then under consideration. The main demands were the extension to Puerto Rico of most of the provisions of the Bill of Rights of the United States Constitution; a wholly elected legislature; power to legislate on all local matters; the retention of the power to override the Governor's veto by a resolution of two-thirds of the legislature; the continued inapplicability of the internal revenue laws of the United States; the appointment by the Governor of all the government secretaries, with the advice and consent of the insular Senate; the limitation of public offices to Puerto Rican residents; and the abolition of the federal court (which was generally seen at the time as unduly interfering with local legislation and jurisprudence), its jurisdiction to be absorbed by the Supreme Court of Puerto Rico.[11]

Even this remarkable document, in which the two continuously warring parties pleaded for more fundamental changes to the Foraker Act than were then considered, failed to move Congress. Resentment against the federal court, even by the pro-statehood party, was so great that a year later, on April 18, 1916, the House of Delegates unanimously requested again its abolition.[12] A few weeks before approval of the Jones Act in February 1917 the House of Delegates repeated the request, this time suggesting that at least federal jurisdiction should be curtailed.[13]

Throughout this period the local Republican party favored many reforms similar to those sponsored by the Unión, culminating in the joint request of 1915 and the House resolutions already discussed. The republicanos differed from the unionistas in seeking the immediate incorporation of the island as a step toward statehood and in pressing for American citizenship through a process of collective naturalization. They criticized with great firmness, however, the restrictive nature of the Jones bill, which in 1916 Barbosa still considered undemocratic, and decided to accept it only under condition that the grant of American citizenship not be delayed.[14]

Santiago Iglesias (1870–1939), a Spanish carpenter who migrated to Puerto Rico after spending some time in Cuba, was the most important labor leader in Puerto Rico until his death.[15] He was a close friend of Samuel Gompers, the president of the American Federation of Labor (AFL), for which he served as labor organizer, and greatly influenced the approval of several basic amendments to the Foraker Act. Iglesias was a staunch opponent of any limitation to the right to suffrage and to the requirement of owning property as a condition for serving in the legislature. He favored statehood for Puerto Ricans, as did the AFL under Gompers, but thought that political leaders in Puerto Rico were obsessed with the status issue and fought mainly instead for inclusion of the law mandating a maximum eight-hour working day in the proposed bill of rights and other measures favorable to labor. He endorsed American citizenship because of the benefits that it could bring to the cause of labor. Among the political leaders of the time Iglesias is now considered the most liberal and progressive, at least in social and economic matters.

The first bill filed by Jones as Chairman of the House Committee on Insular Affairs followed the broad outline of his 1912 bill.[16] This 1914 bill foreshadowed most of the basic features of the Jones Act. John D. Shafroth, an influential Democrat from Colorado and chairman of the Senate Committee on Pacific Islands and Porto Rico, filed a bill on his own.[17] Yager and the Bureau of Insular Affairs had influenced the drafting of this bill and generally preferred it to the others. The Shafroth bill offered American citizenship to Puerto Ricans, but by the process of individual naturalization. It contained no punitive provisions aimed at those who did not choose to become American citizens. Individual naturalization was considered as a way to refute the Unionist charge that American citizenship was being forced upon Puerto Rico. The Bureau initially favored this method, but later endorsed Jones's proposal for collective naturalization.

The republicanos opposed both the Jones and Shafroth bills throughout the whole process of enactment of the second organic act, favoring another proposal before the Shafroth committee, the Saulsbury bill, which incorporated Puerto Rico to the United States as an implicit step toward statehood but did not have the slightest chance of approval.[18] At no time had McKinley, Roosevelt, Taft, or any appreciable group of Congressmen endorsed the idea of incorporation.

The Senate held hearings in 1914 on the Shafroth bill. Governor Yager backed it, preferring the bill's individual naturalization process, and he vigorously warned against endorsement of the collective naturalization method to be employed by Jones. "It is highly important at the present time," Yager stated, "that Congress should not even appear to force American citizenship upon anyone in Puerto Rico, and any effort to do so will create division and strife in the island."[19] The Governor's advice would go unheeded.

Muñoz Rivera opposed the bill. "The immense majority of my constituents," he said, "aspire to their national independence as an ultimate solution of its local problem."[20] As to the grant of American citizenship, he pleaded for postponement of action: "The majority of Puerto Ricans think that the conferring of American citizenship in any form whatever would interfere with the future declaration of the status of the inhabitants of the island, and I pray Congress to postpone any legislation on this point for a period of a few years so that we may demonstrate our capacity for self-government and Congress may fix a definite solution for the future."[21] The Resident Commissioner also objected to the Governor's absolute veto, the continuation of Congressional power to annul local legislation, and several other provisions.

The Secretary of War favored the individual naturalization method, but differed from Yager in wanting to retain the punitive provisions for those who did not become naturalized. In his view, the United States should not encourage anti-American feelings by allowing part of the population to reject American citizenship.[22]

Although the Wilson administration thought that Jones could have obtained passage of his bill in 1914 or 1915, his priority at the time was the Philippine bill, finally approved in 1916.

In early 1916 Jones and Shafroth reintroduced their bills.[23] Although Muñoz Rivera and Jones did not enjoy a close working relationship, Jones amended the provision concerning the Governor's veto at Muñoz Rivera's suggestion. This would enable the legislature to approve a measure over the Governor's veto by a two-thirds vote, in which case the bill would be referred to the President for his approval or rejection within ninety days, a provision which was part of the Philippine bill. This became part of the final Puerto Rican act. Muñoz Rivera was also asked to choose between the Commissioner of Education and the Treasurer as the second department head to be appointed by the President (the Attorney General was the first). According to Luis Muñoz Marín, his father unfortunately chose local control of the treasury instead of taking over educational policy. The President would continue to appoint the Attorney General and the Commissioner of Education until Muñoz Marín became the first elected Governor of Puerto Rico in 1949.

The suffrage limitations wanted by the Governor and the Bureau of Insular Affairs remained in the Jones bill, and the issue was the subject of the most debate. Jones, sensing great opposition to the bill by many who doubted the capacity of the Puerto Rican people to govern themselves, came to see the proposed limitations on the right to vote as essential in order to convince enough Congressmen that there was little danger in granting Puerto Rico an elective Senate.[24] The House of Representatives finally approved the bill on May 23, 1916.

The Senate Committee then took up consideration of the Jones bill and reported it out with several amendments. The Senate committee disagreed with the provision, added by Jones, which would forever ban the naturalization of those who should decide not to accept American citizenship initially. As to suffrage, the committee believed that this right should be restricted, but that those who had acquired the right to vote before enactment of the new organic act should be allowed to continue to vote for ten years.[25] After the bill left the committee Shafroth tried for seven months to bring the bill to the floor. Such was the lack of interest in the measure, however, that debate did not start until January 30, 1917, close to the end of the session.

Only about a dozen Senators showed any interest in the debates. Shafroth himself was not very well briefed on aspects of the bill and, when asked, was not able to say that Puerto Rico had been enjoying male universal suffrage for quite some time. Senator Warren G. Harding from Ohio, as well as several colleagues, thought that the bill went too far in granting Puerto Rico self-governing powers that, in their opinion, no state or territory had ever had.[26] Senator Fall from New Mexico, a former Secretary of the Interior (New Mexico had been admitted to the Union only five years before), was against giving the people of Puerto Rico the right to vote, universal or limited, and against the concession of American citizenship. He thus explained his position to the Senate: "The trouble with the great United States today is that we have among our numbers alien citizenship, not true American citizens. You say we are a melting pot for all the nations of the earth. Yes, sir; and we have had an overdose of it. We have not been able to digest it."[27] Senator Vardamann, from Mississippi, a member of the committee, confessed that "I really had rather they would not become citizens of the United States. I think we have enough of that element in the body politic already to menace the Nation with mongrelization."[28]

Senator Robert La Follette of Wisconsin insisted on an amendment to the effect that the provisions of local law concerning the qualifications of electors could not be changed unless the Legislative Assembly should so provide, a condition which in fact guaranteed the continuation of male universal suffrage. La Follette proposed further, and contrary to the administration's desires, that no property qualifications could be required of any voter. Shafroth tried to convince him to drop the amendment or soften his stance, but La Follette then proposed a tougher amendment, causing the time of debate to expire.

Three days later, and ten days before the end of the session, Shafroth was again able to bring the bill up for discussion. By then he had been forced, together with the administration, to accept La Follette's position and in that form was approved by the Senate. The conference committee also had to agree, as protracted debate on that issue in the House was generally thought to mean the death of the bill. Approval of the conference report was hurriedly obtained, and on March 2, 1917, the bill became law. A few weeks earlier President Wilson had appeared before Congress to ask for the declaration of war against Germany, and selective service laws soon followed. Years later, baseless charges would be leveled at the United States because of a supposed connection between the declaration of war and the approval of the Jones Act.

The Jones Act, in all, represented a modest step forward on the long road toward self-government. Puerto Rico was permitted to have an elective Senate, but subject to strong safeguards: the Governor's veto and the President's final say in the event that the Legislative Assembly was able to override the veto, and, for good measure, the right of Congress to annul any insular law at any time. The scope of local legislation, moreover, remained narrow. Under the territorial clause Congress could, and often did, legislate for Puerto Rico, something it could not constitutionally do for the states.

Participation in the appointment of some of the government secretaries was obtained through the insular Senate's confirmation power, but Puerto Ricans were not, in practice, appointed to those positions until many years later. Continued control of the governorship, the Department of Justice, the Department of Education, and the Office of the Auditor, all generally filled by nonresident Americans until the 1940s, assured Washington that executive policy was effectively kept out of Puerto Rican hands.

The judicial branch was also carefully maintained out of local reach. The President continued to appoint the justices of the Supreme Court and, instead of direct review by the Supreme Court of the United States, as under the Foraker Act, a right of appeal to the Court of Appeals for the First Circuit was established under the Jones Act, even as to matters of local law, which allowed for greater supervision.

The extreme caution displayed in extending even such a limited measure of self-government is a good indication of the strength of the policies developed in the earlier years. Unlike the Philippines, Puerto Rico was not being groomed for independence. Nor was it being prepared for statehood, like Hawaii. The Jones Act reaffirmed instead the decision to keep Puerto Rico as an increasingly Americanized colony, on the road to self-government, but always to be securely subject to the sovereignty of the United States.

American citizenship was conferred in a most inelegant way. Official Washington did not care about the appearance of coercion that permeated the whole process, for the collective naturalization method was imposed when individual naturalization, together with a larger measure of self-government, was acceptable to the Unión. The evidence, moreover, clearly pointed to the Puerto Rican people's deep regard for its association with the United States, irrespective of the constant shower of humiliating charges that they were unfit for self-government. American citizenship was to be received gratefully, no matter what.

The lingering prejudices of the times, and the dream of empire having begun to fade but its memory being still strong, obscured the vision of the policymakers. American citizenship was granted under the worst possible light and with little thought of what that momentous step could mean in terms of Puerto Rico's eventual status. Its effects would be completely contrary to what Washington intended. It exacerbated the feelings in favor of independence and, in spite of clear expressions to the contrary, it encouraged those who thought that statehood was Puerto Rico's allotted fate. The professed Washington ideal of a contented colony was a mirage. In the next decades the people's sense of unhappiness would grow, divisions would deepen, and the differences over the status problem would seem ever more intractable.

7

The Jones Blues

The start of the Jones era, from 1917 to 1932, was marked by increasing dissatisfaction of all the local parties with the existing regime and by massive indifference on the part of Washington to the local plight.

Key political figures of the preceding period died either just before or soon after passage of the Jones Act. Muñoz Rivera died in 1916, De Diego two years later, and Barbosa in 1921. Their deaths led to the transformation of the parties which they led. Within the Unión, the struggle between the autonomist and the independence factions intensified. The Republican party went through a similar process, the progressives fighting the unconditional wing. Both parties soon gave way to new, unstable alignments.

By 1924 the Unión, headed by Antonio R. Barceló, joined forces with a disgruntled group of republicanos (who had formed a separate party led by José Tous Soto), and together founded the Alianza. Another unlikely alliance was formed among the rest of the republicanos, the Partido Republicano Puro (under the leadership of Rafael Martínez Nadal), and Santiago Iglesias' Socialists, who together founded the Coalición in 1924. Both the Alianza and the Socialists eventually paid dearly for these moves. The Coalición gained power in 1932, but flew apart after the 1940 elections. The Alianza was dissolved in 1929, giving way in 1932 to the Partido Liberal Puertorriqueño, composed of the members of the old Unión. In 1922 a number of independentistas who had been members of the Unión deserted it, because of the removal of independence from its platform, and established the Partido Nacionalista, which in later years turned to violence.

One of the ostensible aims of the Jones Act, to help the cause of the faltering republicanos, failed. The Unión continued to win all the elections after 1917 until its dissolution, as did its successor, the Alianza. The Coalición won the elections in 1932, the first time that a party favoring statehood was in power since

1904. In 1940 the statehooders were again thrown out of power for another twenty-eight-year period.

After enactment of the second organic act, the Unión initially limited itself to ratifying its 1913 and 1915 platforms. The Republican party was more vocal in the call for more reforms. The program announced on May 14, 1917, called for, among other things: the power to override the Governor's veto; the appointment of all department heads by the Governor, with the advice and consent of the Senate; the abolition of the federal court; the elimination of the ban on foreign vessels shipping goods between Puerto Rico and the United States for a period of twenty years; and the election of the Governor by the people or by the Legislative Assembly. As its eventual goal, the party asked for statehood when three conditions were met: the illiteracy rate fell below 30 percent (this goal could easily be reached in less than ten years), Puerto Rico was economically able to afford it, and the people approved it in a referendum.

Full autonomy was the temporary goal on which the unionistas and the republicanos who comprised the Alianza were able to find common ground. By leaving to other generations the solution of the ultimate status of the island, the Alianza aimed to banish the status question from the elections and allow Puerto Rico to concentrate on its economic and social problems, a theme that would be taken up again by the Popular Democratic Party in 1940.

The Socialists emphasized primarily the social and economic problems of the island. Since 1919, while believing in statehood as the ultimate goal, Iglesias favored a number of autonomist reforms, such as the elective Governor and Puerto Rico's power to set its own tariffs and enter into commercial treaties. For Iglesias, anything that could improve the insular economy and bring Puerto Rico closer to the United States standard of living was good for the statehood cause. In this respect, the Socialist wing of the Coalición brought to the fight for statehood an element that was absent, then and now, from the philosophy of the traditional statehood parties, which have usually been against reforms that in any way differ from the treatment accorded the states.

Following the passage of the Jones Act, reforms began to be requested almost immediately after its approval.

Puerto Rican Governor Arthur Yager was worried that the extension by Congress of the selective service laws and the actual start of the draft in 1917, which happened before the expiration of the period set as a final date for refusing American citizenship, would affect the number of people that would desire to opt out. He wrote that "compulsory service, coming so soon after the enactment of the Jones bill, might bring on a campaign of misrepresentation as to the motives of the American Government in granting citizenship, and that the natural desire of many persons to escape the draft might lead [them] to renounce American citizenship."[1] His fears did not materialize. There was no such campaign, as indeed there was no such motive, contrary to what would be alleged by some many years later. Only 288 persons out of a population of well over one million refused the American citizenship conferred by the Jones Act.

The Unión decided to postpone all demands for liberalization of the Jones Act for as long as the First World War lasted, an action that its successor, the Popular Democratic Party, copied in the course of the Second World War. After the war ended in 1918, the Unión formally asked through the new Resident Commissioner, Félix Córdova Dávila, that, in accordance with the principle of self-determination, a plebiscite be held for the people of Puerto Rico to choose a status from among such alternatives as the Congress would be willing to grant (a petition that would be unsuccessfully renewed in 1945 and 1989–91).[2] At that time the republicanos adhered to Barbosa's thesis that the grant of American citizenship had actually turned Puerto Rico into an incorporated territory—a notion that the administration took pains to deny while the Jones Act was being considered.[3] They accordingly thought that to favor independence after the Jones Act constituted treason and that statehood was the only alternative open to the people of Puerto Rico. The Supreme Court of Puerto Rico surprisingly held in 1917, in spite of the legislative history to the contrary, that the island had indeed been so incorporated, a decision which was summarily reversed by the United States Supreme Court.[4] In 1919 the plebiscite proposal was the subject of a House Joint Resolution that was not considered by Congress.[5] Almost eighty years later, after many such proposals, Congress still refuses to commit itself to a referendum on status.

The first bills to provide for an elective Governor were filed soon after. Córdova Dávila's 1920 bill also asked for other reforms, such as the appointment by the elected Governor of all insular officials, the elimination of appeals to the First Circuit, and recognition of the finality of the decisions of the Supreme Court of Puerto Rico on all matters of local law.[6] Córdova Dávila also asked that, if the Treaty of Versailles was ratified, Puerto Rico's right to separate representation in the League of Nations be recognized, as in the case of the British dominions.[7]

The elective Governor bills were not even considered by the Committee on Insular Affairs, so the main parties together pressed in 1921 for the appointment of a resident Puerto Rican as Governor. President Warren G. Harding's answer was to appoint an obscure assistant postmaster from Kansas City, E. Mont Reily, whose wife was a relative of the President's wife.

Reily's appointment caused an uproar in Puerto Rico. As one of his first official acts, Reily appointed an illiterate prison guard from Kansas City as head of the Secret Service in Puerto Rico. The Senate refused to confirm this and some other unfortunate appointments, and Reily threatened the body with recommending that the Jones Act be repealed. When the Senate failed to act and recessed, the Governor went ahead with the appointments. The situation deteriorated to such an extent that on February 25, 1922, the Senate filed articles of impeachment (despite the fact that the Jones Act had not granted it this power). The Senate charged Reily with being incompetent, refusing to execute a number of laws, firing judges without cause, insulting the Puerto Rican flag, and engaging in immoral conduct. The Resident Commissioner attacked him in Congress, but the Governor was defended by several Congressmen. A federal grand jury, in the meantime, recommended that the Governor be indicted for fiscal irregularities. President Harding promptly fired the district attorney who had started to prepare the charges. Puerto Rican opposition grew to the point that the Bureau of Insular Affairs finally recommended that Reily be fired.[8] On February 28, 1923, Harding appointed as Governor the respected chairman of the House Committee on Insular Affairs, Horace M. Towner.

The Reily episode and the increasing official hostility to independence led the Unionist party to adopt a more moderate stance, strike independence from its platform, and concentrate on its autonomist agenda. A bill was accordingly drafted for the establishment of the Associated Free State of Puerto Rico, which was filed on January 19, 1922, by Congressman Philip Campbell from Kansas.[9] The Campbell bill called for several significant changes: the election of the Governor by the Legislative Assembly; the appointment of all government secretaries and judges by the Governor, with the advice and consent of the Senate; the power of the legislature to override the Governor's veto, to impeach the Governor, and to determine the electoral districts; and the election of two Resident Commissioners. The bill did not, however, ask for the adoption by Puerto Rico of its own constitution. The republicanos attacked the Campbell bill as a dangerous step toward independence and advocated legislation sponsored by Representative John I. Nolan of California, to turn Puerto Rico into an incorporated territory of the United States.[10] Both bills died in committee, without hearings being held.

In 1923 the unionistas and the republicanos, chafing under the stern Jones

Act regime, laid down their arms and joined in petitioning Congress for a complete overhaul of the Jones Act. The Legislative Assembly created a joint commission to go to Washington to work toward a new bill.[11] The joint resolution approved by the Legislative Assembly was signed by Governor Towner, who accepted the legislature's invitation to join the commission.

The joint resolution went further than the Campbell bill in most respects. It asked Congress to declare its intention as to the future status of the island and petitioned for full legislative power on all local matters. The commission's efforts brought about the filing of several bills to reform the Jones Act; one, filed by Senator William H. King from Utah, the chairman of the Committee on Pacific Islands and Porto Rico, was passed by the Senate.[12]

In February 1924 the Senate committee held hearings on the various versions of the King bill.[13] Governor Towner, who favored statehood, endorsed it. So did José Tous Soto, the head of the statehood faction within the Alianza. During these hearings Tous Soto advanced an early version of what Luis A. Ferré (a later Governor of the island and head of the statehood movement) was to call "jíbaro statehood." Tous Soto said: "If Puerto Rico should ever come into the Union, it ought to come with her own soul, with her own personality, without surrendering any of her historical traditions, her language, her religion, her laws and the enjoyment of all the blessings of the past."[14] The War Department, however, was against the bill. Secretary John W. Weeks stated plainly: "I do not think the time has come from the standpoint of the people of Porto Rico, to pass this bill."[15]

The King bill was favorably reported out of committee and passed by the Senate on May 15, 1924, with an amendment proposed by the War Department to the effect that the first election for Governor would not take place until 1932, unless the illiteracy rate dropped below 30 percent.[16] Administration officials, however, made sure that the bill was never debated in the House. The people of Puerto Rico would have to wait for twenty-three more years before obtaining the right to vote for their own Governor.

Back in 1924, during the Joint Commission's visit to Washington, Córdova Dávila had endorsed Governor Towner's suggestion (first made in the course of the debates on the Jones bill) that Puerto Rico be given the power to adopt its own constitution, but the Resident Commissioner did not file his bill until 1928.[17] Hearings were not held, but the bill would become a precedent for later proposals to the same effect. In fact, it left a wider margin for the Constitutional Convention to work with than that provided by Law 600, twenty-two years later, which started the process for establishing the Commonwealth of Puerto Rico.

The Alianza tried many other methods for increasing the self-governing powers of Puerto Rico. In its general assembly, prior to the 1928 general elections, it took another tack and declared itself in favor of the admission of Puerto Rico to the American Union as a "Special State," for which purpose an amendment to the United States Constitution was needed. As a Special State Puerto Rico would enjoy all the rights of a federated state, except that its Congressmen would be able to vote only on matters affecting Puerto Rico; the federal laws would not apply to the island unless adopted by the legislature of Puerto Rico; and certain clauses of the Constitution, such as the uniformity and the export and import clauses, would not apply. The idea had originally been advanced in a book by Luis Muñoz Morales, a distinguished legal scholar, and by Towner in 1921, when acting as chairman of the House Committee of Insular Affairs.[18] Towner actually presented a resolution in Congress to so amend the United States Constitution.[19] The constitutional amendment route was thought to have the advantage of quieting debate for a while, making clear that the Alianza was not in favor of independence and perhaps allowing for a few interim reforms. The device did not receive any further attention, although it enraged the powerful independentista wing of the Alianza. During these years, as in the 1980s and 1990s, inconsequential bills with little backing were filed in Congress to gratify this or that Puerto Rican faction.

In 1927 and 1928 the Alianza renewed its efforts to amend the Jones Act along the lines of the King bill. It filed a barrage of bills on the elective Governor measure and other reforms. Congressman Fiorello La Guardia of New York undertook a personal crusade in favor of the elective Governor provision, but with none of the restrictions that appeared in the King bill approved by the Senate four years earlier.[20] At that time, as on many other occasions, before and after, the fashion in Washington was to say that Puerto Rico's problems were economic, rather than political.

None of the bills moved forward. President Calvin Coolidge was firmly against any such reforms. He thought that Puerto Rico was enjoying freedoms for which it was not yet prepared, and that the Treaty of Paris made no promises of any kind to Puerto Rico. He deeply resented, moreover, the charge that Puerto Rico was a colony of the United States, living as it was, according to his lights, under such a liberal government charter as the Jones Act.[21] In such a climate, none of the proposals for reform made by the Alianza, and even those endorsed by the two main parties, could reasonably prosper. The conditions were being laid down for the tragic events of the thirties.

The Alianza won again in 1928, but by a smaller margin. Several months later the Alianza disintegrated. After temporary realignments, the old union-istas within the Alianza started a new party, the Partido Liberal Puertorriqueño, in 1932. Luis Muñoz Marín, son of Luis Muñoz Rivera, was one of the found-ing members. The liberales demanded immediate independence for Puerto Rico.

The conservative faction of the Alianza meanwhile joined the old republi-canos and in 1932 formed the Unión Republicana, which together with the So-cialists continued the Coalición. The new republicanos came out in favor of fuller autonomy as a transition to statehood and, should statehood be denied, independence.

At the end of the twenties and beginning of the thirties a series of books and articles drew attention to the sad economic state of the island. Not only the po-litical, as in the past, but the economic results of the colonial policy followed by the United States in connection with Puerto Rico were being questioned. Muñoz Marín and Theodore Roosevelt, Jr., who governed Puerto Rico from 1930 to 1932, wrote vividly on the subject.[22] In a powerful book, *Porto Rico: A Broken Pledge*, published in 1931, two close observers of the local scene, Bailey W. Diffie and Justine Diffie, pointed out that the United States had failed to fulfill its promise of political and economic betterment for the island. The Diffies brought out the bleakness of the economic picture. Unemployment in 1899 had amounted to 17 percent, twenty years later it was 20 percent, and in 1926, well before the Depression, it had soared to 30.2 percent. In the tobacco factories men earned ten dollars a week, and the women, four. In the sugar in-dustry, salaries fluctuated between forty cents and two dollars a day. The per capita annual income in 1930 was $230.[23]

The poverty of the majority of Puerto Rico's million and a half people who lacked adequate housing, food, clothing, work, education, and medical services contrasted with that of the flourishing American sugar companies established on the island. In 1899 the sugar cane industry used 15 percent of the land avail-able for cultivation. In 1930 that percentage had increased to 44 percent. Taxes on these corporations were kept low, while the dividends distributed to the for-eign shareholders often exceeded their investment.[24] The Diffies thus summa-rized the situation in 1931:

> The problem of the United States in Porto Rico . . . resolves itself into one question: can we govern the Island for its best interests? As long as the United States Government has the ultimate word in policies, the Is-land will be governed for the good of those interests considered "Ameri-

can." Porto Rico is at once the perfect example of what economic imperialism does for a country and of the attitude of the imperialist towards
that country. Ragged, hungry, diseased Porto Rico has just been examined by the President of the United States [Hoover had visited the island
in 1931] and has been given his official approval. Its land owned by absentee capital; its political rights resting in the hands of the United
States Government; its people in the depths of deprivation, it has been
told to help itself. That is the remedy which the President prescribes—
imperialism's answer to problems of its own creation! . . . Porto Rico can
hope for no relief under the existing system.[25]

The Brookings Institution also undertook at the time a study of the Puerto
Rican situation. The writer was also alarmed at Puerto Rico's economic situation: "While the standard of living on the whole thus appears to be somewhat
higher than it was thirty years ago, there is no evidence to indicate that it has
been improving in recent years. Indeed, it is possible that since the war conditions have grown gradually worse."[26] To face the economic crisis, the study recommended repealing the Congressional provision that limited to 500 acres any
corporation's ownership of land in Puerto Rico and extending federal aid programs to the island as if Puerto Rico were a state. At that time, the only legislation of that kind applicable to the island pertained to the establishment of agricultural colleges and agricultural experiment stations.[27]

The Brookings study did not find anything wrong, however, with the political system. It recommended the appointment of native Governors, the creation of an unicameral legislature, the separation of the pre-audit and post-audit functions of the Auditor and, taking a step backward, the abolition of the
Senate's power to confirm the Governor's appointments. The elective governorship seemed too bold a step. According to the study: "The election of the
Governor would almost eliminate American influence and would be very little
different so far as control of local affairs is concerned from independence."[28]

Theodore Roosevelt, Jr., was the first Governor of Puerto Rico who publi-
cized in the United States the intolerable living conditions prevalent in Puerto
Rico and strongly attacked the United States colonial policy, of which his own
father had been one of the principal architects. Born in 1887 and Harvard–educated, he served as Assistant Secretary of the Navy, was an unsuccessful candidate for the governorship of New York, was Governor of Puerto Rico from 1930
to 1932, when he became Governor of the Philippines. He was the first American Governor of Puerto Rico who applied himself to learning Spanish until he

was able to communicate with the people and their leaders without the embarrassment of an interpreter. Roosevelt, upon the repeated refusal of the United States government to pay attention to his requests for aid for ailing Puerto Rico, said publicly in 1930: "There are those who argue that as Puerto Rico does not pay her share of taxes to the Federal government she should not be included in these benefits. To my mind this is a false and shortsighted position. The people of Puerto Rico are citizens of the United States. It is incumbent upon the United States, if the Declaration of Independence means more than empty words, to endeavor to provide all its citizens a fair opportunity in life. It is only by aid of the Federal government that this can be accomplished for our people in Puerto Rico . . . Narrow policies and a great nation go ill together."[29]

Some of the local leaders were distressed by his words because of their possible adverse effect on tourism![30] Roosevelt also criticized the local legislature's improvident use of the meager public moneys in erecting what he considered pretentious buildings, like the Capitol, the insane asylum, the main penitentiary, as well as the failure to find new solutions to old problems. On political status, as he disclosed in his memoirs, he thought that all the alternatives "involve great difficulties. Statehood, I think, though I was able to find no statement to that effect, had been the unconscious aim of previous administrations, particularly those during the early days."[31] He considered, however, that both statehood and independence were problematic and opted, like Taft, for dominion status as an eventual goal, a policy he tried to follow during his governorship.[32] Cultural assimilation also seemed wrong to him. He thus explained the birth of the Americanization policy: "Like most countries, we were convinced that we had the best form of government ever devised in the world and that our customs and habits were the most advisable. . . . The logical consequence, therefore, was that we felt that we could do no higher and nobler work than to model these other people on ourselves."[33]

Walter Lippmann wrote in the prologue to Roosevelt's memoirs that the book was

a confession that the imperialistic dream of 1898 has proved to be unrealizable, that the management of an empire by a democracy is impossible. That this should be said by Theodore Roosevelt is to my mind one of those neat historical turns that the slovenly and inartistic Muse of history so rarely achieves, that it should be said at the end of years of practical experience in colonial administration, of an experience which was by worldly standards highly successful, seems to me most convincing.

. . . For me this book is a personal document which exhibits in striking fashion how alien to the democratic tradition is the whole impulse of imperialism. For here in the history of one family, of the father who was touched with the imperialist vision and of his son who has dealt as governor of our two greatest colonial possessions with the practical consequences, we find as good evidence as we shall find that the conquest of empires and the governing of empires cannot permanently be the ambition of a truly democratic nation.[34]

Dreams may start to fade, but their memory lingers. Roosevelt was one of the few American governors sent to Puerto Rico who clearly saw the contradiction between colonialism and democracy.

During the first years under the Jones Act cracks appeared in the old colonial policy. A good chunk of the empire—the Philippines—was placed on the road to independence. Puerto Rico was supposed to remain forever subject to United States sovereignty, but there were disturbing signs of discontent. In spite of the grant of American citizenship and open official discouragement of independence, great numbers of Puerto Ricans wanted precisely that. The Americanization policy was not working. Puerto Ricans were as resistant to learning English as most of the American governors were to learning Spanish. The supposed virtues of the Jones Act were not being appreciated, either, even by the usually well-behaved republicanos. The natives kept asking for more and more self-government, although to American eyes they were allegedly unprepared to handle the generous portion served to them so far. To make matters worse, the island was not prospering, as it was expected to do, under the tender ministrations of the sugar companies, which accounted for most economic activity. The islanders did not know how to help themselves. After thirty years of American government, little progress had been achieved. Puerto Ricans were living in subhuman conditions.

During these years Puerto Rico had been turned into little more than a plantation. The growth and export of raw sugar, and to a lesser degree tobacco, basically financed by absentee capital, ruled the economy. By the mid-twenties the working class entered a deeper crisis. Unemployment and underemployment were rampant. The local hacendados were shunted aside by the new corporations and trusts. The repression of the nationalist movement was intensified. Local political parties became increasingly alienated from the interests of the deprived sectors of society.

Still, in the rarefied air of the status debate, the twenties produced ideas and attitudes that influenced political developments in the forties and fifties and cleared the way for the nationalist and populist discourses of the following years.[35]

A few observers of the scene in positions of power—Towner, Roosevelt, King, La Guardia—started questioning the traditional United States policy toward Puerto Rico, but their voices were not heard. The bureaucratic wall which protected the territorial turf of the Bureau of Insular Affairs was hard to breach. The cracks in the cement just led the bureau to try to repair and strengthen the old pillars. The islanders pushed incessantly for independence, statehood, or at least fuller self-government. They pleaded with the United States government to disclose at least its intention about the future status of Puerto Rico. All was to no avail. What was needed, according to the bureau, was simply a stronger resolve not to give in for some time to any of the foolish demands for more self-government, to concentrate instead on more Americanization, more effective discouragement of outlandish feelings for independence, and sound exhortations to the natives to help themselves. The President and Congress were too busy to review the reigning preconceptions concerning Puerto Rico, unwittingly encouraging the development of a potentially explosive situation.

The Puerto Rican leadership did not display great vision, either. Their petty squabbles, posturing, strange political alliances, and flitting from one petition to the next lessened the essential dignity of their demands. Theirs was a just cause, but poorly pleaded. The main parties were able to speak with one voice on occasion, but most of the time they were at each other's throats, creating the conditions for permanent dissension and serious estrangement from the realities of the time.

8

The Troubled Thirties

The 1930s are of seminal importance in Puerto Rican history. The squalid economic conditions of the island worsened, and as it began to falter, the old colonial policy became even more rigid. The Americanization policy—abetted by the coming to power of statehood seekers for the second time in the century—reached a fevered pitch. While trying without success to improve the economy, the regime became more impatient and repressive with the believers in independence. In response, the support for independence grew and some of its advocates became radical. Out of this climate of misery and violence came a new political party which would rule for most of the rest of the century.

The more the Jones Act was criticized, the louder it was praised by the officials in charge of its administration. To an even greater degree than the Foraker Act, the Jones Act acquired a sacramental character. It was so strictly constructed that it became a serious obstacle to local governmental action. On one occasion, for example, the legislature passed a law to help the victims of an earthquake. The Attorney General of Puerto Rico ruled the law unconstitutional because, according to him, the Jones Act supposedly prohibited donations to any person, corporation, or community that was not under the control of the government. The same provision was used to invalidate a scholarship program. Another stipulation of the act was that all officials be citizens of the United States. Contrary to normal interpretation of similar clauses in state constitutions, "officials" was held to include all insular and municipal employees. Congress repealed this interpretation four decades later.[1] An act of the legislature to provide incentives to adults who would teach others to read and write was declared by the Attorney General to be in violation of Article 17 of the Jones Act, which stated that the Commissioner of Education "shall superintend public instruction throughout Porto Rico."[2]

Many laws floundered because of supposed violation of the sacred text. In

1932 the legislature approved 116 bills and 163 resolutions. The Governor signed only 44 laws and 52 resolutions, constitutional objections having been raised with respect to most of the rest. The federal court was also a fearful guardian of the organic act. Many laws, especially tax measures, survived the gaze of the Attorney General only to fall by the wayside upon judicial review. The federal court's reading of the Jones Act got to be so outrageous, preventing the enforcement of many local tax provisions, that Congress amended the act to provide that "no suit for the purpose of restraining the assessment or collection of any tax imposed by the laws of Porto Rico shall be maintained in the District Court of the United States."[3]

A reading of the Jones Act and some of its interpretations does not, however, give a complete picture of how Puerto Rico was governed at the time. The interplay of power among the various institutions and officials concerned produced a different constitution.

Through the entire Jones period, first as part of the War Department and beginning in 1933 as part of the Interior Department, the Bureau of Insular Affairs continued silently to accumulate power. Since early in the century it had nurtured the theory, endorsed even by such experienced Presidents as Theodore Roosevelt, William Howard Taft, and Woodrow Wilson, that colonial administration required special expertise and that the bureau was its natural depository. The bureau advised the President about appointments through the appropriate Secretary, who often played a relatively passive role; initiated and monitored legislation, both federal and local; supervised the work of the Governor; passed judgment on local events; and generally served as Puerto Rico's intermediary in Washington, to a higher degree than the Governor, who rarely had access to the President or Congress. The bureau normally had close contacts with the appropriate committees of both the House and Senate and as such had much greater clout than the Resident Commissioner or the Governor. Even Towner, a former chairman of the House committee that handled bills relating to Puerto Rico, was unable to get Congress to act on his recommendations for reforming the Jones Act. Without the bureau's blessing and help it was virtually impossible to push a measure through Congress or get the attention of the White House. Through the years the bureau was also able to secure primary responsibility for the performance of important local functions, such as the sale of bonds, the representation of Puerto Rico before the higher federal courts, and even purchases of some importance by the insular government. In sum, the Governor and other presidential appointees were increasingly, with rare exceptions, the bureau's subordinates, and it was chiefly before the bureau that the local parties had to plead their cause.

The Governor's veto power, especially the item veto, became a strong weapon in his hands, but the strong bailiwicks built by the Attorney General, the Auditor, and the Commissioner of Education curtailed his initiatives to a large degree, besides the bureau's appetite for control. The Governor also soon found that his power to appoint the other four heads of departments, with the advice and consent of the Senate, did not amount to much. The commissioners considered themselves beholden to the political party that backed their appointment.

The relations between the legislature and the Governor were not usually very good. During the 1930s the legislators often appeared to be more interested in getting their candidates appointed to this or that position and engaging in petty disputes with the Governor than in devising good laws. Appropriations were made without regard to budgetary constraints, which forced the Governor to use his item veto power with great frequency and in practice forfeited to the Governor the power over the purse. The thirties were one of the least productive periods of the Legislative Assembly of Puerto Rico.

The federal district court of Puerto Rico and the Court of Appeals for the First Circuit continued their capricious reading of local statutes, without regard to the decisions of the Supreme Court of Puerto Rico. The situation became so intolerable that the Supreme Court of the United States had to admonish the lower federal courts several times. In a 1923 case Justice Oliver Wendell Holmes had already done so: "This court has stated many times the deference due to the understanding of the local courts upon matters of purely local concern. . . . This is especially true of a court inheriting and brought up in a different system from that which prevails here. . . . Our appellate jurisdiction is not given for the purpose of remodeling the Spanish-American law according to common-law conceptions."[4]

The command went unheeded and the Court had to repeat it, to no avail, until it again unanimously ruled in a 1940 case: "As this court recently stated: 'Orderly development of the government of Puerto Rico as an integral part of our governmental system is well served by a careful and consistent adherence to the legislative and judicial policy of deferring to the local procedure and tribunals of the island. . . .' We now repeat once more that admonition. And we add that mere lip service to that rule is not enough."[5] The Supreme Court of Puerto Rico was at the time, however, almost as prone as the lower federal courts to interpret the civil law of the island according to common-law methods and precedents.[6]

The municipalities were not the school of democracy that they were intended to be. The Treasurer of Puerto Rico was supposed to be only an adviser, but he actually supervised a good part of the municipal administration. The Auditor and the Attorney General also exercised great power over the municipalities, as did the Commissioner of Education and the Commissioner of Health. The Governor settled the frequent conflicts between the mayors and the municipal assemblies.

In sum, the small voice that Puerto Ricans had in handling their affairs contributed to the climate of helplessness and hopelessness that permeated the thirties. Cynicism set in and democracy was in a sorry state. As their votes were worth so little, the struggling workers and the army of the unemployed sold their votes to the sugar companies and other bosses. In that kind of society, governed by others, exploited by a few, with an embattled sense of cultural identity, where traditional political action led nowhere, violence started to look good to some.

Although the Liberal party, successor to the Unión and the Alianza, polled by far the largest number of votes in 1932, by joining forces with Iglesias' Socialist party under the common name of the Coalición (but each party keeping its identity and platform), the republicanos were able to return to power for the second time in the century. The republicanos obtained a few more votes than the socialistas, and together they outnumbered the liberales alone. The Coalición won again in 1936, despite the liberales continuing to be the majority party, but it was swept out of power in 1940 by a new organization, the Popular Democratic party.

When they came to power, the republicanos unleashed such an Americanization crusade that their stridency was one of the causes of the Nationalist uprising. They were not happy with the Commissioner of Education, José Padín, a Puerto Rican who questioned the teaching of all subjects in English. They were able to secure from Washington his removal, and the educational policy of the earlier years of teaching everything in English was restored. As to status, in 1934 Resident Commissioner Santiago Iglesias filed in Congress the first bill asking for Puerto Rico to be admitted as a state of the Union.[7] The bill, which Iglesias continued to file session after session, followed the terms of the typical statehood enabling act, without asking for any transition period with special economic measures. The bills were never reported out of committee.

Iglesias continued to have a strong following among the workers. His interest in entering into such an unlikely coalition with the republicanos, who were traditionally backed by American officials and the employer class—the very ones who had persecuted him and fought unionization for decades—was rooted in his belief that by access to power he could improve the lot of the Puerto Rican laborer. His sudden identification with his old tormentors, with whom he nevertheless shared, for other reasons, the belief in statehood as the ultimate status goal, ended by harming his party. The laboring masses would increasingly turn in the forties to the recently established Popular Democratic party.

Finally, after the unfruitful years that its leadership spent as members of the Unión and the Alianza seeking a panoply of autonomist solutions, the Liberal party became in favor of immediate independence. The pro-independence credentials of its principal leader, Antonio R. Barceló, were somewhat tarnished, but the young leaders who joined him were highly vocal and respected in their call for full sovereignty.

The head of the young group was Luis Muñoz Marín, who was destined to play a key role in Puerto Rican affairs from then to the end of the seventies. Born in 1898, the only son of Luis Muñoz Rivera, Luis Muñoz Marín spent most of his infancy, boyhood, and adolescence in the United States and spoke flawless English and Spanish. He returned to Puerto Rico for a time to help Iglesias campaign in the 1920 elections, not because he believed in statehood—he never did—but because he shared Iglesias' socialist ideas. He did not hold his father's party in high regard. He soon returned to the States, where he dedicated himself to journalism and poetry and was an active member of New York literary circles. In 1931 he returned to Puerto Rico to edit a well-known newspaper and a year later ran for Senator on the Liberal ticket and was elected. He was from the start a major figure in the Liberal party. Highly articulate, perceptive, and imaginative, a witty conversationalist, with a physical presence that drew attention to him the moment he entered a room, he immediately attracted a strong following and soon became the most respected Puerto Rican politician in Washington, with personal access to President Franklin D. Roosevelt, Eleanor Roosevelt, and the head of the Bureau of Insular Affairs. He was convinced that independence was the best solution to the status problem, from the point of view of both Puerto Rico and the United States, but his political convictions were often tempered by his concern for the need to improve the standard of living of the Puerto Rican people. His relationships with Barceló and the older leaders of the party were uneasy. His socialist beliefs set him apart from a party that in his mind was getting too close ideologically to the republicanos.[8]

On May 11, 1930, Pedro Albizu Campos, long to be remembered in Puerto Rican history as the heir to the nineteenth-century revolutionary tradition represented by exiled Puerto Rican independence leaders, became president of the old Nationalist party. Born in Ponce in 1891, he graduated from Harvard Law School in 1917, served as an officer in the United States Army until 1919, and entered politics as a member of the Unión and, later, of the Alianza. A highly intelligent, intense, charismatic man and an electrifying public speaker, he did not formally join the Nationalist party until after a speaking trip to Latin America in 1927 and 1928, although he had been preaching independence and the need for a radical organization to fight for it since at least 1926.[9]

The Nationalists were on the ballot in 1932, Albizu seeking a Senate seat. The Liberal and Nationalist parties were both for independence, and the Republican party was also for it should statehood be denied by Congress. The results were disastrous for the Nationalist party, which polled less than 2 percent of the vote; Albizu obtained double the amount of votes that his party did, but still lost. After the elections Albizu Campos denounced the electoral process as a periodic farce and declared that revolution was the only way open for attaining independence.

Several violent incidents had occurred even prior to the elections. The republicanos tried to enact a bill in April 1932, which did not become law, declaring the traditional Puerto Rican flag, which was being used as a symbol by the Nationalist party, the official state flag of the island. Albizu, incensed, called for a public meeting, and at the end of his fiery speech the crowd marched toward the Capitol, where it was repelled by the police. One of the marchers died when the throng pressed him against a stair banister. A few weeks later a nationalist entered the office of Emilio del Toro, the Republican Chief Justice of Puerto Rico, and slapped him. In another speech Albizu threatened the lives of Barceló, Iglesias, and Del Toro and promised to have the chief of police killed should a single nationalist die at the hands of a policeman.

After the elections the outbreaks of violence continued, each more serious. In October 1935 the students at the University of Puerto Rico were holding a meeting to protest a speech by Albizu in which he accused them of being sissies for not fighting for independence. The police guarded the entrance to the university, and when a car with four nationalists went by the police arrested them. In the shooting that ensued the four nationalists, as well as a policeman, died. At the funeral Albizu spoke and repeated his threats, making an appeal to arms should Puerto Rico not be made immediately independent. In January 1936 two policemen were wounded when trying to disarm a nationalist. In February two nationalists killed the chief of police, Francis Riggs. The police took them into custody and murdered them at police headquarters, claiming that they were trying to escape.

Riggs' death increased the level of official repression of the independence movement. General Blanton Winship, then Governor of Puerto Rico, asked the legislature to reinstall the death penalty, which the legislature refused to do. Six weeks after the assassination of the chief of police, Albizu Campos and six other leading members of his party were indicted by a federal grand jury for conspiring to overthrow the government of the United States. The American Civil Liberties Union had protested that such be the charge, instead of murder or conspiracy to commit murder. A few months later a federal jury convicted the accused and they were sent to a federal penitentiary in Atlanta to serve a maximum of fifteen years.

Order was not restored by the removal of Albizu from Puerto Rico. In October 1936, Santiago Iglesias was wounded by a nationalist's bullet. On March 21, 1937, the Nationalist party decided to hold a parade in Ponce, after obtaining the mayor's permission. The chief of police revoked the mayor's permit and sent 150 policemen to Ponce to enforce his order. The nationalists, unarmed, started to march anyway. A shot was heard—it could not be determined whether its source was a civilian in the crowd or the police—and the police fired into the marchers. Nineteen people were killed, two of them policemen, and over a hundred were wounded. Arthur Garfield Hays, a noted attorney sent by the American Civil Liberties Union to investigate what came to be known as the Ponce Massacre, pointed to Governor Winship as the person primarily responsible for the killings.[10]

The next year there were attempts against the lives of Winship and Judge Cooper, who had sentenced Albizu. Things then quieted down until 1950, when several groups of Nationalists started a series of violent acts in Puerto Rico and the United States.

Resort to violence in the thirties was not condoned by the people of Puerto Rico. Independence was still sought by the strongest party on the island, but within a framework of abiding friendship with the United States. The Nationalist party shrunk to a small band of believers in direct action.

Up until police chief Riggs' assassination, Ernest Gruening, the distinguished former editor of the *Nation* and since 1934 director of the Bureau of Insular Affairs, was a close friend of Muñoz and collaborated with the Liberal party. When Riggs was killed, Gruening asked Muñoz, then in Washington, to issue a statement condemning the act. Muñoz refused to do so unless the killing of the two nationalists while in custody was also officially condemned. There was a falling out between Gruening and Muñoz, and Gruening started collaborating with the Coalición.

When Riggs was killed, Senator Millard E. Tydings from Maryland, a close

friend of the slain chief of police, decided to teach a lesson to all those who favored independence. At Tydings' request, Gruening drafted a bill offering independence to the island under punitive economic conditions. The request was
sanctioned at a Cabinet meeting held on March 16, 1936, where Harold Ickes,
Secretary of the Interior, suggested that such a bill be secretly drafted, without
public involvement of the administration.[11] The bill overshadowed recommendations to the President from mainland observers of the local scene that a thorough revision of the Jones Act be undertaken and called for a referendum in
which the people would determine whether they wanted independence.[12] If independence was chosen, all assistance programs would immediately come to an
end; the authority of federal agencies to make loans to Puerto Rican residents
would cease; six months after inauguration of the new government Puerto Rico
would undertake all obligations for its defense; 25 percent of the United States
tariffs would be added each year until the full tariff would come into effect in
four years; Puerto Ricans would have to choose between American and Puerto
Rican citizenship six months after the inauguration of the republic; and hence
Puerto Ricans would be subject to the immigration laws, which would allow only
500 residents a year to enter the United States.

The Liberal party immediately came out for independence, in spite of the
conditions imposed by the bill. The head of the Republican party, Rafael
Martínez Nadal, initially favored it also, but after a while changed his mind and
returned to his traditional pro-statehood stance. Iglesias, however, attacked the
bill in Congress, and Luis Muñoz Marín sought an alternative, which was em-
bodied in a bill filed by Congressman Wilbur Cartwright, from Oklahoma.

The Cartwright bill called for independence, but without the punitive conditions of the Tydings bill.[13] If the people of Puerto Rico ratified the constitution to be drafted for the republic, a bilateral commission would then negotiate
a commercial treaty between the two countries. Puerto Ricans could choose to
retain American citizenship. Those who did not would be subject to the immigration laws.

Although as chairman, Tydings could easily have had the Senate Committee on Insular Affairs hold hearings on his proposal, he laid aside his bill and endorsed a resolution for establishing a fifteen-member commission to study the
matter. Each of the four political parties in Puerto Rico, including the Nationalists, were to appoint one member. The resolution was approved by the Senate,
but the House took no action on it.[14]

From 1937 to 1940 there was little activity in Congress regarding Puerto

Rico's status. Iglesias filed several bills for amending the Jones Act and substituted a bill to turn Puerto Rico into an incorporated territory of the United States for his usual statehood bill.[15]

Puerto Rico was receiving at the end of the twenties a little more than $4 million in the form of direct rehabilitation and $6 million in loans to farmers. Theodore Roosevelt, Jr., then Governor of Puerto Rico, dramatized its need for aid and was the person most responsible for having the island included in a major road building and repair program.[16]

Upon the advent of the New Deal, all parties except the Nationalists favored its extension to Puerto Rico. In August 1933, the Puerto Rico Emergency Relief Administration (PRERA) was established, starting a program to distribute food surpluses and emergency programs to reduce unemployment (which had by then reached 35 percent), as well as direct aid to the needy.[17] By mid-1934 an estimated 35 percent of the population was receiving some form of aid from the PRERA.

From the start, federal relief funds were extended to Puerto Rico in a different manner than to the states. Governor Winship complained in 1935 that Puerto Rico was receiving only one-eighth of what would have been its due as a state under the Federal Emergency Relief Act.[18] Puerto Rico was also excluded from other vital measures, such as Social Security.

Unhappy with the results of the rehabilitation programs established in Puerto Rico, Muñoz Marín proposed that an overall economic plan for Puerto Rico be adopted. The idea was well-received and a federal commission was appointed for that purpose, headed by Carlos Chardón, chancellor of the University of Puerto Rico. Although left off the commission in order not to displease the Coalición, Muñoz took an active part in the deliberations of the group, with the blessing of the federal authorities. The Chardón plan recommended specific measures to combat unemployment, increase the island's gross product, and promote a more equitable distribution of wealth. Its centerpiece was to be the creation of a public corporation to acquire land and operate sugar mills, while distributing land to farmers to grow other products.

The plan was strongly opposed by the sugar interests and the Coalición and was not endorsed by Washington. The Comptroller General of the United States ruled that public monies could not be used for the acquisition of land. In 1935, however, President Franklin Roosevelt created the Puerto Rico Reconstruction Administration (PRRA) by executive order to serve at least part of the purposes of the Chardón plan.

The PRRA, jealously run from Washington to the last detail, undertook a variety of activities, including the establishment of a cooperative (instead of the corporation originally proposed) to acquire and operate a sugar mill. It promoted the organization of other cooperatives; built hydroelectric facilities and a cement plant; planned the establishment of other industries, including a glass plant and a cardboard plant; and instituted health care, education, slum clearing, rural electrification, and other programs. In all, through December 31, 1938, when its liquidation appeared to be imminent, the PRRA spent slightly less than $58 million.

Criticism of the Puerto Rico Reconstruction Administration and of the manner in which the New Deal was extended to Puerto Rico has been harsh. Senator Chester Bowles of Connecticut wrote in 1955:

> For all that it accomplished as the local adjunct of the New Deal in the nineteen thirties, the Puerto Rico Reconstruction Administration early demonstrated the ineffectiveness of a rigid planning, which was benevolently prepared and supervised by a government outside the immediate context of local needs. Thus a decade ago Puerto Ricans learned a lesson which should now be a truism: that if a people are to be saved from whatever danger threatens them, whether it be the militant aggression of communism or the social scourge of poverty and disease, they will in the last analysis save themselves through their own indigenous power, pride and responsibility. If outsiders are to be helpful, their help must take the form of friendly and unobtrusive support.[19]

Rexford G. Tugwell, a member of Roosevelt's brain trust, was even less charitable. He had this to say about the effect of the New Deal in Puerto Rico and the vast slums and misery he found when arriving in 1941 to govern the island:

> This is what colonialism was and did: it distorted all ordinary processes of the mind, made beggars of honest men, sycophants of cynics, American-haters of those who ought to have been working beside us for world-betterment—and would if we had encouraged them. Economically it consisted in setting up things so that the colony sold its raw products in a cheap market (in the mother country) and bought its food and other finished goods in a dear market (also the mother country); there was also the matter of foreign products to be carried in American ships. In that sense Puerto Rico was a colony just as New York and Massachusetts had been colonies. Except for "relief" of one kind or another, which George

III and the others were too foolish to give when it would have been wise, Puerto Rico was just as badly off. And relief was something which the Congress made Puerto Rico beg for, hard, and in the most revolting ways, as a beggar does on a church step, filthy hat in hand, exhibiting sores, calling and grimacing in exaggerated humility. And this last was the real crime of America in the Caribbean, making of Puerto Ricans something less than the men they were born to be.[20]

The New Deal, however, did have a beneficial impact on things to come. It helped to turn Puerto Rico's attention to its economic plight, to temper its obsession with status as the magic solution to all problems, to realize that freedom can take many forms, to nudge political parties toward the realization that economic salvation cannot alone come from the outside, that self-government and self-help go hand in hand. The failed program to rehabilitate Puerto Rico from the outside also provided many of the ideas that fueled the efforts at economic betterment since the forties.

To sum up, the thirties evidenced the failure of the traditional colonial policy toward Puerto Rico. Politically, it did not produce a happy, stable society. The people of Puerto Rico were not content with their assigned lot as supposedly fortunate inhabitants of a perpetual possession of the United States. American citizenship, which did not bring with it equality of treatment, was not enough to hide their sores. Public opinion became tragically polarized, emptily debating which of two then-impossible dreams—independence or statehood—suited Puerto Rico best. Alienation, cynicism, and violence each vied for recruits. By the end of the thirties profound social changes would bring about a massive realignment of the political parties. The thirties paved the way for the shattering of existing political parties by the populist approach of Muñoz Marín.[21]

Culturally, the Americanization policy failed. The people clung desperately to their language and sense of self.[22] And, economically, the island hit bottom. After forty years of United States rule, the economy of the island was in shambles, little better than at the end of the nineteenth century. Attempts from afar to bring about a recovery did not work. The stage was set for Puerto Rico to go gentle into that good night or to find a way to keep breathing.

Dr. José C. Barbosa, father of the statehood movement, organized the Republican party. He served as member of the Executive Council during the Foraker years and was elected to the Senate upon its establishment in 1917. Photo Archives, University of Puerto Rico.

Luis Muñoz Rivera, head of the autonomist movement, in 1904 founded the Unión de Puerto Rico party, which favored autonomy and eventual independence. He served in the House of Delegates from 1904 to 1910, and from then until his death was Resident Commissioner of Puerto Rico in Washington, D.C. Photo Archives, University of Puerto Rico.

José de Diego headed the strong independence branch of the Unión de Puerto Rico. Photo Archives, University of Puerto Rico.

Santiago Iglesias, Puerto Rico's foremost labor leader and an advocate of statehood, with President William Howard Taft. Photo Archives, University of Puerto Rico. Iglesias was born in Spain and came to Puerto Rico in 1898 as an organizer for the American Federation of Labor. He founded the Socialist party, which was in power as a member of the Coalición from 1933 to 1940.

Pedro Albizu Campos, head of the Nationalist movement, became the chief spokesman for advocating independence by violent means. Photo Archives, University of Puerto Rico.

Rexford G. Tugwell, the last American appointed Governor of Puerto Rico, was one of the most effective governors, whether appointed or elected, that Puerto Rico has had to date. Photo Archives, University of Puerto Rico. After his resignation, Jesús T. Piñero, then Resident Commissioner, was appointed Governor by President Truman.

Luis Muñoz Marín served as President of the Senate from 1941 to 1948, when he became the first elected Governor of Puerto Rico. A former believer in independence, he became an autonomist and promoted the establishment in 1952 of the present Commonwealth of Puerto Rico. Photo Archives, Luis Muñoz Marín Foundation.

The Plaza Colón in Old San Juan at the eastern end of the city, 1898. Photo Archives, University of Puerto Rico.

Aibonito in 1900, with the church dominating the scene and the people dressed in Sunday finery. The town was and still is one of the most important in central Puerto Rico. Photo Archives, University of Puerto Rico.

View of Hormigueros, 1900. A small town, close to Mayagüez, in the western part of the island, Hormigueros is famous for its church, shown in the background. Most of the streets of small towns were unpaved. Photo Archives, University of Puerto Rico.

View of Patillas, in southern Puerto Rico, 1900. Photo Archives, University of Puerto Rico.

The Ponce Massacre, 1937. Photo Archives, University of Puerto Rico.

Coffee pickers, 1930s. Photo Archives, University of Puerto Rico.

Washing clothes in river, early 1940s. In the countryside and in many towns, running water was not still available in the forties and fifties. Photo Archives, University of Puerto Rico.

Fetching water, 1946. General Archives of Puerto Rico. Photo by Jack Delano. Many towns had common faucets and families sent their children to fetch water for cooking, bathing and washing clothes. The photographer, Jack Delano, is a distinguished artist and composer who has recorded life in Puerto Rico for many decades and published several books. At the time Delano was working for the Community Education Division of the Puerto Rico Department of Education.

Working the sugar lands, 1946. General Archives of Puerto Rico. Photo by Jack Delano.

A farm worker, 1946. General Archives of Puerto Rico. Photo by Jack Delano.

Farm worker resting, 1946. General Archives of Puerto Rico. Photo by Jack Delano.

Women de-stemming tobacco leaves in a cigar factory, 1946. General Archives of Puerto Rico. Photo by Jack Delano.

A San Juan slum, 1946. El Fanguito, the largest slum (later destroyed), was largely built on swampland, and the houses could be reached only by rowboat and were connected by planks. General Archives of Puerto Rico. Photo by Jack Delano.

Young worker and his wife and children, 1946. General Archives of Puerto Rico.
Photo by Jack Delano.

Country store, 1946. General Archives of Puerto Rico. Photo by Jack Delano.

Woman in her kitchen, 1950s. General Archives of Puerto Rico. Photo by Jack Delano.

The mountain town of Barranquitas, hometown of Luis Muñoz Rivera, 1995. Photo from *Puerto Rico desde el cielo.*

Ponce's central square, 1995. Photo from *Puerto Rico desde el cielo*.

A San Juan square, 1995. Photo from *Puerto Rico desde el cielo.*

Panoramic view of Old San Juan, 1995. Part of the old wall is in the foreground, showing one of the gates giving access to the sea. At right, foreground, is La Fortaleza palace, the fortress residence of Puerto Rico's governors. Photo from *Puerto Rico desde el cielo.*

San Juan suburbs, 1995. To the left is the Condado, a hotel and residential area. To the right is Santurce and beyond, Hato Rey, the financial district. Photo from *Puerto Rico desde el cielo.*

9

The Elective Governor Act

Out of the deep depression, both economic and spiritual, of the thirties a new Puerto Rico began to emerge. Let us look briefly at Puerto Rico before this change.

By 1940 the population had climbed to 1,869,255, almost 70 percent of which lived in rural areas, not much different than at the start of the century.[1] Only nine towns had a population in excess of 10,000. The birth rate was alarmingly high, 38.7 for every thousand inhabitants, as compared to 38 in 1900. Improved health conditions had reduced the death rate during that period from 27.1 to 18.4 per thousand, which was still inordinately high when compared to the 10.8 then prevalent in the United States. Life expectancy was only 45.12 years for men and 46.92 years for women.

Per capita income was $121 a year, about the same as forty years earlier. The coveted factory jobs at the sugar mills paid an average of thirty and a half cents an hour. The sugar cane cutters earned half of that.

Slightly more than 50 percent of the school-age population attended school, just 7.3 percent more than twenty years before. The illiteracy rate was 31.5 percent. The education budget amounted to $6,121,035, of which $385,450 represented federal grants. All federal assistance to the island in 1940 totaled $2,994,000.

Industrialization was almost nonexistent. Out of a work force of 601,990, construction workers numbered 16,037, and those employed in service organizations, 1,799. The tourism industry had not developed; San Juan had only one adequate hotel. Government services were deficient. Few towns had sewer service. Running water and electricity were absent from most of the countryside. Through the Aqueduct and Sewer Service Authority, established in the early forties, the government of Puerto Rico started a vast program for bringing water and sewer service to town and country, but it took many years. Hospitals and doctors were scarce. The roads were few. The number of motor vehicles was 12.8 per thousand people, as compared to 131 per thousand in Hawaii.

The Great Depression hit the island hard. Total exports in 1931 were $94.8 million and in 1940 amounted to $90.9 million. Imports increased by half during the same period and reached $100.5 million in 1940. The prices for the main crops—sugar, tobacco, and coffee—fell significantly. The total assessed value of property dropped from $337.9 million in 1930 to $311.8 million ten years later.

Luis Muñoz Marín's relations with Antonio R. Barceló and older leaders of the Liberal party became increasingly tense in 1936. Muñoz was then advocating abstention from the upcoming elections, fearing that the backlash from Riggs' assassination would bring about the defeat of the Liberal party and hurt the independence cause. Barceló initially favored abstention, but soon altered his position. At its 1936 general assembly the liberales decided by a one-vote margin to back Barceló and his slate of candidates. On September 25, 1936, Muñoz then founded Acción Social Independentista (ASI), which worked for independence and social justice for the people of Puerto Rico. Its members were free to cooperate or not with the Liberal party in the 1936 elections. ASI carried within it, of course, the seed of a new party. It attracted the most promising leaders of the liberales.

In spite of its internal struggle, the Liberal party still polled by far the largest number of votes of any single party, but by pooling the strength of the Unión Republicana with that of the Socialist party the Coalición won by 44,566 votes. The liberales blamed Muñoz Marín for the defeat, and the grounds were laid for his expulsion from the party on May 31, 1937. By then the Liberal party was fighting for the Cartwright bill, after withdrawing its endorsement of immediate independence, and was favoring a set of autonomic reforms. On June 27, 1937, Muñoz and his followers then founded a new party, the Partido Liberal, Neto, Auténtico y Completo, which later changed its name to that of the Partido Popular Democrático (PDP). The new organization, which meant the coming to power of a new generation, initially favored independence for the island, as well as vast social and economic reforms. In the climate of the times, the two objectives would soon appear to clash. The PDP was squarely against the plantation owners. It drew heavy support from the agregados, the peones (laborers), the reserve labor force, the rural and urban poor, the lower-middle class, the criollo propertied element, and the intellectual elite, entangled then with a romantic vision of old Spanish values.[2] The electorate of the traditional parties was deeply altered. The Liberal and Socialist parties would not survive the changes. The Republican party would be seriously weakened for a long time.[3]

The PDP decided that the strident and sterile debate on status was for the moment distracting attention from even more urgent tasks. It therefore concentrated its efforts on a campaign to educate the poor not to sell their vote; on the promise that political status would not be considered to be at issue in the coming elections; and on the dissemination of a detailed program of social and economic reforms. By that time Muñoz Marín was privately convinced that the PDP would not win should it maintain the independence plank in its platform. Nationalism started to give way to populism.[4]

It worked. The PDP won the 1940 elections in four of the seven electoral districts. The Coalición, although each of its candidates for the legislature received fewer votes than the PDP, was nevertheless able to elect its candidate for Resident Commissioner by a slim margin. A third party, the Unificación Tripartita, composed of what was left of the Liberal party and dissident factions from the Republicans and the Socialists, was strong enough to elect three members to the House, where they held the balance of power until a majority was obtained for approving the reform package to which the PDP had been pledged.[5]

From then on Muñoz Marín and his Popular Democratic party swept all elections for the next twenty-eight years. The enormous power entrusted to Muñoz and his party made possible a long-range program of economic and social change, which in turn facilitated the attainment of greater powers of self-government, the achievement of an elective Governor, and the establishment of the present Commonwealth under a constitution of its own adoption. At the same time it contributed to the development of serious problems: swift and heavy urbanization, massive emigration (as the rate of improvement in living conditions did not match rising expectations), and delay in building a more pluralistic society.

The last appointed American Governor, a remarkable man named Rexford G. Tugwell, played a key role in changes to come. Tugwell was sworn in as Governor on September 19, 1941. An economics professor at Columbia and other universities, he was a member of Roosevelt's inner circle who served in various capacities at the Department of Agriculture. Under severe congressional attack from the start, he eventually left federal government service and became chairman of New York City's Planning Commission under Mayor Fiorello La Guardia. Offered the directorship of the Division of Territories by Interior Secretary Harold Ickes, Tugwell indicated his preference for the governorship of Puerto Rico. He was driven by three main concerns: his realization of the urgent need for economic betterment of the island; his desire to streamline the government to facilitate such purpose; and his interest in leading Puerto

Rico out of its status dilemma. Happily, these were also the main goals of Muñoz Marín. A period of fruitful collaboration was to follow, with only occasional disagreements as to the way to achieve them.

The New Deal did not truly arrive in Puerto Rico until Tugwell became governor. Tugwell strengthened the conviction of the new leadership that Puerto Rico had to help itself but, at the same time, unwittingly fostered a sense of overdependence of the people of Puerto Rico on the United States. A few years later Muñoz Marín, in talking about the need for less dependence, unsuccessfully tried to set more modest goals. Federal assistance totals were yet modest, but it is during Tugwell's tenure and Muñoz Marín's early years that Puerto Rico started a systematic quest for an ever-increasing amount of federal funds.[6]

Tugwell helped turn the Puerto Rican government machinery into an engine of change. He cut the Auditor and the Attorney General down to size and retrieved part of the powers usurped by them. Most important, he brokered the establishment of a Bureau of the Budget, a Planning Board, and a Bureau of Statistics—all unknown until that time in Puerto Rico—and laid the groundwork for the eventual creation of a civil service. He also popularized the use of the public corporation device as a flexible instrument of executive action and battled to demythologize the Jones Act and portray it as a limited, rather shortsighted charter, unresponsive to the realities of the times. The public corporations set up during his governorship in the power production, aqueduct, sewer, transportation, and economic development fields did much to create a sounder economic infrastructure for the island, although the effect would later start petering out.

Tugwell initially favored statehood for the island. He used to say privately that as an American he preferred independence, and as a Puerto Rican, statehood. Later in his governorship he was for "some sort of union with the United States." Contrary to most of his predecessors, however, he thought that the Jones Act was colonial in character and should be amended in depth, albeit incrementally. Change should come gradually, he thought, especially because of the role that Puerto Rico was then playing in the security system of the Caribbean area.[7]

Early in 1942 Tugwell privately recommended to President Franklin Roosevelt that steps be taken to allow Puerto Ricans to elect their own Governor. A presidential commission was soon established to suggest such changes as would be necessary for that purpose.

This was much less than what Muñoz Marín had been seeking. Muñoz believed that, as soon as the Second World War ended, there should be either a plebiscite or a constitutional convention to resolve the status issue once and for all. The self-determination rhetoric had already been revived since August 14, 1941, when Winston Churchill and Roosevelt had proclaimed in the Atlantic Charter that "They respect the right of all peoples to choose the form of government under which they will live, and they wish to see sovereign rights of self-government restored to those who have been forcibly deprived of them."[8] This declaration rekindled the status debate in Puerto Rico, increased its expectations, and initially led the PDP to formulate demands which the government of the United States was not yet ready to meet.

On March 9, 1943, President Roosevelt recommended to Congress that Puerto Ricans be allowed to elect their own Governor and announced the establishment of a commission to advise the President on the amendments to the Jones Act required to that end. Harold Ickes, Abe Fortas (Under Secretary of the Interior), Tugwell, Muñoz Marín (then president of the Senate of Puerto Rico), Martín Travieso (associate justice of the Supreme Court of Puerto Rico), and members of other parties, were some of its members.[9]

Muñoz Marín was not sure about the wisdom of setting up this commission. He thought that an amendment of the Jones Act just for the purpose of providing for the election of the Governor could delay for years a fuller revision of the Jones Act. Muñoz unsuccessfully tried to expand the commission's agenda and finally agreed to participate in its deliberations in the hope that the members could be convinced to endorse other changes. Specifically, he hoped to obtain a block grant for general government purposes to be used in exchange for a reduction of federal expenditures, the level of which had started to worry him deeply, and he wanted a date to be set for the people of Puerto Rico to exert their right to self-determination.[10] He recommended to that end that a constitutional convention be called to propose to Congress Puerto Rico's final status choice.

On February 10, 1943, Muñoz had obtained a concurrent resolution from the Legislative Assembly demanding an end to colonial rule in Puerto Rico and the recognition of the right to self-determination once the war ended. Clashes within the commission occurred, however, from the start. Muñoz objected to the creation of the office of High Commissioner as a supervisor of affairs in Puerto Rico and suggested that, at the most, a Coordinator of Federal Agencies in Puerto Rico be appointed, instead. This provoked an irate response from Abe Fortas, who would later become an advocate for a different approach to the Puerto Rican problem. Fortas said: "Now, the United States will retain sover-

eignty over Puerto Rico. The United States will continue to be supreme in
Puerto Rico, and that is flat. There is just not any question about it. We might
just as well quit if we are not going to proceed on that basis, and you might as
well have that very clearly in mind that the United States, under this scheme,
will continue to be supreme in Puerto Rico."[11]

Charges of colonialism were then deeply resented—exactly as now, more
than half a century later. A typical exchange in the course of the deliberations
was the following, which occurred when Muñoz realized the administration's
unwillingness to face up to the need of a complete overhaul of the Jones Act
(which still has yet to happen).

> *Muñoz Marín:* The colonial situation is rotten. By rotten I don't mean
> terrible. I mean it is rotten. It just can't go on much longer.
> *Fortas:* What do you mean by the colonial system? Do you mean the way
> it is administered?
> *Muñoz Marín:* The business of the people of Puerto Rico being to a
> greater or lesser degree ruled by authorities that do not derive their pow-
> ers from their consent.[12]

Muñoz Marín's pounding on the issue had an educational effect. At his request, the commission finally recommended, first, that Congress should state
in the first section of the proposed bill: "It is further declared to be the intention of Congress that no further changes in the Organic Act shall be made except with the concurrence of the people of Puerto Rico or their duly elected representatives."[13] The search for recognition of true bilateralism, still incomplete,
started in earnest at that time. An attempt to lay the groundwork for Commonwealth status was being made.

The commission further recommended that the Governor be elected and
that he should make all appointments entrusted so far to the President, although
the President would have the power to annul any law of the Legislative Assembly. This ran counter to Roosevelt's convictions, as he thought that the Auditor
should continue to be appointed by the President.[14] The creation of the post of
a Commissioner General of the United States in Puerto Rico, opposed by
Muñoz, was also recommended.

In late 1943 Senator Millard E. Tydings filed the bill proposed by the commission.[15] Twenty-eight years after the filing of the first bill in 1919, the elective Governor proposal finally won bipartisan support. Senator Robert A. Taft
thought that the bill represented "not a very long step, but an important step,
in the direction of giving the people of Puerto Rico the right of self-govern-

ment." As to the ultimate status of Puerto Rico, Taft said in the course of the debates: "I suggest that instead of granting independence to Puerto Rico we might ultimately make Puerto Rico a sort of an autonomous dependency in which we retain our diplomatic and military status under an arrangement by which we would give certain definite contracts to the Puerto Ricans with respect to tariff and economic relations, which would insure their prosperity."[16]

The bill was approved by the Senate, but its chances in the House of Representatives were not good. Congressional hostility toward Tugwell kept climbing. Muñoz Marín, unhappy with the limited nature of the bill, asked Ickes to let the bill die, stating that he was preparing other proposals that he would later discuss with the Secretary. Ickes answered that the House was not likely to approve the bill and expressed his concern that Muñoz would not back reintroduction of the bill in 1945.[17]

After the victory of his party by a landslide, in 1945 and 1946 Muñoz Marín was keenly interested in convincing Congress of the importance of agreeing to a formula for finally decolonizing Puerto Rico. This led to the filing in 1945 of the Tydings-Piñero bill, which called for a status plebiscite binding on Congress. (This bill will be discussed in the next chapter, as it is properly part of the history of Commonwealth status.)

At the start of 1947, given the tepid reception given to the Tydings-Piñero bill and Interior's continued interest in the elective governor legislation, Muñoz backed again an elective Governor bill.[18] The bill was much simpler than the one recommended by the 1943 Presidential Commission. Mindful of the delicate ecology of the Jones Act, the drafters omitted the provision, suggested by the commission and excluded by the Senate, that no changes in the organic act would be made except with the concurrence of the people of Puerto Rico, nor did they attempt to amend the act in other respects. The idea was to keep the bill as simple as possible and to attempt soon afterward a full revision of the Jones Act.

The Department of the Interior took pains on its part to make clear that by enacting the bill Congress would not be surrendering any part of its precious power over Puerto Rico. Muñoz Marín did not attend the hearings. The House committee report on the bill evidenced the continued strength of the old colonial policy, with its emphasis on the gradual extension of self-governing powers (should the natives prove themselves worthy of such generosity) and its fear of shedding even a slight portion of its sovereign powers over the political destiny of others. The report stated, in language that was essentially repeated in 1950, when greater powers would be sought: "The changes which would be made by the enactment of H.R. 3309 would not alter Puerto Rico's political or fiscal relationship to the United States. Congress does not surrender any of its constitutional authority to legislate for Puerto Rico or to review insular laws. Neither would this legislation prove an obstacle to a subsequent determination by the Congress of the permanent political questions."[19]

As approved by the House, the bill allowed the President of the United States to retain the power to appoint the justices of the Supreme Court of Puerto Rico and the Auditor. The U.S. Senate concurred, except that it provided for the creation of the office of Coordinator of Federal Agencies in Puerto Rico, a position that was never filled. The House concurred and the bill was signed by President Harry Truman on August 5, 1947.[20] In 1948 Muñoz Marín was elected Governor of Puerto Rico.

10

The Establishment of the Commonwealth

Commonwealth status has often been described as an extraordinary invention that sprang from nowhere to end all debate between statehood and independence advocates. Such an apocalyptic view, which has led some to hold that there is nothing wrong with Commonwealth status as it is and that further changes are unnecessary, does not represent an accurate reading of history and has done much to distort the understanding of Commonwealth status. Commonwealth status is better seen in a more modest light, as part of the autonomist movement which in the case of Puerto Rico has its roots in the nineteenth century. It is an important part of such movement, but Commonwealth status has not yet fully met autonomists' demands. Commonwealth, with all its faults, has served Puerto Rico well, but attempting to hide its shortcomings and pretending that all is well in the oldest colony in the world does a disservice to both the people of Puerto Rico and the government of the United States.

Commonwealth status is based on two central elements: compact and constitution. The compact idea goes back to the Autonomic Charter of 1897. The Charter stated in very clear terms that it could not be amended except at Puerto Rico's request, however, and there is still dispute over the exact meaning of the legislation which so far has served as the basis for Commonwealth status. The latest expression of the compact principle when Commonwealth status was being discussed had been the report of the 1943 Presidential Commission. The second main idea, the adoption by the people of Puerto Rico of its constitution, goes back to demands by the Alianza starting in 1924 and culminating in a 1928 bill, as well as to statements by Senator Teller in the course of the debates surrounding the Foraker Act in 1900 and Congressman Towner in 1916.[1] Throughout the years these two aspirations were repeatedly set forth. The immediate precedent of the cornerstone of Commonwealth status, Public Law 600, was the Tydings-Piñero bill of 1945, which united the two ideas.[2]

The organization of the 1943 Presidential Commission to consider changes to the Jones Act leading to the elective governorship worried a strong group of independence advocates within the Popular Democratic party, who viewed it as a delaying move and urged Senator Tydings to file a new independence bill, which he did. That step led to the creation by such leaders of a Congress for Independence on August 15, 1943, to support the second Tydings bill, with amendments to ease Puerto Rico's transition to independence. Such was the strength of this movement that an absolute majority of the Legislative Assembly of Puerto Rico signed a declaration backing the Tydings bill. Muñoz Marín did not sign the declaration, but he wished the Congress well "in expressing to the people of the United States the ideals which unquestionably are those of the majority of Puerto Ricans."[3] The second Tydings bill did not progress, but the groundwork for a new party had been laid. The leaders of the Congress for Independence had begun to doubt Muñoz Marín's commitment to independence. As they became more convinced of Muñoz Marín's change in ideas, they met on July 25, 1946, to create a new political party to support independence, which two years later would officially be established as the Partido Independentista Puertorriqueño.

In the meantime, in its platform for the 1944 elections, the Popular Democratic party again stated that status would not be an issue, but that a plebiscite on status would be held after the war ended. The PDP won by a landslide, even though the Unión Republicana Progresista, the Socialist party, and the Liberal party agreed on common candidates to oppose it. The PDP swept all senatorial districts and thirty-four of the thirty-five representative districts.

Soon after the elections, on January 10, 1945, Tydings filed his third independence bill. Muñoz Marín testified at the Senate hearings and emphasized that self-determination should be the guiding principle and that Congress should accordingly make known which status alternatives were acceptable to it, for the people of Puerto Rico to choose. Senator Tydings reacted favorably to Muñoz Marín's proposal and asked him to submit an alternative bill. This is the background of the Tydings-Piñero bill, filed on May 16, 1945, by Tydings in the Senate and in the House by Jesús T. Piñero, a PDP leader elected Resident Commissioner in 1944 and appointed Governor of Puerto Rico in 1946.[4]

The Tydings-Piñero bill called for a referendum on independence, statehood, and what was called an Associated State or a dominion. Each status was defined in detail. The independence option was drafted in more generous terms than the previous Tydings bills. The statehood section was a typical enabling act, with no transition period, as then put forth by its proponents.

The main elements of the Associated State were the following. The people of Puerto Rico would hold a constitutional convention for drafting a constitution of their own, to be submitted to Congress for its approval or rejection. Once approved, the United States would relinquish all sovereignty over Puerto Rico, but could retain property rights on military bases and other installations. Instead of a common citizenship, there would be reciprocal citizenship rights. The citizens of the Associated State would not be citizens of the United States, but would have U.S. citizenship rights when traveling to the United States or abroad. The citizens of the United States would be able to travel freely to Puerto Rico. Puerto Rico would have its own immigration policy otherwise.

A common market would continue to exist. All federal assistance laws, past and future, would continue to apply. No provision was made as to other laws, except that United States declarations of war and related legislation would continue to bind Puerto Rico and the internal revenue laws would not apply. Puerto Rico would be able to enter into commercial and other kinds of treaties, except those of a military nature, and could have diplomatic representation of its own. Finally, no change in the relations between the United States and Puerto Rico could be effected except by mutual consent.

The Tydings-Piñero bill never got out of committee, yet, with all its naiveté in light of the times, it is important for understanding the process by which the Commonwealth of Puerto Rico was established. The bill had three basic components: it represented an attempt to advance self-government through the recognition of the right of the people of Puerto Rico to adopt a constitution of their own; it explicitly placed the relations between the United States and Puerto Rico on a mutual consent basis; and it proposed substantial changes in such relations. As will be seen, Public Law 600 of 1950 was clear as to the first objective, murky as to the second, and completely omitted the third. Law 600 was thus a truncated version of the Tydings-Piñero bill. The story of the past forty-odd years is partly the story of the autonomista attempts to complete what was originally sought in this bill, to unmistakably place the relations between the United States and Puerto Rico on a basis of mutual consent and to eliminate the remaining colonial connotations in such relations.

The experience with the Presidential Commission of 1943, the process of adoption of the Elective Governor Act, and the failure of the Tydings-Piñero bill had a sobering effect on Muñoz Marín and the PDP. The government of the United States was clearly not in the mood for a fundamental reform of its relations with Puerto Rico, in spite of all the talk about self-determination in the Atlantic Charter and in the Charter of the United Nations. The decision was accordingly made by the PDP to design a simpler approach to the problem and pare down the party's aspirations for the short term.

Status thus became an issue in the 1948 general elections. Arrayed against the Popular Democratic party were the Statehood party (the new name of the Unión Republicana Progresista), the recently organized Independence party, and remnants of other organizations. The leader of the Nationalist party, Pedro Albizu Campos, had been released from jail on June 3, 1943, and returned to Puerto Rico on December 17, 1947. He was publicly accusing Muñoz Marín of treason for having betrayed independence.

Muñoz Marín ran for Governor. The Statehood, Socialist, and Reformist parties backed a common candidate, Martín Travieso, Chief Justice of the Supreme Court of Puerto Rico from 1944 until shortly before the elections. The PDP won all the senatorial and representative districts, obtaining 61 percent of the vote, as compared to 13.7 percent for the Statehood party, 10.3 percent for the Independence party, 10 percent for the Socialists, and 4 percent for others.

The drafting of what was to be Law 600 by Muñoz Marín, the new Resident Commissioner, Dr. Antonio Fernós Isern, and their advisers, started a year after the demise of the Tydings-Piñero bill. The advisability of tackling the problem of the applicability of federal laws in Puerto Rico without its consent was then under serious consideration. A model for some of the discussions was the British Statute of Westminster, which stated that no British law would apply to the dominions, except at their request or with their consent, and that the dominions could repeal any British law until then applicable to them.[5]

The drafts started to more closely reflect the final product in early 1950. By January 10, the task of writing the constitution was being entrusted to a constitutional convention, instead of to the legislature. Formal contact was established with the Division of Territories of the Department of Interior, which had been watching the proceedings with a jaundiced eye and felt somewhat slighted by not having been consulted beforehand. As happened with the Elective Governor legislation, the division was most anxious to make clear that the proposed petition for Puerto Rico to draft its own constitution did not effect any fundamental change in its relation to the United States. The division was particularly wary of any attempt, as in the discussions of the 1943 Presidential Commission, to inject the compact idea. The division actually offered to draft the bill, as it had been accustomed to doing. The offer was ignored and the ensuing muted tension had its effect on the committees' reports, as the division had excellent contacts with the chairmen and their staff.[6]

By February 20 the requirement that the constitution be subject to approval by Congress had been inserted, and internal debate was raging on whether the compact idea should be expressed in the clear language of the Northwest Ordinance of 1787. The Ordinance stated that its provisions were adopted "as articles of compact between the original States, and the people and States in the said territory, and forever remain unalterable, unless by common consent."[7] Resident Commissioner Fernós Isern was in favor of the principle of bilateral relations, but thought that such a phrase was unnecessary, that the principle could be derived from the procedure to be followed, subjecting the proposed legislation to approval by the people of Puerto Rico, and that bold reiteration could imperil passage of the bill. A compromise was reached by stating in the draft that the act was being approved "in the nature of a compact."

As late as March 3 the question of whether Congress should be given the power to approve the constitution was still being debated. The final version was produced ten days later and in that form was filed by Fernós.[8]

The bill was, as planned, a short one "to provide for the organization of a constitutional government by the people of Puerto Rico." After a brief preamble stating that Congress had progressively recognized the right of self-government of the Puerto Rican people and that "under the terms of these Congressional enactments an increasingly large measure of self-government has been achieved," the first section stated: "Fully recognizing the principle of government by consent, this Act is now adopted in the nature of a compact so that the people of Puerto Rico may organize a government pursuant to a constitution of their own adoption."

The second section provided that the act would be submitted to the voters of Puerto Rico for acceptance or rejection through a referendum. Should the act be approved, the legislature was authorized to call a constitutional convention to draft a constitution for Puerto Rico. This constitution would provide, it was further stated, a republican form of government and include a bill of rights.

The third section provided for transmission of the constitution to Congress by the President of the United States upon the condition that he found that the constitution conformed to the provisions of the act. Upon approval by Congress, the constitution would become effective immediately in accordance with its terms.

The fourth section sustained, under the name of the Puerto Rican Federal Relations Act, the provisions of the Jones Act that were not repealed by section 5. Section 5 repealed most of the sections of the Jones Act which dealt primarily with the establishment of a local government for Puerto Rico.

The Senate held preliminary hearings on the subject of the bill the same day it was filed, March 13, 1950. Muñoz Marín testified without referring to any fundamental change being effected in the relation between Puerto Rico and the United States. Senator Joseph C. O'Mahoney from Wyoming, chairman of the Interior and Insular Affairs Committee, wanted to register a stronger defense against the charge of colonialism being constantly leveled against the United States. He remarked: "I would like to have it clearly on the record that the relationship between the Federal Government of the United States and Puerto Rico, since the island came under the jurisdiction of this Government, has never been one of colonial exploitation of the people." Muñoz Marín replied, contrary to his often expressed position: "That is correct, and the Federal Government has at times been more helpful than at other times, but at all times its attitude has been one of helpfulness toward Puerto Rico."[9]

At the House hearings the next day Muñoz did clarify his views on this matter, however, in an exchange with Congressman Lemke, who asked whether he preferred a self-government as a possession or territory of the United States. Muñoz answered: "Certainly not as a possession, sir. I do not believe that Americans can be possessions of other Americans." Later he made a statement to Lemke which was quite damaging to the compact theory: "You know, of course, that if the people of Puerto Rico should go crazy, Congress can always get around and legislate again. But I am confident that the Puerto Ricans will not do that, and invite congressional legislation that would take back something that was given to the people of Puerto Rico as good American citizens." Resident Commissioner Fernós compounded the damage by adding: "I would like to make two comments: One, the road to the courts would always be open to anybody who found that an amendment to the constitution went beyond the framework laid down by Congress; and, secondly, the authority of the government of the United States, of the Congress, to legislate in case of need would always be there."[10]

In the course of the several hearings held and in the reports filed, the Department of the Interior and the various committees took pains to state that the bill would not change Puerto Rico's relationship to the United States. Interior Secretary Oscar Chapman wrote: "It is important at the outset to avoid any misunderstanding as to the nature and general scope of the proposed legislation. Let me say that enactment of H.R. 7674 will in no way commit the Congress to the enactment of statehood legislation for Puerto Rico in the future. Nor will it in any way preclude a future determination by Congress of Puerto Rico's ultimate political status. . . . The bill under consideration would not change Puerto Rico's political, social, and economic relationship to the United States."[11]

Resident Commissioner Fernós agreed with this at the same time that he emphasized the compact theory. On the one hand, he stated that S. 3336 "would have the nature of a compact. In this respect it follows the precedent established by the Northwest Ordinance, albeit its terms are not identical." But, on the other hand, he affirmed that S. 3336 "would not change the status of the island of Puerto Rico relative to the United States. . . . It would not alter the powers of sovereignty acquired by the United States under the terms of the Treaty of Paris."[12]

Both the Senate and the House reports said that "The measure would not change Puerto Rico's fundamental political, social, and economic relationship to the United States."[13] The measure sailed smoothly through Congress, and on July 3, 1950, President Truman signed it into law.

Ever since the debates on Law 600 in Congress, and increasingly in the course of the referendum for its acceptance or rejection, the charge that the vaunted compact between Puerto Rico and the United States was a sham—that Law 600 did not, and constitutionally could not, create such a thing—caused the PDP to take care that the record from then on firmly emphasized the compact theory. The PDP also made sure to counter the parts of the legislative record which so far negated the claim that the relations between the United States and Puerto Rico were based on the principle of government by consent. Muñoz Marín's speeches during the referendum campaign and the constitutional convention reflected this approach, as well as his efforts after the referenda on Law 600 and the constitution.

The referendum on Law 600 was held on June 4, 1951. The Independence party resolved to vote against the law. The Statehood party was divided; the older leadership was for it and the younger, led by Miguel Angel García Méndez and Luis A. Ferré, against. The party finally decided not to take an official position and let its members vote their conscience. The Socialist party was in favor of the law.

The Nationalist party, however, was alarmed. It branded Law 600 as an attempt by the United States, abetted by Muñoz Marín, to perpetuate Puerto Rico's colonial condition. On October 30, 1950, bands of nationalists attacked seven towns and captured one of them, Jayuya. On the same day five men unsuccessfully tried to force their way into the Governor's official residence to kill Muñoz Marín.[14] On November 1 two nationalists tried to assassinate President Harry Truman at Blair House in Washington, D.C. More than 4,000 National Guard soldiers and officers had to be mobilized in Puerto Rico. In all, twenty-eight people, including nine nationalists, were killed, and forty-nine people were wounded in the island. In 1954 nationalists sprayed bullets at the United States House of Representatives from the spectators' gallery and wounded five Congressmen. The nationalists were apprehended, convicted, and jailed.

In the course of the campaign Muñoz Marín stated time and again his understanding of Law 600: that it consecrated the principle of compact and that it and the Federal Relations Act could not be amended without the consent of the people of Puerto Rico. The opposition countered these statements, claiming that Puerto Rico continued to be a colony of the United States. Law 600 was finally approved by 76.5 percent of the vote in the referendum.

The members of the constitutional convention were selected at elections held on August 27, 1951. The candidates backed by the PDP got 80 percent of the vote, compared to 11.5 percent for the Statehood slate and the rest for the Socialists. Of ninety-two delegates, seventy were from the PDP, fifteen from the Statehood party, and seven from the Socialist party. The Independence party chose not to be on the ballot.

The convention met from September 17, 1951, to February 6, 1952. The constitution followed the main lines of a typical state constitution, with some interesting innovations. The bill of rights, largely patterned after the Universal Declaration of Rights approved by the United Nations and the American Declaration of the Rights and Duties of Man, approved at Bogotá by the Organization of American States, was generally broader than the usual state constitution, a fact that created problems when the constitution was considered by Congress. The article dealing with the legislative power also had a striking provision. As the Popular Democratic party had proved to be so powerful at the polls and the minority parties had been able to elect only a token number of legislative representatives, the PDP delegates themselves requested a device to ensure that, no matter how many votes were polled by the majority party, the minority parties would together always be able to elect at least one-third of the members of each chamber. The article dealing with the judicial power was also innovative, and the constitution of Puerto Rico became the second constitution within the United States (after that of New Jersey) to provide for full unification of its court system. The body politic created by the constitution was named the Estado Libre Asociado de Puerto Rico, which should have been translated "the Free Associated State of Puerto Rico," but was instead dubbed, by convoluted and misleading interpretation of the Spanish terms, the Commonwealth of Puerto Rico.

The fact that the Commonwealth's constitution had to be approved by Congress had a dampening effect on efforts to break new ground. Muñoz originally thought that the constitution could be used as a means to propose to Congress some of the desired changes in the relations between the United States and Puerto Rico, but early in the course of the constitutional convention the idea was discarded as impractical. Such amendments were left for another, more propitious time—which never came. All the delegates did was approve a resolution at the end of the debates, emphasizing the bilateral nature of the relationship by stating that the Commonwealth was established "within the terms of the compact entered into by mutual consent, which is the basis of our union with the United States of America." The resolution also included the somewhat innocuous statement that "The people of Puerto Rico reserve the right to propose and to accept modifications in the terms of its relations with the United States of America, in order that these relations may at all times be the expression of an agreement freely entered into between the people of Puerto Rico and the United States of America."[15]

Eighty-nine of the ninety-two convention delegates approved the constitution, which was submitted to a referendum on March 3, and passed by 80 percent of the votes cast.

The constitution was sent to President Truman on March 12, 1952, for transmittal to Congress. The Governor's draft letter of transmittal to the President, a subject of intense bilateral discussion (as was the proposed answer), stated that, although much progress had been made through the years toward the achievement of self-government, "a vestige of colonialism remained: the relationship between the United States and Puerto Rico, although increasingly liberal, was established by unilateral action, even if always taken after consultation with Puerto Rican leaders. The present process is based on bilateral action through free agreement. No doubt opinions may differ as to the details of the relationship, from both the Puerto Rican and the American points of view, but the principle that the relationship is from now on one of consent through free agreement, wipes out all trace of colonialism."[16]

On April 22, 1952, the President stated in his letter of transmittal of the Constitution to Congress: "With its approval [the constitution's], full authority and responsibility for local self-government will be vested in the people of Puerto Rico. The Commonwealth of Puerto Rico will be a government which is truly by the consent of the governed. No government can be invested with a higher dignity and greater worth than one based upon the principle of consent."[17]

The matter was far from settled. In its report favoring approval of the constitution, the House committee repeated its standard disclaimer to the effect that no change was being effected thereby in the relations between the United

States and Puerto Rico.[18] Muñoz Marín was incensed at what he considered a continued and blatant attempt to keep Puerto Rico as a colony, subject to the untrammeled will of Congress. He spoke at the Senate hearings:

> Although colonial status has been gradually disappearing, there has been lacking the basic moral element of freedom, which is consent based on free agreement. Kindness, even justice, unilaterally bestowed, may denote an anticolonialistic spirit, but it does not finally and decisively create an anticolonial status. The principle of compact contained in Law 600, specifically and in fact that it required approval by the Puerto Rican people, fully wipes out that moral lack. As we see it, we are not engaged in taking "another step in self-government—this is self-government." . . .
>
> Nothing short of self-government can be by its own nature, and by the dignity of human freedom a subject for solemn agreement. We are establishing a status that is not federated statehood, but is no less than federated statehood. . . .
>
> It is unthinkable that a free people, a people worthy of American citizenship, should deliberately go to the polls and vote for a status that they conceive as one of inequality. . . .
>
> In order best to understand what the constitutional process means to the people of Puerto Rico, I think I should point out the significance of the wrestling with the problem of political status that has gone on in the soul of our people. You gentlemen may have forgotten how colonialism lacerates the spirit of those who suffer it, because it has been such a long time, and so many generations, since you were subjected to it. Let me tell you that the feeling that they are considered inferior—especially if they feel quite sure that they are not—is a festering sore in the human spirit—the feeling that a man has the right to do without your authorization what he has not the right to do others unless with their authorization, is not conducive to the free play of constructive energies.[19]

The gnawing feeling that these words were not fully heeded in the course of establishing the Commonwealth of Puerto Rico, that the resulting relationship still had not been adequately purged of all its colonial connotations, clearly impelled Muñoz Marín to dedicate the rest of his years to efforts to add to the powers of the Puerto Rican people within a framework of association with the United States.

The Constitution was mauled in the process of its approval by Congress. Many Congressmen were unhappy with several provisions. At the end, Congress required that section 20 of the bill of rights be eliminated, despite the fact that it was closely modeled on the Declaration of Human Rights approved by the United Nations at the behest of the United States and others. Section 20 recognized, among others, but as aspirations or goals, depending on the progressive development of the economy, the right to social protection in the event of unemployment, sickness, old age, or disability; the right to obtain work; the right to an adequate standard of living; and the rights of mothers and children to special care and assistance. Congress was also unhappy with another provision requiring attendance at elementary public schools to the extent permitted by the facilities of the state. Representatives thought that the rights of nongovernmental schools were being trampled and that a quite superfluous amendment was required.

Senator Johnston from South Carolina harbored serious doubts about allowing Puerto Ricans the right to amend their constitution without the approval of Congress, reservations shared by many other Senators. He accordingly proposed an amendment to the effect that "no amendment to . . . the constitution of the Commonwealth of Puerto Rico shall be effective until approved by the Congress of the United States." The amendment was approved by the Senate. The reaction in San Juan was explosive. The majority of the members of the constitutional convention sent a cable to the conference committee, stating that "to do justice to Puerto Rico and the United States, self-government deserves to be fully and not meagerly or doubtfully recognized."

The amendment was deleted in conference, after a compromise was reached—a provision be added to the constitution to the effect that "Any amendment or revision of this constitution shall be consistent with the resolution enacted by the Congress approving this constitution, with the applicable provisions of the Constitution of the United States, with the Puerto Rican Federal Relations Act, and with Public Law 600."

In the House there had been another close call. Congressman George Meader from Michigan proposed an amendment to make sure that Congress was not divesting itself of any of its power over Puerto Rico under the territorial clause of the United States Constitution and that no compact was being entered into. The amendment stated: "Nothing herein contained shall be construed as an irrevocable delegation, transfer or release of the power of the Congress granted by article IV, section 3, of the Constitution of the United States." The amendment, which would have been rejected by the constitutional convention, was defeated, but only on procedural grounds.[20]

On July 3, 1952, President Truman signed the resolution approving the

Constitution, subject to deletion of section 20 and the clarification of the provision on compulsory education, and four days later the constitutional convention met and approved the conditions imposed by Congress.[21] On July 25, 1952, after such a harrowing ordeal and a tawdry record, the Commonwealth of Puerto Rico finally came into being.[22]

The Big Sleep

The original United States policy toward Puerto Rico changed in the first half of the twentieth century in some significant ways, although several basic elements were still present. As in the early twentieth century, Puerto Rico was not being groomed at the beginning of its second half for independence or statehood. Puerto Rico was to be held instead in perpetuity, or as long as needed, firmly under the control of Congress, as a useful guardian of eastern access to the Panama Canal, a key part of the security system for the Caribbean area and the southeastern coast of the United States, and a well-located place for naval, air, and electronic installations.

By the start of the fifties there was some occasional talk about self-determination, but nothing was done. It was rather safe rhetoric, as there seemed to be no groundswell of public opinion in Puerto Rico in favor of separation from the United States. Nevertheless, independence was discreetly frowned upon, and the independence movement, which had shown itself to be capable of violent (if disorganized) action in the thirties and again at the start of the fifties, was closely monitored and even covertly harried. Gradual and somewhat hesitant extension of increasing doses of self-government was still the prevalent policy, but without surrendering any part, or at least any vital part, of Congress' vast powers over the island.

The rights to elect a Governor and to adopt an internal constitution regarding matters of strictly local concern, closely resembling the state constitutions, were finally granted after many years, but basically in the spirit of the old gradualist policy, although there was some sense that something quite singular was being created. No territory or possession had ever enjoyed such rights. Puerto Rico was being granted powers as extensive as those of any state and, yet, it had characteristics that set it apart, such as its exemption from federal income taxes and the devolution of custom duties and internal revenue taxes on certain products. The United States and Puerto Rico were drifting into uncharted seas, which perhaps accounts for the unease displayed by the keepers of the territorial grail and their fretful insistence on asserting at each possible junction, even while the waves of change were crashing against the old policy, that everything remained as it always was.

By the end of the forties, the policy of governing Puerto Rico from afar was gone. Already during Tugwell's governorship, Puerto Rico was given enormous leeway in setting its internal course. Upon Muñoz Marín's election as Governor, intervention by the Department of the Interior in local affairs soon became a thing of the past. The change in policy paid off. From 1941 to the 1960s Puerto Rico was transformed, largely by local initiative, from a rural to an industrialized society, poor by United States standards but economically at the vanguard of Latin America and, above all, one of the most solid democracies in the Caribbean.

Already by the 1950s, the bureaucratic obsession with holding full power over Puerto Rico in the European imperialist fashion made no sense. That power was not being used for the traditional purpose of exploiting the colony. The questionable prestige of creating an empire had lost its glitter. The *mission civilisatrice,* the desire to civilize other people and bring them up to one's image, had been rightly forgotten. Americanization ceased to be a United States policy goal in Puerto Rico in the late forties. Puerto Rico spent decades in the melting pot, at high heat, and never melted. What was the reason then for the quasi-pathological insistence on keeping Puerto Rico on parole, with electronic devices on hands and feet to forewarn of any suspicious movement, claiming that the self-governing powers so far granted could at any time be unceremoniously taken away?

One explanation is that old policies never die, or at least die an agonizingly slow death, while in a coma and brain dead, but another lies in the climate of the times. The chill of the Cold War was setting in. Communism was found lurking under every stone. Puerto Rico had sporadic nationalistic and socialistic tendencies. Why tempt the gods? When Fidel Castro revealed his true colors in 1960, the reasons for not tinkering further with the political status of Puerto Rico seemed to grow stronger.

To Puerto Ricans of the fifties and later, however, who were conscious of the deficiencies of Commonwealth status as it emerged from the legislative wringer, keeping Puerto Rico in a state of subjection did not seem to be as much a conscious policy as just plain, unplanned inattention, unstudied indifference. Muñoz Marín and other leaders accordingly decided to try to engage in a franker discussion between Puerto Rico and the United States as to what had been accomplished and what was needed to rid Commonwealth status of its remaining colonial connotations. This decision led to the 1953 proceedings at the United Nations, started at Puerto Rico's request, and to the various attempts since then to decolonize Puerto Rico once and for all.

The initial discussion of the Puerto Rican case at the United Nations shall first be considered in this chapter; later events at the U.N. will be examined in the next. The story of other efforts to improve the political condition of the island after 1952 to the present shall then be told.

Article 73e of the Charter of the United Nations required any country in charge of a non-self-governing territory to transmit information to the U.N. periodically on the political and economic conditions prevailing therein. Pursuant to a 1948 resolution, the General Assembly had also indicated its desire to be informed of any change in the constitutional status of a non-self-governing area as a result of which the administering country thought it necessary to discontinue sending such information.[1] Since its approval there had been dissension as to the meaning of the charter and the 1948 resolution. The eight countries still administering non-self-governing territories, including the United States, held that the decision on whether a territory had ceased being a colony was for them to decide, and others claimed that it was up to the General Assembly of the United Nations to judge.

The process for excluding Puerto Rico from the United Nations list of non-self-governing territories was started by a letter from Governor Muñoz Marín of Puerto Rico to President Truman asking him to cease transmitting information under article 73e of the Charter. The Governor's letter and the President's eventual communication to the United Nations were the subject of protracted confidential discussions with the Department of the Interior and the Department of State. The ensuing debate provided an opportunity to thrash out the varying views as to what Commonwealth status meant and was intended to accomplish.

The first draft of the proposed communication from the Governor to the President, discussed with both departments, minced no words.[2] In addition to stating that "However happy the relationship was in fact, the people of Puerto Rico were not satisfied to remain in a status which, in theory although not in practice, reflected the taint of colonialism," the draft went on to say that the people of Puerto Rico were now self-governing and that "their status and the terms of their association with the United States cannot be changed without their agreement." The negotiators at the Department of the Interior and the Department of State were aghast at the use of the term *colonialism*.[3] Nor did they agree with the view that there was a compact between Puerto Rico and the United States. James P. Davis, director of the Division of Territories of the Interior Department, came to San Juan to discuss the matter further. At the same time, Vernon D. Northrup, Acting Secretary of the Interior, wrote to Dean Acheson, Secretary of State, insisting that Puerto Rico should still be considered a territory of the United States. The government of Puerto Rico held fast to its position.

On January 29, 1953, the Department of State notified the United Nations that it would no longer transmit information on Puerto Rico under article 73e. The memorandum in support of such notification, which was not filed until March 21, glossed over the differences between the United States and Puerto Rico on the meaning of Commonwealth status. Puerto Rico's position was expressed through reference to Resolution No. 23 of the constitutional convention, which stated its understanding of the meaning of Commonwealth status, but the United States carefully refrained from endorsing such an interpretation.[4] The government of Puerto Rico was not pleased with the result, and serious consideration was given to requesting the United States to withdraw its claim that Puerto Rico had ceased being a non-self-governing territory. This option was finally discarded for two reasons: it did not seem proper to embarrass the United States before the world, and, especially, conversations on the presentation of the case before the United Nations still held the prospect of full agreement on the meaning of Commonwealth status.

The debates at the United Nations occurred before three entities: the Committee on Information on Non-Self-Governing Territories, the Fourth Committee, and the General Assembly. There was from the start evident skepticism at the U.N., as there is now, as to whether Puerto Rico had ceased being a colony, a fact which unquestionably helped in the final and full acceptance by the United States delegation, in its discussions with the representatives from Puerto Rico, of Puerto Rico's interpretation of its relationship to the United States. The Puerto Rican case, however, became a battleground for much more than the issue of Puerto Rico's status. The real issue was actually who had the power to judge whether a given territory had indeed become fully self-governing. At a time when the General Assembly had not yet resolved what factors were to be used for ruling that decolonization had truly taken place, the Puerto Rican case was a means for the General Assembly to assert its power to issue such a judgment, as against the contention of the eight colonial powers that such was their prerogative. Puerto Rico was the first case in which the issue was joined and votes cast in the General Assembly.

The United States argued with increasing force against the charges that Puerto Rico's colonial status had not changed, finally adopting in full the position of the Puerto Rican government. Mason Sears, United States delegate to the Committee on Information, spoke without compunction about the compact between Puerto Rico and the United States. "A compact," he said, "is far stronger than a treaty. A treaty can be denounced by either side, whereas a compact cannot be denounced by either party unless it has the permission of the other."[5]

After several further discussions and appropriate clearing by the State Department, Frances P. Bolton, the American delegate to the Fourth Committee of the United Nations, made the following key declaration:

> The Federal Relations Act to which reference has been made has continued provisions of political and economic union which the people of Puerto Rico have wished to maintain. In this sense the relationships between Puerto Rico and the United States have not changed. It would be wrong, however, to hold that because this is so and has been so declared in Congress, the creation of the Commonwealth of Puerto Rico does not signify a fundamental change in the status of Puerto Rico. The previous status of Puerto Rico was that of a territory subject to the full authority of the Congress of the United States in all governmental matters. The previous constitution of Puerto Rico was in fact a law of the Congress of the United States, which we called an Organic Act. Only Congress could amend the Organic Act of Puerto Rico. *The present status of Puerto Rico is that of a people with a constitution of their own adoption, stemming from their own authority, which only they can alter or amend. The relationships previously established also by a law of the Congress, which only Congress could amend, have now become provisions of a compact of a bilateral nature whose terms may be changed only by common consent.*[6] (emphasis supplied)

When the report of the Fourth Committee came up for a vote at the General Assembly, opposition to the proposal that information on Puerto Rico should cease was still extremely strong. In the course of the debate, Ambassador Henry Cabot Lodge (grandson of the turn-of-the-century Senator) saw fit to make the following declaration to assure some wavering votes: "I am authorized to say on behalf of the President that if, at any time, the Legislative Assembly of

Puerto Rico adopts a resolution in favor of more complete or even absolute independence, he will immediately thereafter recommend to Congress that such independence be granted. The President also wishes me to say that in this event, he would welcome Puerto Rico's adherence to the Treaty of Rio de Janeiro and the United Nations Charter."[7]

On November 27, 1953, the General Assembly approved by a vote of 26–16, with eighteen abstentions, Resolution 748 (VIII), which considered it appropriate that transmission of information on Puerto Rico should cease.[8] The General Assembly stated, "the people of the Commonwealth of Puerto Rico . . . have achieved a new constitutional status," adding that the assembly "recognizes that, in the framework of their Constitution and the compact agreed upon with the United States of America, the people of the Commonwealth of Puerto Rico have been invested with attributes of political sovereignty which clearly identify the status of self-government attained by the Puerto Rican people as that of an autonomous political entity." The United States opposed the provision in the resolution which affirmed "the competence of the General Assembly to decide whether a Non-Self-Governing Territory has or has not attained a full measure of self-government." On that issue the United States was defeated 34–19, with seven abstentions.

There was little sense of triumph among the PDP leadership after the United Nations vote and even second thoughts as to whether it had been wise to ask that Puerto Ricans be declared a self-governing people. The Federal Relations Act remained untouched. Consent to its terms was far too broad. Among many other things, how could the continued power of Congress to legislate for Puerto Rico unilaterally on an extraordinarily wide range of matters be consonant with the principle of government by consent? The legislative record of Law 600 was not good, either. There was little evidence that Congress would go along with the interpretation placed on Puerto Rico's status at the United Nations by the United States government. There was a long way to go before Puerto Rico could objectively be held to have ceased being a colony of the United States.

As it happened, in addition to Congress, even the executive departments of the government of the United States soon lost all memory of what had so solemnly been proclaimed at the United Nations. They behaved as if no compact of any kind existed and as if Puerto Rico continued to be a territory or possession of the United States, completely subject to its sovereign will. Puerto Rico leaders would spend the rest of the century unsuccessfully trying to convince the United States to allow full decolonization.

There were two schools of thought initially within the government of

Puerto Rico as to how to proceed to the second stage of full autonomy, attempted in the Tydings-Piñero bill and largely obtained in the Autonomic Charter, but left pending in Law 600. Some thought that the most appropriate way was to keep whittling away, bit by bit, without fanfare, at the remaining rough edges of the old organic act, now the Federal Relations Act. Others favored a thorough overhaul of the largely outmoded and deficient Federal Relations Act and the negotiation of a more advanced, unambiguous compact, which would truly decolonize Puerto Rico.

The first approach was tried briefly in a joint resolution filed March 4, 1953, by Resident Commissioner Fernós.[9] It amended or did away with some provisions that reduced the scope of self-government, including Congress' setting of the debt margin of the government of Puerto Rico and its municipalities, and the anomaly of subjecting the decisions of the Supreme Court of Puerto Rico to revision by the Court of Appeals for the First Circuit, instead of the United States Supreme Court. The bill was abandoned in favor of a broader approach.

At the time, the chief objectives of the autonomist movement were the following: raising the standard of living of the Puerto Rican people as fast as possible; reducing the functions of the United States government in Puerto Rico to those considered mutually essential to the continued association between the two peoples; limiting the right of Congress to legislate for Puerto Rico without the latter's consent, except in such areas as defense, including declarations of war and military service, citizenship, the common market, and the like, which would be entrusted to the United States; recognizing Puerto Rico's power to participate in selected international organizations and activities; and developing a formula for Puerto Rico to contribute, according to its means and increasingly as conditions allowed, to the United States treasury.[10]

These were not idle musings. The PDP had polled over 60 percent of the vote at the 1952 elections, but the Independence party had grown impressively, polling 125,734 votes out of 664,947 and becoming the second strongest party in the island; the Statehood party obtained only 85,172 votes. A greater measure of self-government was constantly being demanded. Events in the Caribbean, closely followed in Puerto Rico, were also indicating that the British, Dutch, and French colonies were swiftly moving toward full decolonization at a faster rate than Puerto Rico (see chapter 13). Finally, the Puerto Rican leadership was becoming increasingly worried about excessive dependence on United States largesse, without a corresponding effort by Puerto Ricans to develop a better work ethic and also contribute to their fellow citizens. A thorough review of the relations between the United States and Puerto Rico seemed to be in order.

Work on a complete revision of the Federal Relations Act accordingly began, although it was subordinated for the moment to improving the economic
conditions of the island.[11] Puerto Rico's efforts to help itself were well re-
warded. With the assistance of the United States in maintaining a legal structure that permitted Puerto Rico to become an attractive place for American and
worldwide investment, the rate of growth of the gross product of Puerto Rico
soon reached and stayed in double digits for a considerable number of years. The
island was able to develop first a manufacturing base and then a service economy; vast slums were eliminated; education expanded; health conditions improved; tourism blossomed, even though the government of Puerto Rico had to
show the way to reluctant investors by building the first world-class hotels itself. Although lagging behind politically, Puerto Rico became in those years a
shining example of how a people could start lifting itself out of despair.[12]

After completion of the preliminary studies for the reform of the Federal
Relations Act, a task to which Harvard professor Carl J. Friedrich and others
contributed significantly, a resolution was enacted by the Legislative Assembly
of Puerto Rico in 1958 requesting changes in the Federal Relations Act. It asked,
among other things, that the Commonwealth of Puerto Rico be described in a
way that would not permit any possible charge that it was a "possession" or "territory" of the United States; that a mechanism be established so that the Commonwealth of Puerto Rico could gradually assume, as its economic condition
would warrant, federal functions being carried out in Puerto Rico that were not
essential to the nature of the association; that a better system be adopted to rule
the applicability of federal laws to Puerto Rico; and that Puerto Rico's right to
decide whether it would be included in commercial treaties negotiated by the
United States be recognized.[13]

This resolution served as the basis for the Fernós–Murray bill filed in early
1959 by Fernós and James E. Murray, chairman of the Senate Interior and Insular Affairs Committee.[14] There was great hostility to the bill from the start.
At the Senate hearings Muñoz Marín reminded the committee of the declarations made by the government of the United States before the United Nations
and repeatedly noted, as did the bill itself, that the relationship between the
United States and Puerto Rico was based on a compact. Senator O'Mahoney
interrupted Muñoz: "Do you regard Public Law 600 . . . do you call that a compact?" Muñoz answered: "Senator, the law that you have mentioned, plus its acceptance by the people at the polls, plus Law 447, in which the Congress approved the Puerto Rican constitution—those three actions, Senator, I
undoubtedly and unequivocally regard as a compact, which gave great dignity

to the people of Puerto Rico and great prestige to the American Union as a whole." O'Mahoney then relented, stating: "Well, it was intended to do that. I can speak from personal knowledge because I was here when that was done and played some part in it."[15] Senator Henry (Scoop) Jackson also questioned Muñoz on the subject, but remained unconvinced that there was a compact or even constitutional authority to enter into one.

Many departments objected to several provisions of the bill, especially those changing in any significant way United States–Puerto Rico relations. The Department of State, however, found it acceptable,[16] and the Department of Justice had no trouble with the issue as to the power of the United States to enter into a binding compact with the people of Puerto Rico.[17] Despite the favorable views of State and Justice, the bill's chances of passage seemed dim, and the government of Puerto Rico discreetly asked the committee chairmen to allow the bill to die a peaceful death.

Upon the election in 1960 of President John F. Kennedy, the decision was made to enter into wide-ranging discussions with the White House on a revised compact. The new President was most agreeable to the idea and appointed a group of trusted advisors to meet representatives from the Puerto Rican government and consider ways to improve the present status and purge it of all possible undesirable connotations. United States members of the group, which was to function outside the glare of publicity, were Adolf Berle, a former member of Roosevelt's brain trust and Kennedy consultant; William Bundy, from the Department of Defense; Abram Chayes, State Department counsel; Richard Goodwin, then at the Department of State; Nicholas de B. Katzenbach, Assistant Attorney General and soon to be named Attorney General; Harold Reis, a high official in the Department of Justice who was acquainted with Puerto Rico's problems; Arthur M. Schlesinger, Jr., the historian; and Lee C. White, Legal Counsel to the President. It was a dream team to undertake serious, high-level discussions on Puerto Rico's status. Muñoz Marín headed the small Puerto Rican delegation.

Several meetings were held over the following months, the first at the Hay-Adams Hotel in Washington on February 14, 1962, and the rest in secluded places in Puerto Rico.[18] The legal feasibility of the compact and of the ideas being proffered on the development of Commonwealth status were amply discussed, and Reis was charged with preparing a memorandum on the subject. The conclusion was that the more reasonable reading of the constitution of Puerto Rico was that Congress could permanently divest itself of part of its territorial powers and that "It may therefore be possible to work out a relationship under which Puerto Rico could be in a position to conduct commercial relations with foreign nations, participate in international organizations and perhaps attempt to gain admission to the United Nations."[19]

The nature of the bill to be presented to Congress was then discussed in very great detail, the Puerto Rican delegation submitting the first draft. Among the many matters discussed, it was agreed that the best approach to the division of powers would be for the United States to exercise in Puerto Rico only such powers as be expressly delegated to it in the compact, the people of Puerto Rico to retain the rest. Defense and other matters deemed vital to the security of the United States, including the holding of the necessary military bases, would remain as they were, and the United States would be entrusted with all other functions considered necessary to permanent association with Puerto Rico. Federal laws relating to such functions would continue to apply to Puerto Rico as if Puerto Rico were a state. No other federal laws would apply, except with the consent of the people of Puerto Rico. Federal assistance legislation would apply only to the extent that Congress would so determine unilaterally and could be discontinued at any time. Puerto Rico would contribute to the cost of federal services in Puerto Rico by assigning a percentage of its national income to the United States treasury. Each function then exercised by the United States in Puerto Rico was the subject of protracted study and discussion. A formal commission was to be appointed to negotiate the compact and submit it to the Congress for approval or rejection. If approved, it would then be submitted to the people of Puerto Rico in a referendum in which the people would also have the opportunity to petition Congress instead for independence or statehood.

On April 30, 1963, Congressman Wayne N. Aspinall of Colorado introduced the bill, which created a United States–Puerto Rico Compact Commission, composed of members appointed by the President of the United States, the President of the United States Senate, the Speaker of the House, and the Governor of Puerto Rico.[20] The commission was asked to draft a "compact of permanent union between the government of the United States and the people of Puerto Rico," pursuant to such principles as "the recognition and reassertion of the sovereignty of the people of Puerto Rico"; "the permanence and irrevocability of the union between the United States and Puerto Rico on the basis of common citizenship, common defense, common currency, free market, common loyalty to the values of democracy, and of such other conditions as may be considered, in the compact, of mutual benefit to the United States and Puerto Rico"; "the specific definition of the powers of the United States with respect to Puerto Rico and the reservation of all other powers to the people of Puerto

Rico"; "the participation by the people of Puerto Rico in the powers exercised, under the compact, by the Government of the United States, in matters affecting Puerto Rico, in a measure proportional to the scope of such powers and the adoption of a formula under which the people of Puerto Rico would contribute, in a manner compatible with the stability and economic growth of Puerto Rico, to the general expenses of the United States Government."

The bill was savaged at the hearings. Several Congressmen were skeptical about the existence of any compact between the people of Puerto Rico and the United States, and even about its constitutionality, should a compact ever be agreed upon. The following exchange between Congressman John P. Saylor of Pennsylvania and Muñoz Marín was typical of the difficulties being experienced. Saylor commented that Congressman Fred L. Crawford of Michigan, chairman of the committee when Law 600 was being considered, said that nothing had been offered Puerto Rico but the opportunity to vote on a local constitution, and that there was no intention of entering into any compact with the people of Puerto Rico, adding a few choice comments of his own. Visibly angered, Muñoz answered: "Congressman, I have had a great friendship for Mr. Crawford and I have a great respect for his memory, but I would not agree with him on that. If he was right, then Puerto Rico is still a colony of the United States. If it is still a colony of the United States it should stop being a colony as soon as possible for the honor of the United States and for the sense of self-respect of the people of Puerto Rico."[21]

For several months efforts were made to preserve the main features of the bill, but to no avail. On October 7, 1963, the committee reported out the bill, recommending amendments that much diminished its significance. A commission was created—not, as requested, to draft a compact under a set of specific guidelines for later consideration by Congress and the people of Puerto Rico with a three-way referendum to follow—but just to take "into account all factors which may have a bearing on the future relationship between the United States and Puerto Rico . . . and . . . formulate . . . such recommendations with respect thereto as it may deem advisable in the light of its study." In the Senate the bill was described as purely investigatory, there being so much controversy as to what Commonwealth status meant, and it was also stated that the Congress was in no way committed to take action once the commission rendered its report. In such fashion the bill became law on February 20, 1964.[22]

The Status Commission was composed of an equal number of members from the United States and Puerto Rico and had a distinguished secretariat headed by Ben Stephansky, former United States ambassador to Bolivia. Its first meeting took place in June 1964, but work did not start in earnest until after the election in November. Muñoz Marín decided not to run for a fifth term as Governor, and Roberto Sánchez Vilella, his top assistant for many years, ran instead. The PDP again won, polling 58.6 percent of the vote against 34 percent for the Statehood party and less than 3 percent each for the Independence party and the Christian Action party (a short-lived sally of the Catholic bishops in Puerto Rico into partisan politics).

The final report of the commission was filed in 1966. It concluded on the legal factors affecting the status problem that "The policy governing the relationship between the United States and Puerto Rico is and should continue to be based on the principles of mutual consent and self-determination," and that "We can see no constitutional bar to prevent Congress under the existing Constitution of the United States from entering into innovative forms of relationships within the Federal structure including a binding relationship." On the economic factors it decided that "An immediate or abrupt change in political status would involve serious economic risks and dislocations. These could be offset by special economic and financial arrangements which, in the case of Statehood, would involve assistance well beyond the levels Puerto Rico is today receiving." The transition period for statehood was estimated at no less than fifteen years and much longer for independence.[23]

The commission finally recommended that a plebiscite be held among the three status formulas and that one or more ad hoc committees be appointed to recommend to Congress the appropriate measures to implement the results. The plebiscite was held on July 23, 1967. Commonwealth status, not as it stood, but purged of its colonial connotations, polled 425,081 votes against 273,315 for statehood and 4,205 for independence. Except for its brief periods of glory in 1900–1904 and 1933–1941, statehood continued to be a minority movement. The low vote in favor of independence is explained by the fact that the Independence party as such boycotted the plebiscite.

All this would come to nothing. Self-determination was supposedly the order of the day, but Congress did not pay the slightest attention to the expression of the popular will in Puerto Rico, even though the plebiscite was held upon the recommendation of the commission set up by Congress itself.

Not renominated for a new term as Governor in 1968, Sánchez Vilella founded his own political organization, and the weakened PDP lost that year by a slim margin to the newly founded New Progressive party (NPP), the successor to the Statehood party. This temporarily derailed the plans for negotiating a new compact pursuant to the plebiscite mandate. Instead, in 1970 Governor

Luis A. Ferré, a respected businessman and patron of the arts, organized jointly with President Richard M. Nixon an ad hoc committee to study the possibility of granting Puerto Ricans the right to vote in presidential elections. The committee rendered a favorable report, which was not acted upon.[24]

The electoral triumph of the NPP, with 42.4 percent of the vote, brought an end to twenty-eight years of uninterrupted PDP rule. From then on the two parties would alternate in office, although the NPP did not receive 50 percent of the vote until 1996. In 1972, the PDP, led by a young Senator and former Attorney General, Rafael Hernández Colón, won again. Carlos Romero Barceló (former mayor of San Juan and grandson of the former president of the Liberal party, Antonio R. Barceló), who succeeded Ferré as president of the NPP, became Governor in 1976 and was reelected in 1980. In 1984 and 1988 Hernández Colón won the governorship for a second and third terms, until his retirement. In 1992, Pedro Rosselló, a distinguished physician, defeated former Senator Victoria Muñoz Mendoza, daughter of Muñoz Marín. Rosselló was the first NPP Governor to call for a second status plebiscite, held in 1993. All his predecessors had talked for years about the need for one, but nothing had been done before then out of fear of a second rejection of statehood, which was indeed what happened. Dr. Rosselló was reelected in 1996.

Soon after his election in 1972, Hernández Colón discussed with President Nixon the creation of a new ad hoc committee to draft a completely new compact, in deference to the mandate of the 1967 plebiscite. The group was constituted on September 20, 1973, and was co-chaired by Luis Muñoz Marín and Senator Marlow Cook, from Kentucky.

This time the draft of the revised compact encountered greater difficulties than the Kennedy group's version had. The United States delegation even had difficulties with the concept that Puerto Rico's relationship to the United States was in many ways unique and that in some areas it could have greater powers than a state, as well as problems with the possibility of a binding compact.

At the request of the group another draft compact was prepared by the Puerto Rican delegation and circulated to various federal government agencies. The reaction of the Department of Justice was again favorable to the constitutionality of a compact which could not be changed except by mutual consent.[25] The State Department favored participation of the Free Associated State of Puerto Rico (the name used in the draft instead of "Commonwealth") in international organizations concerned with social, economic, educational, scientific, technical, and cultural matters, with the approval of the State Department on a case-by-case basis and, where appropriate, by Congress. It had no objection, either, to the establishment of a separate immigration system for Puerto Rico.[26] The Department of Defense also had no objection to the sections pertaining to security and defense.[27]

Other agencies strenuously objected to several provisions of the compact. The Department of the Interior, in traditional fashion, stated that the proposed compact "appears to weaken the sovereign relationship of the United States to Puerto Rico by granting Puerto Rico certain exceptions that do not apply to the several states or territories."[28]

The White House staff was against the proposed compact well before it received the agency's comments. As early as May 1975, Norman E. Ross, the assistant in charge of following up on the work of the committee, wrote to James Cannon, Assistant to the President on Domestic Affairs: "The proposal contains several far-reaching provisions which would give Puerto Rico significantly greater autonomy than that enjoyed by the States, in the area of Federal regulatory statutes and their accompanying federal regulations. On the other side of the administrative fence, the proposal would establish Puerto Rico as an equal partner with the States in the distribution of social and economic aid. . . . Such a proposal, if not significantly modified, will be embarrassing to the President, the Congress and the American people." The sole issue before President Gerald R. Ford, in Ross' opinion, was how to "diplomatically terminate the activities of the Advisory Group with an 'acceptable' report."[29]

The United States delegation obtained several amendments to the draft, but it clearly wanted to bring the matter to a close as soon as possible, as advised by the White House. On October 1, 1975, the group rendered its report to the President.[30] The White House sat on the report, without transmitting the proposed compact to Congress. On February 10, 1976, Cannon recommended to the President to continue to delay his response.[31] Ford accepted the recommendation.[32] Impatient with the delay, Resident Commissioner Jaime Benítez had already filed in Congress a bill to turn the proposed compact into law.[33]

On October 1, 1976, shortly before the elections, a memorandum to Cannon from one of his assistants suggested, among several options (all against the proposal of the Advisory Group), that a statement be made to the effect that "there are only two ways for Puerto Rico to go—complete independence or statehood." After Ford's defeat at the polls by Jimmy Carter, Cannon recommended to the outgoing President that he should put an end to the process by declaring his belief that the appropriate status for Puerto Rico was statehood.[34]

So much for self-determination. On December 31, 1976, President Ford issued a statement: "After studying the comments and recommendations, and giving deep thought to this important proposal, I have concluded that the proposed Compact, significant and important though it is, does not advance as rapidly as it might freedom and opportunity for the American citizens of Puerto Rico. I believe that the appropriate status for Puerto Rico is statehood. I propose, therefore, that the people of Puerto Rico and the Congress of the United States begin now to take those steps which will result in statehood for Puerto Rico."[35]

Even the pro-statehood leadership in Puerto Rico was aghast. Resident Commissioner-elect Baltasar Corrada del Río said that the statement "probably hurt the cause of statehood by proposing that it be granted without previously consulting its people." Romero Barceló, newly elected Governor and a staunch statehood supporter, dismissed the idea of holding a referendum during his term as Governor. It was clear at the time that if a plebiscite on status was called, statehood would lose, even though the NPP had won the elections. A few days later, letter bombs to President Ford, President-elect Carter, and Governor Barceló were intercepted, and three bombs exploded in Manhattan.[36]

Nearly twelve years passed without further action on this matter. On January 17, 1989, at the initiative of Governor Hernández Colón, the presidents of all three political parties agreed on a procedure for solving Puerto Rico's nagging status problem. They signed a letter to President Bush and the Congress, requesting that the people of Puerto Rico be consulted "as to their ultimate political status and that the consultation should include the guarantee that the will of the People once expressed shall be implemented through an act of Congress."[37] Senator Bennett Johnston, chairman of the Committee on Energy and Natural Resources (which was in charge of Puerto Rican affairs), agreed and filed three versions of a bill. The leadership of the three parties concurred in preferring S. 712, which called for a plebiscite on the three status formulas, as defined by each party and revised by Congress, the preferred status to become law without further action. Almost half a century later, the Tydings-Piñero approach was being revived.

After extended hearings and amendment of the initial bill, the Senate committee filed a favorable report. No action could be taken by the Senate in 1989 because the Finance Committee, needing further information on the cost of each option, could not report out the bill. Preliminary figures from the Congressional Budget Office indicated that statehood would be the costliest option by far, requiring disbursements for 1995 alone of $9 billion.

On April 5, 1990, the Congressional Budget Office filed a report on the economic impact of the various options set forth in S. 712, concluding that under statehood there would be a 10–15 percent reduction in the gross product of Puerto Rico by the year 2000, and a loss in the private sector of 50,000–100,000 jobs.[38] The Senate Finance Committee reported out the bill, heavily amended, on August 1, 1990, but refrained from endorsing it.

In the meantime, on May 9, 1990, members of the House Committee on Interior and Insular Affairs filed a different type of bill. The House bill, which was not self-executing like the Senate bill, defined the three traditional status options in a very general way, called for a referendum, and then provided that members of all Puerto Rican parties would negotiate with Congress on the implementation of the winning formula.[39] The bill was well received by the committee and approved by the House on October 10, 1990. Later that month the leaders of the three political parties in Puerto Rico urged Senator Johnston to consider the House bill, with amendments. An impasse was reached and there was no further action in 1990.

In the next Congress Senator Johnston and Congressman Ron De Lugo from the Virgin Islands again filed their bills. This time the House leadership decided not to back the bill that had been approved the year before. The Senate Committee on Energy and Natural Resources meanwhile voted again on the Senate bill. Seven Republicans and three Democrats voted against the bill because of objections to statehood. The bill was defeated 10 to 10 on February 27, 1991. Chairman De Lugo stated that the House committee would not act on any bill unless the Senate moved first. The legislation was dead. In four decades of incessant work it had been impossible to wake the government of the United States out of its big sleep.

Pedro Rosselló, new president of the NPP, convincingly defeated Victoria Muñoz Mendoza for the governorship in 1992 after eight years of PDP rule under Hernández Colón. Rosselló obtained 938,837 votes, for a total of 49.9 percent of the vote, against 45.8 percent for Muñoz Mendoza and less than 5 percent for Fernando Martín, the Independence party candidate. Carlos Romero Barceló became Resident Commissioner by an even slimmer margin. The Popular Democratic party was divided, and deeply in debt. The NPP platform had promised a plebiscite should the party win the elections. Enthusiasm ran high. For the first time in the twentieth century, the statehood movement felt sufficiently powerful to put statehood to the test. A plebiscite was called for November 14, 1993. Large sums were spent in the campaign. Statehood was depicted as the only way to guarantee and increase federal assistance, as well as to make sure that citizenship could not ever be taken away from Puerto Ricans.

The results stunned the statehood party. There was a greater voter participation than in the 1967 plebiscite, reaching an astounding 73.6 percent of the registered voters, or 2,312,912 votes. Commonwealth won in five of the eight senatorial districts and in fifty-three of the seventy-eight towns. It received 823,258 votes, against 785,859 for statehood.

At the end of April 1994, the White House appointed an inter-agency group to look into Puerto Rican matters. Its agenda was unclear, and nothing has yet happened on enhancing Commonwealth status.

Puerto Rico and the United Nations from 1960 to the Present

On November 27, 1953, the same day that the General Assembly of the United Nations decided that the United States could cease sending information on Puerto Rico, the list of factors for determining when a colony has achieved full self-government was approved. The Puerto Rican case had just been decided and was not analyzed in the light of this list.

The list was later refined and finally resulted in Resolution 1541 (XV), approved by the General Assembly on December 15, 1960, the first of two resolutions which are at the core of decolonization debates at the U.N. The General Assembly recognized three ways of achieving full self-government: independence, free association with an independent state, and integration to an independent state. The basic conditions for achieving the status of free association were that: (a) free association should be the result of the free choice of the territory involved; the association must respect the individuality and cultural characteristics of the people involved and reserve to them the right to modify its status by democratic means and in accordance with the appropriate constitutional processes; and (b) the associated territory must have the right to determine its internal constitution without outside interference.

The resolution was approved by a vote of 69–2, with twenty-one abstentions. South Africa and Portugal were the countries that voted against. Spain had also voted against in the Fourth Committee, but later abstained. The United States and the other administering countries, as well as the Soviet Union and China, were among those that abstained. The only Latin American country that did not vote in favor of the resolution was the Dominican Republic.[1]

The day before the approval of this resolution, the General Assembly had approved Resolution 1514 (XV), the other key document, which declared the inalienable right of all peoples to independence and called for a swift and unconditional end to colonialism in the world.[2] The resolution was adopted by a vote of 89–0, with nine abstentions: that of the United States and the other seven countries in charge of administering nations. (The Dominican Republic was the only nonadministering nation to abstain.) The resolution declared that all peoples have the right to self-determination and independence; that the lack of preparation in the political, economic, social, or educational fields should not serve as a pretext to deny a people's right to independence; that in the trust territories and in all other territories that had not yet attained their independence immediate steps should be taken to transfer to them all sovereign powers; and that all states should strictly observe the provisions of the U.N. Charter and of the Universal Declaration of Human Rights on the basis of full respect for the sovereign rights of all peoples and nonintervention in their affairs.

The composition of the United Nations had radically changed since the early fifties. In 1953 the organization had fifty-one members. In matters of special importance to it, the United States could normally count on the votes of forty-one of these: twenty from Latin American republics, nine from Western Europe, two from Asia, two from Oceania, three from Africa, four from the Middle East, and Canada. In 1955 twenty-four new members were admitted, which reduced the enormous majority enjoyed by the United States. In 1960, the decolonization process had advanced and sixteen new African republics became members, which meant the loss by the United States of even a simple majority on certain important matters, especially those relating to colonialism. The disparity increased in the following years with the admission of many more peoples with a recent colonial past. Decolonization took on an importance that it had not yet attained in the early fifties. The 1953 resolution concerning Puerto Rico began to be looked at with greater skepticism.

In 1961 the General Assembly, worried as to the lack of action after the approval of Resolution 1514 (XV), appointed a committee to oversee compliance with its terms.[3] The United States voted in favor of such a move and agreed to become a member of the committee, which came to be known as the Decolonization Committee or Committee of Twenty-Four.

By 1965 Cuba asked, at the behest of independence advocates in Puerto Rico, that the case of Puerto Rico be added to the agenda of the Decolonization Committee. The United States opposed the request on the basis that, in view of the 1953 resolution on Puerto Rico, the committee lacked jurisdiction to consider the case. The committee postponed action on the matter.

In 1972 the motion was made by Cuba that the Puerto Rican case be included in the agenda of the General Assembly. United States Ambassador to the United Nations George Bush objected on the ground that such an act would constitute undue intervention in a United States domestic matter.[4] The General Committee, which controls the agenda of the General Assembly, voted against such inclusion 10–5, with eight abstentions. The General Assembly approved the recommendation of the General Committee 56–27, with thirty-eight abstentions.

The next year the request was repeated, but this time the petition was for inclusion of the Puerto Rican case on the agenda of the Decolonization Committee, on the basis that Puerto Rico's right to self-government had not yet been recognized and the conditions of Resolution 1514 (XV) had not been met. The committee, in plain repudiation of the United States position, resolved to ask its Working Group to look into the procedure that should be followed for the resolution to be complied with.[5] The vote was 12–0, with ten abstentions. The General Assembly overwhelmingly approved the report of the Decolonization Committee by a vote of 95–5, with ten abstentions.[6] The United States, which had already resigned as member of the committee, voted against the resolution, together with four of the remaining colonial powers in the world.

From 1973 to 1977 the Decolonization Committee approved yearly resolutions reaffirming "the inalienable right of the people of Puerto Rico to self-determination and independence," requesting that the United States abstain from taking any steps to impede the exercise of such rights, and deciding to keep the matter under permanent review.[7]

Up to then, only groups favoring independence had been appearing yearly before the Decolonization Committee to request that Puerto Rico be decolonized, their efforts being somewhat blunted by the active intervention of Cuba in supporting their efforts. In 1978, however, the situation dramatically changed, and colonialism was denounced by all political parties in Puerto Rico. Governor Romero Barceló and former Governor Hernández Colón appeared before the committee and complained about the political condition of Puerto Rico.

Romero Barceló paid lip service to the official line that the committee was meddling in the internal affairs of the United States and Puerto Rico. But he then stated in strong terms that, in the light of the political condition of the island, which still had colonial vestiges and did not meet the aspirations of the Puerto Rican people, it was understandable that members of the committee who could be deemed to be impartial should desire to study the Puerto Rican case.[8]

Hernández Colón spoke next in much plainer terms. He severely criticized President Ford's violation of Puerto Rico's right to self-determination when he refused to respect the 1967 plebiscite, as well as the intervention of some of President Carter's assistants in Puerto Rican local politics. He then stated that the

General Assembly should, given the terms of Resolution 748 (VIII), require the United States to recognize Puerto Rico's right to attain full self-government and guarantee its right to participate in the exercise of United States rights in Puerto Rico and to be represented in international organizations.

Following these and other testimonies, the Decolonization Committee approved a strong resolution, stating that the resolutions of the United Nations on decolonization should be respected.[9]

The 1978 proceedings had a beneficial effect. On August 2, 1979, a concurrent resolution was approved by Congress, stating that because "certain other governments lacking in a clear understanding of the United States relationship with Puerto Rico have questioned the status of Puerto Rico and the extent to which its citizens enjoy the right to self-determination," it was resolved "that the Congress takes this opportunity to reaffirm its commitment to respect and support the right of the people of Puerto Rico to determine their own political future through a peaceful, open, and democratic process."[10] This resolution would mean little in the following years.

In 1980 the General Assembly adopted a Plan of Action to reaffirm its commitment to Resolution 1514 (XV) on the twentieth anniversary of its adoption.[11] The new resolution declared that colonialism in any of its forms and manifestations was incompatible with the United Nations Charter, Resolution 1514 (XV), and the principles of international law; restated its obligation to oversee compliance with such declaration and principles; and urged all nations to cooperate with the Decolonization Committee in proposing measures to free the remaining colonies. The resolution was adopted by a vote of 121–6, with twenty abstentions and eight absent. The United States voted against.

Emboldened by such action, the Decolonization Committee asked the General Assembly in 1981 to include the Puerto Rican case directly in its agenda. In his column in the *New York Times* Tom Wicker wrote: "In his 1980 campaign Ronald Reagan promised to take the lead in obtaining statehood for Puerto Rico. But the promise was abandoned and the Reagan Administration now faces the embarrassing possibility that the next United Nations General Assembly will declare the island one of the world's few remaining colonies, and demand that something be done about it."[12]

The committee repeated its recommendation the next year.[13] The United States was, however, able to defeat the recommendation at the General Assembly by a vote of 70–30, with forty-three abstentions.[14] It was a remarkable diplomatic feat, given the general opinion as to Puerto Rico's subordinate condition. Reviewing the work of the General Assembly in 1982, United States Ambas-

sador to the United Nations Jeane Kirkpatrick considered that vote as the greatest United States victory at the UN that year, together with rejection of the attempts to expel Israel from that body.

In 1989 Pedro Rosselló, then vice president of the statehood movement, testified before the Decolonization Committee. Speaking in his personal capacity,
Rosselló recited the reasons why Puerto Rico should still be regarded as a colony
of the United States and energetically urged the United Nations to demand that
Puerto Rico be decolonized, abandoning the traditional position that this was
an internal matter over which the United Nations had no jurisdiction.[15] Again
in 1991, this time as president of the NPP, Rosselló repeated his charges.[16]

Although inspired at times by questionable motivations and fueled by blind
hostility to the United States, rather than by genuine concern about the shortcomings of Puerto Rico's political condition, the debates at the United Nations
on this issue have helped to highlight the colonial nature of the island's present
relations with the United States. Mistakes have been made on all sides in the
handling of the issue. The many nations with a recent colonial past share too
narrow a view of how self-government can be fully achieved. Resolution 1514
(XV), with its insistence on independence, does not take due account of the
many faces of freedom, and Resolution 1541 (XV) at times places more emphasis on the formalities of self-government than on its substance.

On the other hand, the refusal of the General Assembly so far to place the
Puerto Rican case on its agenda has been made solely on jurisdictional grounds
and only after strenuous diplomatic efforts by the able Americans who have
served as ambassador to the United Nations. The stubborn truth is that there is
general agreement, even among leaders of all three parties in the island, that
Puerto Rico is still a colony of the United States, its government claiming and
exercising full sovereignty over Puerto Rico, legislating and otherwise acting for
the island without its consent, questioning the existence of a true compact and
its content, and consistently ignoring the results of plebiscites.

13

Decolonization in the Caribbean and in Micronesia

The Caribbean carries the dubious distinction of being the first area of the New World to be colonized and the last to become free. A brief look at what has happened in the Spanish, British, French, and Dutch parts of that region in comparison to Puerto Rico shows that the roads to liberty have been many: independence, integration to the metropolis, and full autonomy in association with the metropolis. Other former colonies have fared fairly well along those paths, but Puerto Rico has tried them all and so far has found them blocked. Although Puerto Rico is among the most politically stable entities in the region, in terms of status it lags pitifully behind. Puerto Rico also has has a smaller degree of self-government than most of the former members of Trust Territory of the Pacific Islands.

As respects the former Spanish territories, the two South American countries with a Caribbean coast, Venezuela and Colombia, both fought successfully for their independence against Spain starting in 1810 and became fully independent a few years later. The Central American republics with access to the Caribbean Sea (all but El Salvador) also attained their early independence. During the colonial period, Panama, Costa Rica, El Salvador, Honduras, Nicaragua, and Guatemala were part of the captaincy general of Guatemala which, like that of Puerto Rico, was part of the viceroyalty of New Spain (present-day Mexico). The captaincy general of Guatemala became independent in 1819. After being part of the short-lived Mexican empire of Agustín de Iturbide, the Republic of the United States of Central America was established in 1823, and in 1839 the five states which composed it—Guatemala, El Salvador, Costa Rica, Honduras and Nicaragua—became separate republics. Mexico, after eleven years of fighting, formally became independent in 1821. Panama was part of Colombia until 1903.

South and Central American countries bordering the Caribbean basin were therefore the first continental peoples of the region to be decolonized. In the early nineteenth century there consequently remained in the area four colonies, all non-Hispanic: British Guiana, Dutch Guiana, French Guiana, and British Honduras.

Little remained of the vast Spanish island empire in the Caribbean by the early nineteenth century. The British, French, and Dutch had taken over by that time all of the Lesser Antilles and two of the Greater Antilles, Hispaniola and Jamaica. The part of Hispaniola known as Haiti was ceded by Spain to France in 1697. When Haiti wrested its independence from France in 1804, the Spanish part of the island, Santo Domingo, also was taken over by the rebels and became a part of the empires of Toussaint L'Ouverture and Jean-Jacques Dessalines. The Spaniards retook control of Santo Domingo in the 1810s, but in 1821 Santo Domingo proclaimed its independence. A year later, Jean-Pierre Boyer again united Hispaniola under the Haitian flag until 1844, when the present Dominican Republic came into being.

Cuba and Puerto Rico were thus the only remaining Spanish colonies in the Caribbean after the Latin American Wars of Independence. Cuba became free as a result of the Spanish-American War, although subject for many years to the strictures of the Platt Amendment imposed by the U.S. Congress, and Puerto Rico was left in lonely splendor as the only colonial remnant of the once mighty Spanish empire in the New World.

In the other three groups of territories in the Caribbean belonging to the British, the French, and the Dutch (Denmark and Sweden also secured properties in the area, but their presence never became significant), life was as hard as in Puerto Rico during the early centuries of Spanish rule. It was not until the Second World War that these peoples started advancing swiftly toward decolonization.

Representative institutions had existed on some of the British Caribbean islands since the seventeenth century.[1] Representation, however, was limited to the small white elite in the form of participation in an advisory body to the Governor, usually named the Executive Council, and in a quasi-parliamentary institution generally known as the Legislative Council. Severe property and literacy qualifications were imposed on the right to vote, thus limiting political participation to large landowners and affluent merchants. This type of representative government, called a Crown colony, had many forms, and not all the British colonies in the Caribbean (or elsewhere, for that matter) enjoyed all the institutions described.[2]

From the upper reaches of representative government a colony could move to the higher stage of responsible government. It was only after the Second World War that the British Caribbean colonies started inching toward the system of responsible government, which was reached by degrees until the totality of the legislative body was elected and a majority of the Executive Council was appointed and could be discharged by the legislative body and was in charge of the executive departments.

True democratic participation was not possible, of course, until the limitations on suffrage were removed. This never happened in the British Caribbean under the Crown Colony or other type of representative government. The arrival of universal male suffrage was agonizingly slow. The first British Caribbean colony to be allowed universal suffrage was Jamaica, and this did not happen until 1944. Some other British colonies, like Bermuda, did not have it until the sixties. The Dutch colonies suffered a worse fate. As late as 1936 only about 2 percent of the population of the Dutch Antilles had the right to vote. Universal suffrage was not in place until 1948. The French colonies enjoyed male universal suffrage for the first time in 1848, and Puerto Rico also had it sporadically since 1812, but intervention by the mother countries often made a farce of the right.

The system of responsible government did not come close to full self-government. The British Parliament retained plenary powers over the colonies, just like Congress claims to have over Puerto Rico. The Crown appointed the Governors and the members of the upper courts. Laws approved by the colonial legislatures could be disallowed by the Crown, through the Governor's reserve powers, and could be annulled by Parliament.

In 1956 the United Kingdom promoted the establishment of the Federation of the West Indies, uniting ten of its Caribbean colonies: Jamaica, Trinidad, Barbados, Antigua, Montserrat, St. Kitts-Nevis-Anguilla, Dominica, Granada, St. Lucia, and St. Vincent.[3] It was not a success, for many reasons. One was that the British Caribbean colonies lacked a true common past, for each was accustomed to dealing directly with Great Britain, but not with each other. There were great differences in the composition of their populations, their economies, and their goals. The federation died in 1962, at which time Jamaica, followed by Trinidad the same year and by Barbados in 1966, opted for independence with Britain's blessing.

After failed efforts to keep together what was left of the Federation, in 1967 Parliament created for the six remaining members the status of Associated State, an advanced version of Puerto Rico's Commonwealth status which followed the requirements of the list of factors and Resolution 1541 (XV).[4] The United Kingdom's powers were limited to defense, foreign relations, citizenship (at that time there was no freedom of movement between the islands and the United Kingdom), and such other powers as the Associated States would entrust it; the rest of the powers remained with the islands. Following the trail blazed by the Dominions in the thirties, no British law would apply to the Associated States except at their request or with their consent. The parliament of any Associated State could repeal any British statute. No local law could be declared null because of incompatibility with British legislation, except as to matters entrusted to the United Kingdom. Finally, the Associated States had the right to denounce at any time their agreement with the United Kingdom and opt for independence.

The status of Associated State stopped satisfying some of the peoples concerned a few years later. In 1974 Granada opted for independence. By 1983 the rest of the Associated States had also declared their independence, happily assisted by Great Britain. Twelve of the British Caribbean colonies are now independent countries: nine of the ten former members of the Federation; British Guiana, which became independent as Guyane in 1970; the Bahamas, which became independent in 1973; and British Honduras, now Belize, which became a republic in 1983. Six others—Montserrat, Anguilla (which separated itself from St. Kitts-Nevis), the British Virgin Islands, the Cayman Islands, the Turks and Caicos Islands, and Bermuda—by their free decision have desired to continue to be British colonies, each enjoying different levels of self-government.

The twelve formerly British Caribbean nations are today part of the African, Pacific and Caribbean Group (APC) in the United Nations and periodically negotiate with the European Community preferential treaties known as the Lomé Conventions.[5] There have also been many attempts at economic integration of the group.

The early colonial history of the French colonies of Martinique, Guadeloupe, and French Guiana is similar to that of the Spanish Antilles.[6] Excessive concentration of power in the metropolis and its representatives and the monopoly of commerce by a small number of metropolitan ports marked both regimes.

The French Revolution had its impact in Haiti, unleashing events that led to independence, but its effects on the three other territories were minimal.[7] The legislative assemblies which were then established were short-lived. Slavery was outlawed in 1794, but restored in 1803, until its final abolition in 1848.

As in Puerto Rico, rights in the French colonies were often won and lost several times. Universal male suffrage was instituted in 1848, at the start of the Second Republic, lost with the restoration of the Empire in 1854, and recovered in 1870. At that time the French Caribbean territories were given the right to representation in the French parliament, the National Assembly, a right which Puerto Rico enjoyed in the Cortes from 1812 to 1814, from 1820 to 1823, and from 1870 to 1898.

Like Spain, France oscillated, as an answer to unvarnished absolutism, between a regime of special laws and partial integration to the metropolis. Independence was abhorred and efforts toward autonomy were persecuted. During this time France, like Spain, was mindful of keeping all basic colonial governmental functions—executive, legislative, and judicial—firmly in its hands, and it did not commit itself to economic assistance of any consequence. Thus integration to France came to be identified politically in the first half of the twentieth century with the opportunity for greater self-government and economic development. The political parties that demanded and finally obtained integration in 1946 were the Communist and Socialist parties.

The Assimilation Law of 1946[8] turned the French Caribbean territories into departments, the basic French political unit,[9] roughly equivalent to, though with important differences, a Spanish province and an American state, in equality of conditions to others. Assimilation meant that the islands' inhabitants had a right to be represented as any other department in the French parliament, a right which they had enjoyed anyhow, with interruptions, since the last third of the nineteenth century. The executive branch remained in the hands of prefects appointed by the French government, and the various metropolitan French ministries continued to exercise direct authority in the overseas departments. Departmentalization did not entail the acquisition of a local legislative body. The Caribbean departments tried to establish one, but in 1982 the attempt was declared contrary to the constitution of the Fifth Republic.[10] Overseas and metropolitan departments are entitled only to general and regional councils with limited powers, similar to those enjoyed by the colonies. The entire judicial branch also continued to be ruled by national legislation.

Although, politically, the achievement of departmental status did not mean much in terms of added powers of self-government, it did make a significant difference in economic assistance levels. French governmental transfers—in the form of investment in the infrastructure, increased employment in the public sector, and welfare payments—represent roughly two-thirds of the gross income of Martinique and Guadeloupe and more than three-fourths of that of French Guiana. Grants and subsidies to local governments are generous. In 1982 social expenses per capita in the overseas departments amounted to 1,539 francs, as compared to 661 for the metropolitan departments.[11]

Departmentalization has not quieted the status debate in the French Caribbean; indeed, political parties have reversed their roles. The rightist parties (former opponents) are now the defenders of departmentalization, whereas its initial supporters, the leftist parties, together with the center parties, denounce it. Departmentalization grew in popular favor for many years, reaching an 80.8 percent approval rating in 1981, but then it started to decline. By 1988 the rightist parties became a minority in the general councils of Guadeloupe and Martinique, for the first time in twenty years. In the regional elections of 1992 the conservative parties in Guadeloupe obtained only fifteen of the forty-one seats in the Council. In Martinique they received only sixteen out of forty-one and in Cayenne a mere two out of thirty-one. In 1986 the advocates of independence for Martinique were not able to elect a single member of the General Council. In 1992 they elected nine.

There is also unhappiness in the French Caribbean concerning cultural issues. Many French Caribbean intellectuals and others feel that, in spite of the common language, their culture is being threatened. Such culture, anchored in concepts like *négritude* (Aimé Césaire) and *antillanité* (Edouard Glissant), is deemed to be quite different to the French. The feeling of cultural identity with France does not seem to be strong.

To members of other Caribbean areas, the French experiment with departmentalization is generally regarded as achieving decolonization on only a semantic plane. That view is increasingly shared by many in the French Caribbean overseas departments.

The Dutch founded many colonies in North and South America and the Caribbean basin. The ones that survived the longest were the latter, composed of Dutch Guiana (later Surinam), and the Dutch Antilles, composed of two groups of islands, the Leewards (Curaçao, Aruba, and Bonaire), and the Windwards, which chiefly included St. Eustacius (Statia), Sint Maarten, and Saba. Their early history is quite similar to that of the French islands.

The Statute of the Realm, approved by the parliaments of the Netherlands, Surinam, and the Netherlands Antilles, entered into effect on December 26, 1954, after years of negotiation. It established a new constitutional relationship between the Netherlands and its Caribbean territories, which acquired thereby a considerable degree of autonomy within a new kingdom composed by them and the mother country.[12]

The Realm was entrusted with jurisdiction over defense, foreign affairs, the common citizenship, and certain other specific matters, the rest being reserved to the former colonies. Even in the field of foreign affairs, the Realm may not negotiate or denounce economic or financial treaties which affect its Caribbean members without their consent. The Antilles can also become members of international organizations.

Although the inhabitants of the Dutch Antilles and the Netherlands share the same citizenship and there is free movement within the Realm, no resident of the Antilles may serve in the armed forces of the Realm, except by law of the Antilles. The Realm does not have constitutional organs separate from those of Holland, but the statute provides for participation of overseas representatives in the deliberations of the Dutch Parliament and the Council of Ministers. On judicial matters, the Dutch Supreme Court has the final say, but in cases affecting an overseas member of the Realm, the member may request that a judge representing it be added to the Court.

As in the case of the Puerto Rican Autonomic Charter of 1897 and the 1931 Statute of Westminster for the British Dominions, the Statute of the Realm may not be amended without the consent of the Antilles. As concerns economic matters, the Antilles contribute to the expenses of the Realm according to their resources. In contrast to the American and French practices, the financial aid provided by the Dutch to their overseas territories has been modest. The Netherlands Antilles never developed the sense of economic reliance fostered in Puerto Rico and the French dependencies.

As regards internal government, in 1954 the Dutch Caribbean territories acquired the right to adopt their own constitution, subject to certain conditions. The Crown appoints each overseas Governor, who executes both the laws of the Realm and the local laws, but may postpone their execution until the Dutch monarch decides. Upon the recommendation of the Council of Ministers, the monarch may annul all or part of any law or administrative act of the Antilles government.

In cultural terms, the Netherlands and the United States were the only colonial powers that did not succeed in imposing their language on their major Caribbean possessions. The Netherlands, like the United States for a number of decades, imposed its language for instruction in the Antilles. Dutch is at present the language of official government communication between the Antilles and the Netherlands, but the language of Curaçao, Aruba, and Bonaire, even the language of government, is Papiamento (a Portuguese-based language with a vast amount of Spanish, Dutch and African terms), while English has been for centuries, and continues to be, the language of Sint Maarten, Statia, and Saba.[13]

The Statute of the Realm functioned well for a number of years, but demands for greater autonomy and even independence eventually grew. Contrary to France, the Netherlands started, like Great Britain, a policy of withdrawal from the Caribbean basin. In 1975 Surinam opted for independence. In 1986, when Aruba decided to separate from the Netherlands Antilles, it was granted *status aparte*, with full right to participate as an equal part of the Realm, but upon the condition of becoming independent in 1996. At Aruba's request, this date has been postponed indefinitely, the majority of the people being in favor of greater autonomy in association with the Netherlands, although there are groups that still favor independence, and a tiny element would like Aruba to become a province of the Netherlands.

Thus Puerto Rico's state of subordination and its paucity of self-governing powers, as compared to other Caribbean areas, is indeed uninspiring, if not shameful. On the road to independence it has made no progress as compared to the British territories; on the road to integration and equality with the metropolis it has been badly outdistanced by the French territories; and on the road to autonomy it is shockingly behind the Netherlands Antilles. This is unfortunately the face that the United States and Puerto Rico are presenting to the whole world. How could such a thing ever come to pass? How can the nation most identified, and rightfully so, with the values of freedom and equality in the world keep such a shoddy political ghetto as Puerto Rico, for all to see and wonder, right in its own backyard?

The comparison with Micronesia is not very flattering, either. Micronesia is the general name for the former Trust Territory of the Pacific Islands (essentially the Mariana, Caroline, and Marshall Islands, although the geographic term also comprises the islands of Nauru and Kiribati, both independent). It consists of some 2,200 very small islands, an area of some 700 square miles (less than half the size of Rhode Island) spread over three million square miles of ocean (about the size of the continental United States). The population in 1990 was about 200,000, divided into six ethnic groups that speak nine languages. Micronesia is now composed of four political entities: the Commonwealth of the Northern Mariana Islands, the Federated States of Micronesia, the Republic of the Marshall Islands, and the Republic of Palau. The first chose a form of Commonwealth status. The last three negotiated compacts of free association with the United States.

The Mariana Islands (also known as the Ladrones) include Guam, which was ceded by Spain to the United States in 1898 with Puerto Rico under the Treaty of Paris, and is now an unincorporated territory of the United States. The Northern Marianas stretch northward 400 miles from Guam. They consist of twenty-one small islands, only six of which are inhabited. In all they measure 184 square miles, compared to Guam's 209. The principal islands, in order of size, are Saipan, Tinian, and Rota. The population of the Northern Marianas in 1990 was 43,345, of which roughly 39,000 lived on Saipan.[14]

The Marianas are closer to Asia than to the United States, located about 1,250 miles from Tokyo, 1,500 from Manila, 3,300 from Honolulu, and 5,400 from San Francisco. Magellan sighted the Marianas and landed in Guam in 1521, but it was not until 1688 that the Spanish started settling these islands and other parts of Micronesia. In 1899 Germany acquired the Northern Marianas from Spain. Soon after the outbreak of the First World War, Japan occupied the Northern Marianas and in 1920 obtained a mandate from the League of Nations over the whole of Micronesia. In the course of the Second World War, Japan used Saipan and Tinian as bases for attacks against United States interests. The United States captured these islands in the summer of 1944. The atomic bombing missions against Hiroshima and Nagasaki were flown from Tinian. On July 18, 1947, the United States took over administration of the Marianas, together with the rest of Micronesia, as one of the eleven territories in the United Nations trusteeship system.[15]

The United States expressly disclaimed sovereignty over Micronesia.[16] Although Micronesia was never formally considered to be a territory or possession of the United States, it was treated as such.[17] Micronesia was administered by the United States Navy until 1951 and, with the exception of U.S. Navy administration of the Northern Marianas from 1952 to 1962, has been administered by the Department of the Interior.[18]

Termination of the trusteeship was considered beginning in the sixties. In 1964 the Congress of Micronesia was established by order of the Secretary of the Interior, and negotiations for terminating the trust were started in 1969.[19]

Starting in 1961 the Northern Marianas were interested in union with Guam, the inhabitants of which had been made citizens of the United States in 1950, and the majority of whom were *chamorros*, like the rest of the residents of the Marianas. Guam rejected the proposed union in a 1969 plebiscite. The Northern Marianas continued to be represented in the Joint Committee on Future Status set up by the Congress of Micronesia to negotiate for the Trust Territory as a whole. In 1970, however, the Congress of Micronesia spurned an offer of Commonwealth status patterned after the Puerto Rican model and insisted on a freer relationship with the United States. Interested in a perfected Commonwealth status, the Northern Marianas asked for separate status talks.

Negotiations between the United States and the Northern Marianas began in December 1972 and were concluded on February 15, 1975, with the signing of a Covenant to Establish a Commonwealth of the Northern Marianas in Political Union with the United States of America. Five days later the covenant was approved by the people of the Marianas in a plebiscite. On July 1, 1975, at the same time that Puerto Rico's proposed revised compact was being rejected by the White House, President Ford transmitted the Marianas covenant to Congress, which approved it on March 24, 1976.[20]

The covenant is quite explicit as to where sovereignty lies. Section 101 states that the Northern Marianas, upon expiration of the trusteeship agreement, will become a Commonwealth "in political union with and under the sovereignty of the United States of America." In spite of the fact that the territorial clause is not listed among the provisions of the United States Constitution that apply in the Marianas and that certain sections of the covenant may not be modified except with the consent of the government of the Marianas, the legislative history of the covenant indicates that the Congress understands that it is vested with plenary powers over the Commonwealth. A Senate report, for example, stated: "Although described as a commonwealth, the relationship is territorial in nature with final sovereignty invested in the United States and plenary legislative authority vested in the United States Congress. The essential difference between the Covenant and the usual territorial relationship, such as that of Guam, is the provision in the Covenant that the Marianas constitution and government structure will be a product of a Marianas constitutional convention, as was the case with Puerto Rico, rather than through an organic act of the United States Congress."[21] In budget procedures and most other ways the Commonwealth of the Northern Mariana Islands is treated as a territory and its government reports to the President and the Congress through the Office of Territorial and International Affairs of the Department of the Interior.[22]

The first article of the covenant also provides that "the United States will have complete responsibility for and authority with respect to matters relating to foreign affairs and defense affecting the Northern Mariana Islands."

Consultation procedures on all matters affecting the relationship between the parties are established. The last section of the first article contains a partial recognition of the principle of government by consent, the United States agreeing that certain "fundamental" provisions of the Covenant may be modified only with the consent of both governments.

Article II of the covenant allows the people of the Northern Marianas to approve a constitution and amend it without approval by the government of the United States. Article III grants American citizenship by the method of collective naturalization to various groups, especially people born and domiciled in the Northern Mariana Islands who were citizens of the Trust Territory of the Pacific Islands or domiciled for a certain period of years.

In article IV of the covenant a United States District Court for the Northern Mariana Islands is established, attached to the same circuit as Guam (the Ninth). Its jurisdiction is the same as that of other federal district courts, except that the District Court for the Northern Mariana Islands has jurisdiction regardless of the value of the matter in controversy and can also act as the court of last resort in local matters. A Supreme Court for the Northern Mariana Islands was created in 1989.

Section 501(a) of Article V spells out the provisions of the United States Constitution that apply within the Northern Marianas. Other provisions of the Constitution of the United States "which do not apply of their own force within the Northern Mariana Islands" will be applicable therein only with the residents' consent and that of the government of the United States. What this means is not exactly clear. Given the awesome scope of Congressional power over the Northern Marianas, several clauses of the United States Constitution omitted from the covenant list obviously apply, such as the supremacy and the commerce clauses. For the same reason, the omission of the territorial clause from the list seems to lack significance. Equivalent power is recognized in the government.

Contrary to what the courts so far have decided with reference to Puerto Rico, the Congress of the United States may legislate municipally for the Northern Marianas, provided that the Marianas are specifically named therein.[23] All other federal laws apply to the Northern Marianas as they apply in Guam or to the states, as Congress may decide. Exceptions are the immigration, coastwise shipping, and minimum wage laws, which do not apply to the Northern Marianas, unless the Congress determines otherwise at some future point (section 503). Such laws did not apply to the former Trust Territory, either.

The covenant provides that the United States income tax laws shall apply in the Northern Marianas as a local territorial income tax, as is the case in Guam and the Virgin Islands, the proceeds going to the local treasury. The Commonwealth may impose additional taxes as it sees fit. This mirror tax technique ended with the Federal Tax Reform Act of 1986.[24] Since then, the Northern Marianas have imposed local taxes and grant a 95 percent rebate of federal taxes on income derived from Northern Mariana sources.[25]

The Northern Marianas are not included in the customs territory of the United States. The Northern Marianas may levy duties on goods imported into the territory from any area outside the customs territory of the United States and impose duties on exports from that territory. Imports from the Northern

Marianas into the customs territory of the United States are subject to the same treatment as imports from Guam. This means that goods produced in the Northern Marianas (where at least 50 percent of the value has been added in the Northern Marianas) can enter the United States customs territory free of duty, a system also used in the Virgin Islands. Customs and excise taxes levied by the United States on goods imported into its customs territory go into the treasury of the Northern Marianas. The government of the Northern Marianas may rebate United States customs and excise taxes.

Article VII of the covenant pledged an initial period of seven years guaranteed annual levels of direct grant assistance for budgetary support for government operations, capital improvements, and economic development, adjustable each year according to the percentage change of the United States Department of Commerce composite price index. The total initial pledge was for $14 million a year. After the initial seven-year period, the annual level of payments continues until Congress otherwise determines. The United States also pledged in the covenant to make available to the Northern Marianas the full range of federal programs and services available to the territories.

The Covenant provides that the Northern Marianas shall lease to the United States for a term of fifty years, renewable by the United States for another fifty years, 17,799 acres on Tinian Island (about two-thirds of the island), 177 acres at Tanapag Harbor on Saipan Island, and the entire island of Farallón de Medinilla, among other areas. Farallón de Medinilla has been used by the United States Navy for target practice since 1970. The United States also reserved the right to acquire other property for public purposes in the Northern Mariana Islands by eminent domain.

The United States refused to allow the Commonwealth of the Northern Marianas a delegate or Resident Commissioner with the right to sit in Congress, as Guam, American Samoa, the Virgin Islands, and Puerto Rico have. The covenant provides instead for a Resident Representative to the United States, with a two-year term of office. In further aggravation, the Resident Representative reports to the Department of the Interior, a fact resented by the Northern Marianans.[26]

In conclusion, the United States has been severely criticized for allegedly encouraging the separation of the Northern Mariana Islands from the rest of Micronesia.[27] Separation has also been considered as entailing the elimination of independence as a viable alternative for the Northern Marianas.[28]

Serious questions have been raised, and rightly so, as to the compatibility of the Northern Mariana covenant with United Nations decolonization criteria.[29] The United States government has not taken steps to distinguish the Northern Marianas from an unincorporated territory.[30] Northern Mariana leaders have at times charged that the Commonwealth has not been given the autonomy the covenant promised them.[31] Predictably, because of the very shortcomings of the covenant, its legislative history reveals a compulsion on the part of the United States to deny time and again that the Commonwealth of the Northern Mariana Islands is a colony of the United States.[32]

The policy reasons behind the covenant were thus described in a report by the Senate Foreign Relations and Armed Services Committee:

> The Administration feels that the Agreement is mutually beneficial. Its witnesses affirmed that the United States is not only a Pacific power (with Alaska and Hawaii extending territorial responsibilities far into that ocean), but that it intends to remain so. Guam, long a United States territory, houses important military bases essential to the nation's defense. Its isolated position will better be protected by the land lease arrangements on Tinian and Saipan. Equally important, to promote the cause of peace and stability in the Pacific Ocean, the Marianas must be denied to others. If the Northern Marianas were to separate from the United States under some other political arrangement, they could freely negotiate a lease of their lands to some other Pacific powers. Finally, although no expansion of the training and storage facilities is presently planned, the fifty-year renewable lease over 18,000 acres provides for such if necessary.[33]

These objectives could easily have been met by an arrangement less colonial in nature.

Still, several features of the covenant go beyond what Puerto Rico now has. It is clearer than the Puerto Rican "compact" in trying to describe the relationship between the Northern Marianas and the United States. It sets forth an area which is unambiguously subject to the principle of government by consent. There is greater, although not complete, precision as to which provisions of the United States Constitution apply. The Northern Marianas have an exemption from the coastwise shipping and immigration laws, something which Puerto Rico has unsuccessfully tried to obtain for decades. The Commonwealth of the Northern Mariana Islands enjoys, at least on paper, the right (denied to Puerto Rico) to be consulted on all matters affecting its relationships with the United States. On the other hand, the covenant provides for less self-government in certain areas and unabashedly keeps the Commonwealth of the Northern Mariana

Islands subject to the almost unrestricted power of the Congress, just as any other long-suffering territory or possession. Although Northern Mariana leaders, like many of their Puerto Rican counterparts, dutifully hold that the territorial clause of the United States Constitution does not apply to the Commonwealth, the Department of the Interior stoutly maintains that it does, a position that naturally turns the covenant into something of a mirage.[34]

As respects other parts of Micronesia, after over fifteen years of negotiations, in 1986 the Compact of Free Association Act of 1985 was approved, whereby the remaining governments of the former Trust Territory of the Pacific Islands—the Republic of the Marshall Islands, the Federated States of Micronesia, and the Republic of Palau—became free associated states.[35] The peoples of the three areas during that period rejected the alternatives of independence, commonwealth, territorial status, and continuation of the status quo. All had voted in 1983 in favor of the proposed compacts. The compacts with the Republic of the Marshall Islands, the Federated States of Micronesia, and Palau took effect, respectively, on October 21, 1986, November 3, 1986, and October 1, 1994. As the effective date of the Covenant with the Northern Mariana Islands, concluded on February 15, 1975, was tied up with part of these events, its effective date was November 3, 1986.[36] The compact with Palau did not come into effect until 1994 because of a provision of the Constitution of Palau which required a 75 percent approval vote on any agreement which conflicted with its prohibition on nuclear weapons and waste materials. The United States refused Palau's request to delete the offending clauses from the proposed compact and, after seven unsuccessful plebiscites, the people of Palau resolved the issue by instead eliminating the anti-nuclear provisions from their constitution. Palau received $447 million in aid from the United States, as promised, after voting for free association.[37]

The Republic of the Marshall Islands consists of two chains of very small, scattered islands, none bigger than one square mile, with a total area of 70 square miles and an estimated population in 1992 of 50,004. Some of the better known islands or atolls are Kwajalein, Eniwetok, and Bikini. The Marshalls were the first territory taken from the Japanese by the United States in the Second World War. The Federated States of Micronesia are part of the Caroline Islands and comprise the states of Truk, Pohnpei, Yap, and Kosrae, each consisting of several islands, with a combined population of slightly over 100,000. The Republic of Palau is also in the Carolines. It consists of more than 200 islands, with a total area of some 185 square miles. Most of the population of about 15,000 inhabitants is concentrated on the island of Koror.

The preamble to each compact recognizes that the peoples of the Trust Territory of the Pacific Islands "have and retain their sovereignty and their sovereign right to self-determination" and that their entering into a compact of free association with the United States "constitutes an exercise of their sovereign right to self-determination." Even though the Trust Agreement has not been properly terminated by action of the Security Council of the United Nations, the courts have held that at least de facto foreign statehood status has been achieved.[38]

The compacts recognize the capacity of the three island governments (hereinafter referred to as the Free Associated States or FAS) "to conduct foreign affairs and shall do so in their own name and right, *except as otherwise provided in this Compact*" (italics added).[39] The compacts impose serious restrictions in that respect. The most important one is that the FAS "shall refrain from actions which the Government of the United States determines, after appropriate consultation with those Governments, to be incompatible with the authority of and responsibility for security and defense matters" in or relating to the Republic of the Marshall Islands, the Federated States of Micronesia and Palau. In recognition of such authority and responsibility, it is also agreed that the FAS "shall consult, in the conduct of their foreign affairs, with the Government of the United States." The compacts further provide that the FAS must have United States support to apply for membership or other participation in regional or international organizations. In the course of the compact negotiations, the United States considered the FAS ineligible for full membership in the United Nations because of the defense authority vested in it.[40] All of the FAS, however, are now full members of the United Nations.

Contrary to the case of the Northern Mariana Islands, the citizens of the FAS are not citizens of the United States. They can, however, travel freely to the United States, establish residence as nonimmigrants, and accept employment, but they may not establish the residence necessary for naturalization. Likewise, any citizen or national of the United States may enter, reside, and work in the free associated states. The governments of the United States and the FAS may establish "representative offices" in the capital of the other "for the purpose of maintaining close and regular consultations on matters arising of the relationship of free association and conducting other government business."

The United States accepted responsibility in the compacts for compensating citizens of the FAS for losses or damage to person or property resulting from the American nuclear testing program conducted in the Northern Marshall Islands between 1946 and 1958. The United States tested sixty-six nuclear devices at Bikini and Eniwetok during this period. The claims were settled for $150 million in 1985.[41]

The United States provides grant assistance to the FAS over a fifteen-year span (fifty years in the case of Palau) at a total estimated cost of $2.7 billion, with a provision for partial adjustment for inflation, or $300 million less than the level of assistance at the time the compact was agreed upon.[42] The level is highest during the first five years of the compact and is scaled down then and again at the tenth year. The United States, in consultation with the Micronesian entity concerned, determines the procedures for the periodic audit of all grants and other assistance under the contract.

Thirteen years after the effective date of the compact, the parties begin negotiations regarding those provisions of the compact which expire on its fifteenth anniversary and their future political relationship. The separate agreements are usually not subject to this termination period. The negotiations can last for only two additional years (section 231), and economic assistance continues during this time. The fifteen-year period is clearly aimed at guarding United States government investment in the area for a reasonable period against unilateral termination rights. Unilateral termination rights by the FAS do not affect certain provisions of the compact and the separate agreements, especially in the area of security and defense.

The Free Associated States are not included in the customs territory of the United States, but they may export products to the United States duty-free essentially as if they were insular possessions. Articles not so covered are entitled to most-favored treatment (sections 241–243). The FAS uses United States currency, but it may institute another currency, the terms of the transitional period to be agreed with the government of the United States (section 251).

All FAS citizens living in the FAS are exempt from most United States income taxes. The FAS are also treated as possessions for certain purposes of the Federal Internal Revenue Code, thus allowing the establishment of tax incentive programs analogous to those Puerto Rico had until 1996.[43] Moreover, if such provisions are amended or repealed after January 1, 1980, it was agreed that they would continue to apply to the FAS for two years during which the United States and the FAS shall negotiate an agreement which shall provide benefits substantially equivalent to those obtained under such provisions.

Under Title III of the compacts the government of the United States has full authority and responsibility for security and defense matters in or relating to the FAS. To that end it may foreclose access or use of the FAS to any third country for military purposes and may establish military areas and facilities subject to separate agreements, most of which were simultaneously negotiated together with the compacts. Within these areas the United States may conduct "the activities and operations necessary for the exercise of its authority and responsibility under this Title."

Unless otherwise agreed, the United States cannot test by detonation or dispose of any nuclear or toxic chemical or biological weapon. It cannot test, dispose of, or discharge any other radioactive, toxic chemical, or biological materials "in an amount or manner which would be hazardous to public health or safety." Any such material or substance may, however, be stored within the FAS "in an amount and manner which would not be hazardous to health or safety," subject to international guidelines accepted by the government of the United States. In case of a national emergency declared by the President of the United States, a state of war, or an impending attack on the United States or the FAS, the United States may store any toxic chemical weapon or any radioactive materials intended for weapons use in the FAS (section 314).

Specific arrangements for the establishment and use of military areas and facilities in the FAS are set forth in separate agreements. The United States may request additional military areas and facilities, which requests shall be considered sympathetically, but no provision for the exercise of eminent domain power by the United States is made.

The United States shall not include any of the FAS as named parties to a formal declaration of war, without their respective consent. FAS citizens are not subject to involuntary induction, but are eligible to volunteer for service in the Armed Forces of the United States. In case of disputes concerning the implementation of these provisions, joint committees are established to consider them. If any unresolved questions remain, the FAS may raise them personally with the Secretary of Defense.

The compacts may be terminated several ways: by mutual agreement of the United States and any of the FAS, or by unilateral action of the United States or any of the FAS.

In the event of termination by unilateral act of the United States, for which six months' notice must be given, assistance and security and defense rights and obligations, together with certain other provisions, remain in full force until the fifteenth anniversary (the fiftieth in the case of Palau) after the effective date of the compact (sections 442, 452).

Unilateral termination by any of the FAS requires approval by the people of the respective area in a plebiscite, for which at least three months' notice must be given to the government of the United States. Termination shall not occur before three months after the plebiscite. Should any of the FAS so terminate the compact, a large number of provisions continue in effect, including those related to security and defense, until the fifteenth anniversary (the fiftieth in the case of Palau) of the effective date of the compact, except that economic and program assistance would be discontinued unless otherwise agreed (sections 442, 453). The separate agreements relating to security and defense remain in force according to their own terms. In the case of the Marshall Islands, for example, the Military Use and Operating Rights Agreement lasts for up to thirty years from the effective date of the compact and the Mutual Security Agreement cannot be terminated or amended except by mutual agreement.[44]

The compacts of free association have been strongly criticized. The present military need for these Micronesian islands has been questioned.[45] The acquisition of large areas of land in such a land-scarce region, necessarily affecting Micronesian life and aspirations, has been termed extravagant.[46] The massive impact of the military testing in the Kwajalein Missile range is considered a potential problem.[47] The failure to explore adequately other alternatives—such as international neutralization, the negotiation of a bilateral treaty, or less restrictive long-term agreements—to safeguard United States interests in the area has been deplored.[48] The open discouragement of independence along the long years of negotiation—in the Marshalls the United States did not favor a plebiscite which included such an option—has been decried.[49] Above all, the extraordinary length of time in negotiating a new status for the former members of the Trust Territory of the Pacific, almost two decades, as compared to the action taken by the other nations operating trusts under the United Nations trusteeship system, and the failure of the United States to follow proper trust termination procedures, has caused dismay. There is general agreement that the proper forum for terminating such a trust is the Security Council of the United Nations. The United States has circumvented the Security Council and limited itself to informing only the Trusteeship Council, a friendlier forum, a fact that has led some to argue that the present compacts are either void or voidable under international law.[50]

The compacts have been generally denounced as failing to comply with the decolonization standards established by the United Nations, the most glaring violation being, according to students of the FAS process, the refusal to permit true unilateral termination.[51] The device of separate agreements has been used in such manner that the scope of unilateral termination has been greatly narrowed and at times erased. The FAS compacts have in these and other respects been unfavorably compared to free association compacts entered into with other similarly small territories, such as the British Associated States and the Cook Islands. The citizens of the Cook Islands are also citizens of their former administering nation, New Zealand, a fact that has not prevented them from enjoying far greater powers of self-government than the FAS. New Zealand is also responsible for defense and foreign affairs, but the Cook Islands have an untrammeled right to unilateral dissociation, with no subsidiary agreements with different termination dates to stand in the way. During the 1970s the Cook Islands became more involved in external affairs and by 1980 achieved full freedom to conduct its own affairs. The goal of strategic denial, of preventing the Cook Islands from being used for military purposes by other foreign states, is served by treaty.[52]

With all their faults, the compacts executed by the United States with the Free Associated States of Micronesia still evidence a welcome disposition to break away from old territorial molds. They provide in many respects a much greater degree of self-government than has ever been accorded Puerto Rico by the United States. It is to be hoped, as the time for renegotiating the Micronesian compacts nears, that still longer strides toward decolonization will be taken.

14

Clearing the Way for a Second Look

As the centenary of the landing of American troops in Puerto Rico approaches, the political, economic, and social conditions of the island are nothing that either the United States or Puerto Rico can be proud of. Great strides have been achieved in many areas, but at a high price. In the process, the people of Puerto Rico have, to a deplorable extent, become addicted to handouts, accustomed to conditions of political inferiority, and largely indifferent to the erosion of their national identity.

There was a time when Puerto Rico, in the midst of its industrialization efforts, was among the developing countries with the highest long-term rates of growth. This has changed. From 1991 to 1996 Puerto Rico's rate of growth was well behind those of many other developing areas. In spite of massive infusions of aid, poverty levels are also atrocious, below those of several other Caribbean islands. Unemployment is rampant, usually fluctuating between two and four times the United States figure. The school dropout rate before the twelfth grade is 30 percent, as compared to 11 percent in the United States in 1993.[1] The homicide rate in Puerto Rico for 1994 was three times that of the United States (27.5 per 100,000 inhabitants, as compared to 9) and topped that of the worst state, Louisiana (19.8 per 100,000).[2] In 1957 Puerto Rico's murder rate per 100,000 had been 5.4.[3] Puerto Rico's role in the drug trade is also frightening. The island has been designated by the United States Justice Department as one of seven areas having particularly severe problems with drug trafficking and is considered the prime point of entry for the South American drug cartels.[4] For example, in 1996 the General Accounting Office reported that Puerto Rico and the U.S. Virgin Islands account for 26 percent of documented attempts to smuggle cocaine into the United States.[5] After all, Puerto Rico is only 658 miles from Barranquilla, Colombia, far closer to South America than to the United States, the nearest point of which is about a thousand miles away.

The people of Puerto Rico for the most part belong to one of two groups. The larger portion of the population is abysmally poor, drug-ridden, in poor health, insufficiently educated, and unemployed, and a smaller group is prosperous, well-schooled, hard-working, and enterprising. The increasing alienation between the two should be cause for great worry.

The political results of almost a century of American rule have also been disappointing. Throughout this period, while other former colonial societies have been achieving freedom in various ways, Puerto Rico has been leading the life of the homeless, exposed to the biting wind of subjection, scavenging for morsels of liberty that may be lying around. In almost a hundred years it has only been allowed—degree by exasperating degree, after begging for them, and always being reminded that the hand that giveth also taketh away—a wholly elected legislature, but with limited powers, an elected Governor, and the right to adopt a local constitution of modest scope. Hovering over all these, however, has been the brooding omnipresence of a turf-minded bureaucracy, fearful that the tiniest shred of sovereignty may be torn away from it, and trying to make sure that the hesitant steps taken so far toward self-government really do not mean any significant change of status, that the old plenary powers over Puerto Rico are still in place. To sanitize such a policy somehow, there has been, for half a century now, incessant talk about the supposed right of the people of Puerto Rico to self-determination, which unsurprisingly has led nowhere; it has served as little more than an excuse for maintaining the status quo. The United States has not made up its mind yet about what its interests in Puerto Rico are and what it is ready to permit Puerto Rico to be. The uncertainty is such that the United States has done the unthinkable and turned a deaf ear to the results of island plebiscites on the kind of relationship that Puerto Ricans prefer. One cannot indulge in heady talk about self-determination—undoubtedly well-intentioned, but which has yet to turn into dialogue and has made plebiscites meaningless—unless one defines the range of possibilities and is ready to listen to the choice of the people.

Such is the present state of confusion that many Puerto Ricans have exhibited a disturbing, but understandable urge to deny that they live in a colony at all. As the virus has attacked many mainland Americans as well, when analyzing Puerto Rico's status, the first step in taking a hard new look at Puerto Rico should therefore be to understand what is wrong with Puerto Rico's present situation—why it has indisputably earned the title of the oldest colony in the world.

It can be said that Puerto Rico is still a colony of the United States for several reasons:

- United States laws apply to the Puerto Rican people without their consent.
- United States laws can override provisions of the Commonwealth Constitution.
- The President of the United States and executive appointees negotiate treaties and take other actions which affect Puerto Rico without consulting it.
- Through the unilateral grant by Congress of diversity jurisdiction, United States courts decide cases involving strictly local matters of law.
- There is no equality or comparability of rights between United States citizens residing in Puerto Rico and those domiciled in the States.
- Congress assumes that it can unilaterally exercise plenary powers over Puerto Rico under the territorial clause of the United States Constitution.
- The United States government contends that sovereignty over Puerto Rico resides solely in the United States and not in the people of Puerto Rico.
- Both Congress and the executive branch of the United States government accordingly act as if there were no compact between the United States and Puerto Rico, and some officials even argue that none is legally possible. In spite of statements to the contrary by the Supreme Court of the United States and the Court of Appeals for the First Circuit, both Congress and the executive branch of the United States treat the Commonwealth in practice as if it were no different than any other territory or possession of the United States.
- Even if the courts eventually hold that there is now a binding compact and that this compact encompasses the Federal Relations Act, the consent extended by the Puerto Rican people in 1950 when accepting Law 600 in a referendum is overbroad. Consent to the unrestricted application to Puerto Rico of all federal laws, past and future, does not thereby erase the colonial nature of such an arrangement. A slave's consent to bondage does not make him a free man. The realization of such a weakness in the Commonwealth structure has been, together with the insistence that Congress is vested with plenary powers over Puerto Rico, what has fueled Puerto Rican attempts in the past forty-odd years to enhance or improve Commonwealth status.
- Puerto Rico plays no role in the life of the international community, ei-

ther directly or indirectly as a participant in the decisions taken by the United States.

- Commonwealth status as it is at present does not meet the decolonization standards established by the United Nations.
- There is no known noncolonial relationship in the present world where one people exercises such vast, almost unbounded power over the government of another.

Those in the United States and Puerto Rico who still cling to the strange notion that Puerto Rico is nevertheless self-governing are simply out of step with the rest of the informed world. There is no question that in the Caribbean, Latin America, and the United Nations itself Puerto Rico is seen as a colony of the United States.

There are several things wrong with this state of affairs. First, the United States government has gone back on its solemn representation to the United Nations in the course of the 1953 proceedings about what Commonwealth status meant. Second, since the sixties it has claimed that the status issue is an internal matter between the United States and Puerto Rico, but nothing has been done about the almost unanimous Puerto Rican demand for change. Third, it is wrong for the United States, a steadfast champion of human rights, to refuse to decolonize Puerto Rico, to ignore even joint efforts by all Puerto Rican parties to be allowed to exercise their right to self-determination in a meaningful way.

The United States should certainly take a new look at such an obsolete policy. It should do so not just because of the possibility of further embarrassment before others, but simply because it is the right thing to do. Because the United States enjoys, and rightly so, so much good will in the world for all it accomplishes for causes that are dear to most people, it is difficult to envision the United Nations voting against it on a matter that it deems important to its prestige. Puerto Rican leaders of all persuasions talk about these questions before others with a heavy heart. They prefer in most cases, out of deference to the country of which they are citizens and in which most of them still have abiding faith in spite of a troubled past, to follow the official line that the matter of Puerto Rico's relations with the United States is none of the United Nations' business.

Allowing the Puerto Rican people to chart their own future course is the right thing to do because the United States itself chiefly provided the moral impulse for recognizing in the Charter of the United Nations and other declarations the right of all peoples to self-determination, and because the United States has been the nation most instrumental in making freedom and democracy a reality for so many. It does the United States no credit to continue to be counted among the few remaining colonial powers in the world given the facts that, when fairly seen, it does not share the aims of such an unsavory crowd and when it can so easily and painlessly shed that false image.

Almost a hundred years after the United States acquired Puerto Rico, is it not time to allow the people of Puerto Rico to attain respectability among the peoples of the world and before the American people itself, as well as to free the United States from well-founded accusations of keeping Puerto Rico, unconsciously or unconscionably, under a state of subjection? What conceivable sound policy reasons justify the refusal of the United States to listen to the unanimous demand of local political parties to accept Puerto Rico as a fully autonomous society in association with the United States, or as a state of the Union, or as a free nation? Why should Puerto Rico continue to be what it was once called at the start of the twentieth century, Mr. Nobody from Nowhere?

It is difficult to say and more so to understand that, in terms of political rights, Puerto Rico is in many ways much worse off now than it was under Spain under the Autonomic Charter of 1897 and, in certain respects, even earlier constitutions. Puerto Ricans had full voting representation in the Spanish parliament. They were full-fledged Spanish citizens, with rights equal to those of mainland citizens. The charter could not be amended without their consent. The local parliament had greater powers of legislation than the present Legislative Assembly. There was a common market with Spain, but Puerto Rico could devise its own tariffs. Spanish commercial treaties could not bind Puerto Rico without its consent. All of these rights were taken away by the United States in 1898, and their equivalent have not yet been attained.

The shortcomings of Commonwealth status in its present form are such that a 1970 offer by the United States to grant Micronesia the same status was spurned because, among other things, Commonwealth status fell "well below the standards of self-government acceptable to . . . the United Nations."[6] The Commonwealth of the Northern Mariana Islands chose this status, but with substantial changes that have been unsuccessfully sought by Puerto Rico so far.

As began to be clear many decades ago, the dream of empire is incompatible with the noble libertarian tradition of the United States. Democracy and colonialism do not mix. In this age of reinventing and deinventing government, the United States should not be in the business of governing others. A firm decision to decolonize Puerto Rico at the earliest possible moment, under whatever formula is acceptable to both sides, is what justice requires and best serves the interests of all.

In order for a true decolonization policy to be developed and effectively implemented, certain singular effects that colonialism has produced should be taken into account in order to surmount them. Several preconceptions and imagined hurdles which obscure the view, the product of times long past, must be cleared away.

The Fragmentation Effect

In addition to economic and social terms, Puerto Rico stands also divided politically, but in more ways. As in many other colonial societies of the past, four distinct groups have emerged: those who want incorporation to the metropolis; those who desire some sort of autonomous relationship with it; those who favor the achievement of independence by democratic processes; and those willing to fight for independence by any means. These four positions were also visible in Puerto Rico under Spanish rule. In this respect Puerto Rico is exactly where it was in the nineteenth century, except that the alienation among the four groups within the same society has become worse. To each of these groups, the views and even the existence of the other three are becoming increasingly intolerable. Communication among these islands, this archipelago of hatred, is becoming more and more difficult with each passing year.

Fragmentation at all levels of the colonized society, an insufficiently studied by-product of colonialism, can thus be observed in Puerto Rico under ideal conditions. This well-preserved fossil of a dead or almost extinct species can best be admired in this Galápagos of the colonial world. In the process of decolonization, fragmentation poses serious problems for both the servient and the dominant societies. To the colonized, the fragmentation process should be reversed to the extent possible and, ideally, a national or community consensus, or, more realistically, at least a common approach to some basic issues, should be forged. This is not easy, but it is not impossible. Barbosa, Muñoz Rivera, and Muñoz Marín, to speak only of deceased statesmen, were able to build political parties with a very wide base and sustained strength through several decades.

To the colonizer, fragmentation means that it cannot just sit back and amusedly wait until the wretched colonials speak with one voice. Once a grenade explodes it is hardly up to the wounded to will themselves into health. The former empire builders have an affirmative duty to act quickly, speak clearly, and take an active role in the decolonization process. To a large degree they are to blame for the incoherence of the colonized, their apparent inability to make up their minds as to what they want. Theirs is the duty of nudging the process along. Mindless talk about self-determination, without concrete action, is not enough.

The jealous holders of others' sovereignty must decide what decolonization options are compatible with the national interest.

It is obvious from the history of United States–Puerto Rico relations that the dream of empire did not last long, that the United States has wished Puerto Rico well throughout the whole period, that what happened when things went wrong is frequently the outcome when a democracy undertakes ventures contrary to its most precious values. The United States has also been groping for a solution to the present untenable situation.

Misunderstanding of the fragmentation effect, however, can lead to a misreading of the present situation and the inclination to impose what can be called the Gregorian requirement.

The Gregorian Requirement

As has been observed, the fragmentation effect hinders efforts by the colonized to speak with one voice and, at times, even to speak intelligibly. The Gregorian chant, monophonic singing, is normally beyond their power. Babbling, mumbling, and especially the creation of bedlam are closer to what they do best. Even so, at various times in Puerto Rican history, great majorities have been amassed in favor of statehood, independence, and autonomy. It is only since the late 1960s that signs of deadlock have been appearing. The parties representing Commonwealth and statehood have alternated in power. The difference between votes received by the two main parties in the 1993 plebiscite was less than 3 percent, none achieving an absolute majority. Compare this to a margin of more than 20 percent in the 1967 plebiscite for enhanced Commonwealth status over statehood, when it polled slightly over 60 percent.

Some distinguished officials and observers of the Puerto Rican scene—who seem not to mind that the status petitions of large majorities, amassed in spite of the fragmentation effect, have been paid no heed in most of the twentieth century—consider that the main parties' present inability to muster a strong majority means that the people of Puerto Rico have given Congress a mandate for the status quo and that, accordingly, Congress must do nothing until a majority develops. The Gregorian requirement is held in good faith, but it is plain wrong. The view does not take into account that, although there naturally are differences as to which status formula should prevail, all parties agree that the present situation calls for change and that decolonization should immediately be effected. Conventional wisdom has failed to realize that decolonization need not wait until a definite choice is made. The *decision* to decolonize is entirely separable from the *result* of the decolonization process. The Puerto Rican mandate and the international duty of the United States is for decolonization to be achieved now. The apparent indecision of the colonized as to which traditional decolonization formula is finally to prevail is no excuse for a refusal to purge the present relationship of its colonial traits.

In this context and generally as respects other issues discussed in this book, two things should be made absolutely clear. First, past inattention to Puerto Rican problems, as well as mistakes in their analysis, do not detract from the credit due the United States for its obvious desire to do what is right for Puerto Rico, heed its wishes to the extent possible, and help improve the lot of its people, which unquestionably has bettered. Second, the Puerto Rican leadership cannot be absolved from its share of blame in creating present misunderstandings. The leadership of the Commonwealth movement has often been guilty of not talking clearly and confusing Congress about the reforms it seeks. The proposal for establishing the Commonwealth was initially presented as relatively innocuous, just a case of the law catching up with reality. The subsequent reforms were often portrayed as simple adjustments required to cure Commonwealth status of minor imperfections. The reforms sought were at times bold and at others marginal or even inconsequential. The Commonwealth leadership never used the word *colonial* to refer to aspects of the Commonwealth relationship,[7] and it was banished from the vocabulary of most of the Commonwealth movement leadership.

The statehood leadership, for its part, has traditionally done its best to compound the confusion, ignoring the results of elections and plebiscites, raising fanciful legal objections to all petitions, accusing others of not being good American citizens and of hiding sinister intentions. The independence leadership has not been free of fault, either. In its desire not to be mistaken for nationalists, it has suffered from an excess of good manners, although not to the extent that the autonomists and statehood supporters have.

All three parties, in short, have been raising such a din, all singing different tunes at the same time and mostly off-key, that Congressional impatience or indifference to the cacophony is in a sense understandable, but not justified. Realization of the consequences of prolonged colonialism for human dignity and the capacity for clear and forceful expression would expose the present pandemonium for what it really is, a by-product of the absence of freedom and equality.

The inequity of the rigorous application of the Gregorian requirement under present conditions does not, however, free the people of Puerto Rico from the need to achieve a more civilized level of discourse in these matters and a minimum of agreement on at least the procedures for finding a way out of the maze in which they find themselves.

The Need for Civility and Balance

Issues having anything to do with political status are so emotionally charged in Puerto Rico that achieving a balanced analysis is about as easy as standing in an open field in the middle of a full-force tropical hurricane. The political discourse has deteriorated to the extent of hindering meaningful communication among the local political parties and creating a spiral of increasing contempt and rage at each other's beliefs. For the sake of the continued health of their society, Puerto Ricans must make a conscious effort to retake the road to civility and balance of judgment. This entails, at a minimum, respect for the opinions of others and achievement of greater detachment in the analysis of matters on which different opinions have developed. Puerto Ricans do themselves a disservice by not agreeing on certain premises that are vital to the solution of the status problem and some of their other dilemmas. Is it not time to recognize objectively that all political formulas in play are equally respectable and (subject to conditions that may be negotiated with Congress) feasible; that the supporters of each are equally honorable and well-meaning and have valid reasons, which we may or may not share, for holding them and actively seeking their implementation? A profound change in the behavior of Puerto Ricans toward other Puerto Ricans and their opinions is vital to successful decolonization and the development of a much-needed consensus in the fight against the other great social and economic problems faced by the island.

Colonialism has left other debris which has also seriously impaired the relations between Puerto Rico and the United States and contributed to the paralysis of the past four and a half decades.

The Devaluation of the Vote

Practices arise in colonial societies that seriously devalue the vote and the meaning of the democratic process. The most devastating is the habit of the losers, whether in elections or plebiscites, to sidle up to the colonial authority and try to obtain from it what they could not win at the polls. Under the Foraker Act the American Governors used to complain that Puerto Ricans did not respect the first principle of democracy: acceptance of majority rule. The same can be said today, perhaps with greater truth. No matter who wins an election or a plebiscite in Puerto Rico, the losers immediately flock to Washington to try to undermine the winner's governing program or the chosen status option. Before the governorship became elective, the sniping protocol also included the practice of flattering the Governor. A number of Governors and Washington bureaucrats and politicians who listened were as much to blame, if not more, than the lobbyists themselves.

This disrespect for the democratically expressed will of the majority, on the side of both those who talk and those who listen, explains in part the futility up to now of nonbinding plebiscites in Puerto Rico. The minorities do not feel obligated by them and neither does Washington, in spite of the rhetoric about self-determination. Washington should not encourage this undemocratic practice, which does little but foster cynicism about the electoral process.

The Thinning of the Skin Phenomenon

Colonialism heightens the sensitivity of the colonizer and, at times, of the colonized. The empire's officialdom usually gets enraged at the charge that it is behaving in a colonial fashion, that it is usurping the right of others to govern themselves, whether for good or for bad. As in the times of Manifest Destiny, the colonizing nation sees itself as engaged in the loftiest of missions, helping others to help themselves. To be charged with the unspeakable practices of colonialism, as happens to the United States every year at the United Nations and every day in Puerto Rico, appears to the colonizer to be just plain defamation and ingratitude, a mark that the colonials are simply unprepared to scale greater heights of self-government and evidence that the rest of the world, with the exception of a handful of nations, enjoys baiting the United States on this issue.

A prerequisite to decolonization is the restoration of plain talk to its pre-eminent position in a democracy. Instead of automatically taking offense at such a charge, its basis should be calmly explored. A prior condition, of course, is to repudiate the notion that any people have a God-given right to govern other peoples. In practical terms, a great nation such as the United States must take such reasonable measures as are required in this imperfect world for its security, but such an end can be achieved by more limited, civilized means. The decolonization of Puerto Rico, through any of the established methods or through other inventive devices, in no way prevents American interests in the Caribbean from being adequately protected. There is no rational reason for keeping Puerto Rico on so short a leash.

As respects the island's residents, the fact that Puerto Rico is still a colony by any objective measure causes all sorts of strange reactions. Both statehood advocates and independentistas curiously believe that repeating such an obvious truth ad nauseam will advance their respective causes. Many autonomistas, on the other hand, wrongly consider that the acceptance of such a fact represents a diminution of Commonwealth status.

The statement that Puerto Rico continues to be a colony of the United States after the establishment of Commonwealth status is neutral in nature. It does not undermine Commonwealth status, as the events of 1950–52, objectively seen, were simply part of a larger, still unachieved process. It does not mean that the people of Puerto Rico have no choice but start marching toward either independence or statehood. When the relationship between the United States and Puerto Rico is termed to be colonial, this in no way represents an attempt to tarnish the image of the United States, nor does it tilt the scales in favor of any given status. It is simply the statement of a regrettable, but demonstrable fact. It implies a call for decolonization, without loading the dice in favor of a given solution. Once this type of prejudice is laid aside, the question as to how to improve the relationship between Puerto Rico and the United States can best be addressed.

The Don't-Play-Favorites-Among-the-Natives Syndrome

In the early stages of imperialism, the representatives of the empire are wont to have colonial favorites, which normally are the most obsequious, complaisant, and sycophantic of their subjects. The incondicionales under Spain and the estadistas of the early decades of the twentieth century are two examples from Puerto Rico's history. In later stages, however, although something of the old habit remains, the tendency is not to displease anybody, not to appear to be taking sides. This is a commendable practice, one that a few Presidents never learned, but the problem is that it cannot be extended, as it sometimes has been, to situations where the will of the people has been democratically expressed. It cannot be invoked to justify inattention to the results of referenda, as happened with the 1967 plebiscite. In matters of status, once the choice is made, you cannot abandon the winner for fear of offending the losers. In politics, like in marriage, you must make a choice and stand by it.

The Unsplittable Sovereignty Atom

Another preconception that has hobbled decolonization efforts is the ancient notion that sovereignty is indivisible, that a nation can divest itself totally, but supposedly not partially, of its control over another. There is, of course, no basis to that strange idea. Sovereignty, like the atom, can be split. There are no limits to the arrangements that can be worked out between a former colonial power and its possessions. The Constitution of the United States is not such a quirky document that it deprives the nation of possibilities open to others to shed an ill-fitting colonial dress.

The availability of a wide range of options, on the other hand, is no argument in favor of a specific formula. The legal possibility of a shared sovereignty is of itself no argument in favor of Commonwealth status. The sovereignty issue is just one among many examples of the colonial propensity in Puerto Rico to argue that all legal avenues are closed, except the one which we favor.

The Tying and Untying of Congressional Hands

Another element of the colonial debris, one connected to the sovereignty conundrum, is the quaint notion that autonomist options based on the mutual consent idea are not open to the United States because supposedly one Congress cannot tie the hands of another. This is, of course, sheer nonsense, as the United States Department of Justice has pointed out on several occasions. Congress can obviously bind other Congresses by granting statehood, independence, or anything in between. The Insular Cases interpreted the United States Constitution to mean that the United States could acquire and govern colonies. It would be simply astounding to hold that it cannot permanently divest itself of the power to govern them to the extent that the national interest should dictate.

Again, the fact that such power exists is in no way an argument in favor of some autonomist solution. It is just an indication that the road is open to many solutions, that status issues should be approached practically, on the determination of what are the respective interests of the United States and Puerto Rico and how can they best be served, without resort to dated legalisms which so far have cluttered the road to decolonization.

On Permanence and Impermanence

An illustration of the manner in which colonialism has warped and tarnished the status debate in Puerto Rico is the series of claims and counterclaims about the "permanence" of the various status choices. One of the statehood supporters' main arguments is that statehood is the one permanent solution, that once Puerto Rico becomes a state of the Union there is no way out. Future dissent can thus be stifled, and it is the only sure way to increased federal aid and eternal enjoyment of American citizenship. Many decades ago the autonomists used to deride such claims, but then they decided to compete with the statehooders in the "permanence" race. They stopped talking about association with the United States and started clamoring for union and later permanent union with the United States. To an unengaged observer of the Puerto Rican scene, the whole uninspired, depressing debate, built on the notion that future generations are not to be trusted and that matters are better settled before the people have second thoughts, is indeed puzzling. It is sad to see how human yearnings for permanence and supposed paradise can be so exploited.

On the Price of Liberty

Another of the most insidious hurdles to decolonization is the belief that in order to attain liberty in any form—through some kind of separation, association, or integration, but especially the first two—justice has to be sacrificed. We have seen striking examples of that in the historical United States stance toward independence since the thirties and toward improved forms of association since the fifties. The playing field was never made level. If Puerto Rico wanted independence or full autonomy in association with the United States, or just increased powers of self-government, it was supposed to pay back in the hard currency of injustice. Existing levels of assistance were possible only under a continued state of subjection; higher levels were attainable only under statehood. The ironical twist was that, although statehood was never envisaged as a viable alternative in American policy toward Puerto Rico in the course of most of the twentieth century, it was thereby encouraged indirectly, and to a degree unconsciously, by overt hostility toward independence for most of that time and by glacial indifference to the possibilities of enhancing Commonwealth status.

Such an unexpected consequence of neglect in formulating a clear policy toward Puerto Rico has unwittingly distorted the status picture since the 1960s by indirectly helping statehood adherents to argue that statehood is the only sure way to enjoy increased Federal assistance and that to vote for any other status option is to vote against a better standard of living. Not unexpectedly, the believers in Commonwealth status have been led to petition for assistance levels equal to those of a state, and the proponents of independence have demanded a long transition period during which generous Federal aid would be continued and American citizenship retained.

This is not to say that separation and association options, in different degrees, may not entail reduced or even gradually diminishing aid formulas, although not to a point where the price of liberty is economic ruin. What this means is simply that a conscious policy should be devised. The fact that Puerto Ricans are American citizens entitles them to certain rights and, arguably, equal rights under most, if not all, conditions. What is wrong is United States indecision. Is it ready to admit Puerto Rico now or later as a state of the Union? If so, under what conditions? Until the United States decides to answer these questions, it makes no sense for the government of the United States to put a price on independence or association that the people of Puerto Rico cannot possibly pay, while at the same time dangling the possibility of greater bounties under a statehood that seemingly it is not yet ready to grant or even promise.

The Etiquette of Liberty

There is the urgent need also for a new approach to decolonization. The procedure should not consist, as up to now, of a series of humble petitions by the aggrieved party, frantically pleading for compassion. This old approach is to a large degree responsible for the exasperatingly slow process of the United States feeding bites of self-government to the colonies. The nature of the question should change. The issue should not be whether further powers of self-government should graciously be extended to the colonies, but rather, what powers do the dependencies want to entrust to the former empire, subject to its consent. Nobody has the right to govern another: it is as simple as that. The change in the starting point can help clear away many false obstacles created by the colonial mindset.

The Lashing-Out Reflex

The acceptance of a radically different starting point also helps to counteract the lashing-out reflex. In the heyday of the colonial policy engendered by Manifest Destiny, for the people of Puerto Rico to speak of independence represented the height of ingratitude, if not malevolence. The United States government of the time demeaned American citizenship by conferring it on the Puerto Ricans for the primary purpose of discouraging independence. Continued talk, and later violent action, produced in the thirties the Tydings mock-independence bill, also aimed at teaching the Puerto Ricans a lesson for asking for the forbidden fruit. Policy should not be built on such an emotional basis.

The charge that the relationship between the United States and Puerto Rico still reeks of colonialism has traditionally been considered offensive to the American government. Year after year the United States spends considerable energy defending itself against such charges at the United Nations. Would it not be far more profitable to examine such charges dispassionately and do something about clothing the Emperor?

Puerto Ricans, on the other hand, should also free themselves from the dangers of unthinking action. Appeals to terrorism or violence of any kind are senseless. Puerto Rico is not confronted at present, as have others, by an evil empire bent on exploiting it and keeping it in chains. Here, St. George lacks a dragon to slay. Although such was not the case some years ago, there is no question now that should Puerto Rico desire independence, the United States would be more than willing to oblige. From the point of view of the United States, Puerto Rico is in many ways such a headache that its independence can appear as a consummation devoutly to be wished. On the Puerto Rican side, there is also the need for calm analysis of the situation and mature weighing of the options that may be open to it, free from recrimination and rancor or calls to arms.

On Closing and Opening Doors

A most distressing mark of many autonomistas, one that unnecessarily complicates the status picture, is their inability to accept that Commonwealth may be to some a transitory form of status. Yet, historically, Commonwealth status was precisely intended to be attractive to both those who viewed it as a final alternative to statehood or independence and those who considered it as a good solution for an indefinite number of years on the road to eventual independence or statehood. In the early forties the conclusion was reached by the autonomistas that the longtime debate between independence and statehood was leading nowhere, that the United States was unwilling to grant either option, and that the issue was unnecessarily dividing the people of Puerto Rico. The search for the fullest autonomy possible, a leitmotif of Puerto Rican politics since the last third of the nineteenth century, was accordingly resumed. Full self-government in association with the United States had the potential of becoming as dignified and "final" an alternative as the others, but it could also, in the long run, prove to be a transition to other forms of liberty, if such were the decision of both parties to the proposed compact. A vote for Commonwealth status was not therefore initially understood to require the permanent renunciation of statehood or independence. The doors were always open to the possibility of other agreements. A powerful consensus was built on such a basis. A large number of the proponents of other forms of status did not feel threatened by such a view of the Commonwealth formula.

But then came the time when the fear of "impermanence" and the thought that Commonwealth would otherwise be lessened in dignity, when compared to other options, led to the attempted closing of doors by Commonwealth supporters. The move also answered the understandable desire to quiet the status debate, which instead became increasingly bitter. At a time when statehood and independence were not *for the moment* realistic options from the point of view of the United States, the autonomistas gratuitously took on the added burden of proving to the electorate that independence and statehood were not *ever* viable options. A little more modesty about the ability to peer into the future could help. Puerto Ricans have much to learn yet about the mathematics of uncertainty, about how often events resist prediction.

On the Virtues of Moderation

As much as there is a need to examine the present United States policy toward Puerto Rico, there is also a dire need for Puerto Rico to take a new look at itself. What does Puerto Rico want? Does happiness mean achieving the highest living standards on earth, or can it be attained at more modest levels? Is there no end to the spiral of rising expectations?

Close contact with the United States has unquestionably been highly beneficial to Puerto Rico. With all its present problems, Puerto Rico has still undergone extraordinary changes for the better. It has become one of the most solid democracies in Latin America and the Caribbean. Corruption at high levels of government is unknown in Puerto Rico, and its leaders have all been people of unquestioned probity. Puerto Rico's standard of living, although it leaves much room for improvement, is among the highest in Latin America.

There has been, however, a downside to such contact. Too many Puerto Ricans envy the Joneses. In matters of consumption they do not know when to say when. The natural aspiration for a better life is being replaced in many by a frenetic desire to consume beyond their means. This tendency toward immoderation is reflected in the attitude of many toward the traditional status options. Statehood, for example, is portrayed by some as a form of instant early retirement, receiving continual grants and doing nothing but basking in the bliss. (It would be like earning a pension for life as a prize for learning to walk.) Others see the culmination of Commonwealth status as a way to receive all the benefits of statehood and few of its responsibilities, and there are those who cannot conceive of independence without munificent alimony.

The Gemini Principle and the Sound Barrier

Finally, two main obstacles to a mature territorial policy have been the notion that all territories should be treated the same way as far as possible—the Gemini principle—and the idea that none should be allowed to break the sound barrier on the road to self-government: the attainment of greater powers than those reserved to the states of the Union. These two concepts are unnecessarily restrictive. Many are the differences among the territories, and many are the ways to self-government, each adaptable, following many patterns, to the necessities and desires of each particular people. As respects the distribution of power within a federation such as the United States, the model answers to special historical circumstances that vary greatly from those affecting peoples with diverse social and economic characteristics, historically related to the federation in different manners. Why trace a single, narrow path, from which nobody can wander, in a field so open to a variety of solutions?

Thus, after denouncing hang-ups from another era and pleading for a look unclouded by them, let us discuss possible ways to devise a happy ending for what so far has been a horror story.

15

Possible Paths to Decolonization

In the past forty-odd years, efforts to free the relations between the United States and Puerto Rico of all colonial connotations have crashed against a thick wall. The policy engendered by the spent dream of empire has long been dead, but its demise is still not officially recorded and no adequate replacement has been structured. Self-determination is supposedly its substitute, but, outside of the context of independence, it has proved to be meaningless, and rightly so. The people of Puerto Rico have a unilateral right to independence, although its terms would, of course, have to be negotiated if special conditions are sought. They certainly do not have a God-given right to statehood or to enhanced Commonwealth status. Self-determination should accordingly be limited to its traditional role: the recognition of the colony's right to break loose at any time, which for so long was denied. As to other status formulas, the United States obviously has a role to play, to decide unilaterally who is to be admitted to its union of states, and when, and to determine which changes to the present status are in its best interests. Continued confusion about what self-determination means, together with uncertainty as to what would be acceptable to the United States under the various status options, can only exacerbate the bickering among Puerto Ricans about the brand of paradise they prefer. The unending debate about status is draining away energy that the people of Puerto Rico should better spend in trying to become less dependent economically.

The question therefore is not for Puerto Rico to make up its mind—it has expressed it in two plebiscites—but rather for the United States to make up its own. It should accordingly do two things at the earliest possible moment: speedily signal its decision to fully decolonize Puerto Rico, and determine which decolonization options best serve its present national interests. These are actually two tasks, which so far have been masquerading as one.

The first step should not, as in the past, be postponed or take up an inordinate number of years, as in the case of Micronesia. Puerto Rico's more than half a millennium of subordination to the will of others is long enough. Nor should the United States continue to shoulder the burden of being what it never was meant to be, a colonial power, however well-intentioned. Timely action is as important as the declared commitment to decolonizing.

How can the first task, the decision to bring Puerto Rico into the modern world, to make it as free as any other society, be promptly accomplished? There are at least four ways: the transfer of sovereignty method, a negotiating commission, a binding plebiscite, or a local constitutional convention on status.

The first is the most dramatic. Congress would simply state in a brief joint resolution that all sovereign powers over Puerto Rico are vested in its people and that negotiations will determine which functions they want to entrust to the United States and the United States is willing to accept. The resolution can become effective immediately, or at such time as an agreement is reached, but not later than a given date, unless the parties should otherwise decide. The divestiture could also take effect in stages. Such sovereignty as would be needed to negotiate a compact of independence, or of admission to statehood, or of association with the United States, would immediately be vested in the Puerto Rican people. To avoid dislocation problems that immediate divestiture would cause, it could be provided that, pending agreement on the treaty, compact, or statehood enabling act to be negotiated, the United States would continue to exercise such powers as it now holds, but as powers expressly delegated by the people of Puerto Rico. Such a transfer of sovereignty is status-neutral, and entirely different from a grant of independence as a negotiating precondition.

There are many possibilities open to creative statesmanship along the lines described. The point is that, whatever form is preferred, there should be no grounds for anyone to claim that Puerto Rico is still a colony of the United States. If there is a situation where the American ability to go to the heart of a problem should be invoked, to swiftly cut Gordian knots of all sizes and shapes, this is it. Bureaucracy's traditional vacillation and penchant for enmeshing itself in all sorts of preposterous legal issues should no longer have a significant role to play. Of seven nations entrusted with the administration of colonies under the United Nations Trusteeship System, the United States was the last to liberate its wards—and questions remain about the freedom of the Commonwealth of the Northern Mariana Islands. It is the last colonial power in the Caribbean that still clings to the notion of plenary powers over people who protest being so treated. Why is this startling state of affairs allowed to continue?

Part of the answer lies in the fact that these matters have been usually relegated to the backyards of policy, far from the glare of national scrutiny. There is not only a need to take a second look at Puerto Rico: The look should be taken at the highest levels of power.

A resolution of the sort described should naturally be made subject to approval or rejection by the people of Puerto Rico at a referendum, unless supported by all three political parties. The resolution, which has many variants, would represent a major shift in United States policy toward Puerto Rico. To those still stumbling around in the colonial fog, the idea would seem unworkable for two main reasons. First, sovereignty is treated by them as a controlled substance, highly addictive stuff that cannot be handed out with abandon; and, second, what havoc would such a move, apparently so contrary to the Gemini principle, raise in other United States territories? Yet there is nothing outlandish or even new in the transfer of sovereignty method. A variation of the idea is in fact the cornerstone of Resolution 1514 (XV) of the United Nations, unanimously approved by the General Assembly, with only nine abstentions. What unspoken terrors lurk in the idea of acknowledging, as others do, the right of all peoples to negotiate for their liberty from a position of dignity and not as tiresome supplicants? As to other United States' non-self-governing areas—the Virgin Islands, Guam, American Samoa and the Commonwealth of the Northern Marianas—don't they also have the right to work out through the suggested or some like procedure the status changes which they are clamoring for, if they so desire, consistent with United States interests?

The second way to signal the start of a final decolonization process would be to appoint a negotiating commission, not the usual type of commission to explore alternatives that have been studied to death. It should be headed by a personal representative of the President, with appropriate rank, and would report directly to the President through a White House body such as the National Security Council, or it could be set up by Congress.

The agenda of the Puerto Rico Status Negotiations Commission, if the result of the 1993 plebiscite is to be minded, would be to negotiate a Compact of Permanent Union with representatives of the Commonwealth formula. Given past experience, the Popular Democratic party would probably insist on the use of that particular terminology, however awkward. To be fair to all sides, the commission's charter should provide that the referendum on the proposed compact should offer the Puerto Rican electorate the opportunity to petition Congress instead for other specified status options. Until the commission reports and changes in the present status come into effect, the powers now exercised by the United States over Puerto Rico would be held as powers delegated by the people of Puerto Rico.

Many variations to the negotiating commission method are possible. There are other ways to set up the commission and define its agenda, as circumstances may require, different times at which Congress may desire to intervene, limitations or conditions to the alternative status formulas that may be necessary to spell out, as the United States interest may dictate. The commission's agenda need not be bound to the 1993 plebiscite results. Its role can be to agree with representatives of the political parties on a procedure for defining the status formulas and submitting them, subject to the approval of Congress, to the Puerto Rican people for them to choose.

The third way, the binding plebiscite, can be linked to the negotiating commission or used independently. If used separately, it should essentially be a reprise of Senator Bennett Johnston's 1989 status bill (S. 712) with such changes as are considered proper. In close consultation with representatives of each status formula or just the formula concerned, Congress would define in separate chapters of the bill the status alternatives to be offered to the Puerto Rican electorate in a new plebiscite, should the Legislative Assembly of Puerto Rico so provide by vote of three-fourths of its members, the chapter chosen to become law without further action by Congress.

Finally, the constitutional status convention idea has been repeatedly discussed in the past. It was first presented by Muñoz Marín in the course of the debates of the 1943 presidential commission and has in the past few years been advanced by others. A constitutional convention on status can serve, perhaps better than a plebiscite, as a method for the people of Puerto Rico to choose a status formula. It also provides the mechanism for negotiating its implementation, which can be through a committee of its own or in many other ways, subject to convention approval and acceptance or rejection of the final product at a referendum. It can also propose to the people the changes to the present constitution that may be necessary. The convention method, when used as a separate mechanism, does not require agreement among the three parties or even with Congress to be set in motion. Also, the format is flexible. The convention can be instructed in the enabling legislation, subject to approval by the electorate, to negotiate the formula represented by a majority of the delegates and to go on to negotiate within a given period the next formulas in the order of their preference, within determinate periods also, should prior negotiations prove unfruitful.

In other words, the constitutional convention method is by itself a singularly effective way to signal the decision to decolonize and to dramatize the solemnity of the negotiation phase. The technique can be used together with, or independently of, the system employed by the United States for this purpose. The constitutional convention method can in fact be employed by Puerto Rico alone to petition for an end to the present situation, possibly as a last resort and independently of any United States action, to emphasize Puerto Rico's plight and the need for full decolonization.

Before deciding which status alternatives are acceptable from its point of view, the United States must define its national interests with respect to Puerto Rico. This is, of course, a purely internal matter for the United States government to determine, but history provides a good indication of what American interests should be served by a new policy toward Puerto Rico.

First, under any status option, the United States must make sure that its security interests are adequately protected. It should be able to retain the bases and other properties in Puerto Rico that are at present being used and are essential for defense purposes. Indefinite retention of Vieques (the largest well-populated island adjacent to and part of Puerto Rico) for target bombing purposes could represent a problem under any status formula.[1] The exercise of eminent domain powers would be impossible under independence and difficult under Commonwealth status.

Second, the United States, as part of its need for a stable Caribbean, has a legitimate interest in a friendly Puerto Rico, in making sure that no nation acquires property there for military purposes and that no regime inimical to it is ever installed or long survives, a matter which was properly addressed in the Micronesian negotiations and by New Zealand in decolonizing the Cook Islands. Such goal of strategic denial can also easily be achieved under any status alternative.

Third, the United States has a vested interest in a democratic Puerto Rico. Puerto Rico's history during the past hundred years should quiet any concerns on that score. Its continued ties to the United States, as desired by all parties in Puerto Rico, would add assurances in that respect.

Fourth, the United States has an interest in a peaceful Puerto Rico. Inconformity with status has in the past bred violence. It could happen again.

Fifth, the United States has an unquestioned interest in a prosperous Puerto Rico. Not only would such a condition add to the stability and democratic health of Puerto Rico and improve its contribution to the Caribbean, Latin America, and the United States itself, but, after all, Puerto Rico is peopled by American citizens. The grant of American citizenship carried with it obligations that cannot be shunned. It just would not do for them to remain unconscionably poor. Why continue to encourage mass migration to the United States in search for a better life? On the other hand, this prosperity should preferably not derive from a shower of grants, but from Puerto Rico's ability to make it on its own.

Finally, in spite of the negation of that goal so far by outmoded policies, the United States has a decided interest in a noncolonial Puerto Rico. Colonialism demeans both the United States and Puerto Rico, diminishes the latter's self-respect, and threatens its stability. To put it bluntly, the present do-nothing policy toward Puerto Rico does not serve any perceivable United States interest and should be replaced at the earliest possible moment.

The issue now before the United States is therefore how best to decolonize Puerto Rico with due attention to its legitimate interests and what status options are at this time compatible with these interests and consequently can be offered to the people of Puerto Rico for them to choose. The traditional status options shall now be considered in the inverse order of preference shown at the 1967 and 1993 plebiscites.

From the point of view of the United States, independence appears to be the easiest way out. It is the least expensive remedy, proper arrangements can be made to safeguard United States interests, and it would be the most respected solution to the present dilemma from an international point of view, statehood having been always viewed with deep suspicion, as has Commonwealth in its present form. The people of Puerto Rico have also stubbornly clung to their national culture and traditions through decades of strenuous efforts to Americanize them. To avoid the economic shock that an immediate grant of independence would cause, a transition period could be worked out.

The problem with independence is that, for some time now, although there have been periods in the twentieth century when the independence parties (the Unión and Liberal parties) commanded a majority, less than 4 percent of the electorate appear to prefer it at present. It placed a poor third in the 1967 and 1993 plebiscites. Although in 1952 the Independence party was the second most powerful organization and the statehood supporters ran a very distant third, their roles have been reversed. The past hundred years underscore, however, the volatility of party affiliation on the island. Puerto Rican society has been subject to processes of social change of such depth and abruptness that party composition and even life span have repeatedly varied. Time and again it has been proved that there is life outside the ruling elites, as less privileged sectors of society have learned to find their voice.

Independence supporters have also been relentlessly persecuted on the island by both the United States and the Puerto Rico governments since the early 1900s. Documentation has been brought to light about extensive covert operations by the Federal Bureau of Investigation to destabilize and discredit independence organizations and hound its leaders.[2] Systematic vigilance and repression of independentistas was common during the Muñoz Marín years. Both the Commonwealth and statehood parties have instilled in Puerto Ricans a deep-seated fear of independence.

The fact that the independence movement has been able to resist these assaults for so long is proof of its hardiness. It should further be noted that election and plebiscite results do not really measure the recovery potential of independence. Puerto Ricans of all persuasions are principally cultural nationalists. The overwhelming majority consider themselves Puerto Ricans first and Americans second. Should the people of Puerto Rico feel that their native language or sense of identity are threatened by statehood, if, for example, a condition to statehood was that English would be the primary language or that public school instruction would be in English, large numbers of statehooders would surely flock to the autonomist and independence options. And, should they be further convinced that the United States has no intention of purging Commonwealth status of its colonial features and insists in preserving the status quo, independence could possibly become again the preferred status of a solid majority of Puerto Ricans, although it would take time and understanding for them to overcome their apprehensions.

Which leads to the subject of political steering. The conventional wisdom is that there should not be and that there is no such thing in colonial governance. Apart from questions of what ought to be done, the historical fact is that the United States has for many decades tried to do just that, at times consciously and at others perhaps less so. It has consciously attempted for most of this century to discourage feelings of independence. It has even prevented the autonomist movement from breaking the sound barrier, to differentiate its powers from those of a state, as local realities may dictate, in the mistaken belief that too much self-government could encourage separatist feelings. The United States has also been, in spite of the care spent in making clear at all junctions that neither the grant of American citizenship nor the moves toward increased measures of self-government represented a promise of eventual statehood, unwittingly responsible for the existence in Puerto Rico of a strong statehood movement, although with ebbs and flows. United States indecisiveness, its delphic talk about self-determination, has allowed statehood to get a third wind, after being twice deflated before, after its brief periods of glory in 1900–04 and 1933–40. The United States is also responsible to a fair extent for the good fortunes of the autonomist movement by its resistance so far to both independence and statehood. Unavoidably, there is also steering just by doing nothing.

As concerns statehood, the nature of the statehood movement in Puerto Rico is not understood well. The movement so far has been cyclical, rather than linear. The fact that it has been steadily gaining adherents in the past thirty years, to the point of winning the 1996 elections by an absolute majority of the vote, which had not happened in the past sixty years, provides no assurance that it will continue to grow. In the course of the twentieth century it has never been able to hold power for more than eight consecutive years, and it has twice faded into insignificance after being the strongest party on the island (it polled 68 percent of the vote in 1902). It has never commanded a majority in a plebiscite, although its support has grown dramatically and statehood may well command a majority the next time around.

Why have the people of Puerto Rico so far behaved that way toward such a respected status, even as recently as the 1993 plebiscite, in spite of the extraordinary welfare levels that it promises and the political equality it would bring within the American Union? Is it unfriendliness toward the United States? Ingratitude? Plain orneriness?

It is none of these, although some mainlanders, misunderstanding the situation, are at times inclined to set Puerto Rico loose or force statehood upon it for its own good. A number of Puerto Ricans advocate violence against the United States because of its behavior in status matters, but the overwhelming majority of Puerto Ricans, including believers in independence, desire strong ties with the United States. The rejection of the statehood alternative so far is basically due to cultural and economic reasons.

The vast majority of Puerto Ricans want to continue to be Puerto Ricans, above all. They have never viewed their American citizenship, which they hold in high regard, as requiring them to cease feeling that way. They are proud of their Caribbean, Spanish, and African heritage, as fiercely proud as the people of Quebec are of their French cultural legacy. They feel that they constitute a distinct society, a people in their own right, a nation, as other peoples in the Caribbean and in Latin America are. A 1996 poll showed that only 25 percent of the people of Puerto Rico consider the United States to be their nation. For the other 75 percent, their nation is Puerto Rico.[3] After four centuries of Spanish rule, Puerto Ricans did not want to be part of Spain, in spite of the common language. For the most part, up to the present they have not wanted to be merged into the United States, either. The retention of Spanish as the primary language of Puerto Rico, with English as an official language also, would in that respect be a precondition to statehood, as has repeatedly been made clear by its proponents.

The language issue has been met by Congress before. When Louisiana was admitted as the eighteenth state in 1812, seven years after Congress ratified its cession by France, a large part of the population spoke either French or Spanish. The enabling act required that judicial and legislative proceedings be conducted in English.[4] In the case of New Mexico and Arizona, with their large Spanish-speaking populations, Congress went further and insisted that school instruction be conducted in English. All state officers and members of the state legislature were also required "to read, write, speak and understand the English language sufficiently well to conduct the duties of their office without the aid of an interpreter."[5] Oklahoma, with its large American Indian population, faced a similar problem. It was admitted to statehood in 1906, also with the condition that instruction in the public schools "shall always be conducted in English."[6]

In Puerto Rico's case this issue should be faced squarely by Congress in order to determine whether the above precedents, to which Congress is not necessarily bound, should be followed. Fairness both to the people of the United States and to that of Puerto Rico requires that there be no equivocation about this.

In this respect the degree of English proficiency in Puerto Rico is important. Only 19 percent of residents can speak English with relative ease, and another 23 percent can speak it with difficulty. To the remaining 58 percent, English might as well be Chinese.[7] The decision should be made whether greater literacy in English should be required as a condition to statehood. On the other hand, the experience of Louisiana, Oklahoma, New Mexico, and Arizona shows that, after statehood, tendencies toward homogeneity take over that normally make languages other than English recede into secondary roles. *E pluribus duum* would not be the necessary consequence of admitting Puerto Rico as a state. A second look at statehood, moreover, could lead to the conclusion that there is nothing inherently unacceptable in the notion of the United States having a state in which Spanish would be the primary language, although there are strong arguments against the establishment of such a precedent.

In the Statehood party's view, Congress is powerless to require that English be the language of public education or of government in Puerto Rico. Legislation to that effect, even if national in character, would not have to be obeyed by the State of Puerto Rico. Puerto Rico could also keep its separate sports identity. Facts such as this, together with the refusal to give up Spanish as the primary language of instruction, government, and daily life, make it somewhat unclear whether the term *statehood* has the same meaning in Puerto Rico as in the United States.

The fact that since 1948 Puerto Rico has participated in the Olympics and other international athletic events under its own flag is generally unknown in the United States. Pride in the fact that Puerto Rico competes not as part of the United States team but against it, as a separate nation, is so pronounced that attitudes toward the status issue are affected by it. Polls show that all the independentistas, 70 percent of all Commonwealthers, and 50 percent of all statehooders insist that no status change should affect Puerto Rico's separate identity in international sports. This naturally would not be permissible under statehood, although the Statehood party claims the contrary. The statehood party claims that this is none of the United States' business, but a matter to be decided solely by Puerto Rico and the International Olympic Committee.

The economic impact of statehood has been another reason for the resistance so far to petition for statehood. United States government studies indicate that statehood would have serious repercussions for the Puerto Rican economy. The Congressional Budget Office concluded the following in a 1990 study of the option of granting statehood with a ten-year transition period, as outlined in the binding plebiscite bill then being considered.

> Those aspects of statehood [that] . . . CBO is able to quantify may eventually bring about a significant reduction in the growth of the Puerto Rican economy. Increased federal transfers (less new taxes) would initially stimulate the economy. Later, however, statehood could lead to slower economic growth than would be expected under commonwealth status because statehood could reduce the growth of investment, output, and employment in the manufacturing sector. This reduction would be initiated because, under statehood, U.S. corporations operating in Puerto Rico would no longer enjoy tax advantages provided by Section 936 of the Internal Revenue Code.[8]

The declines in growth were estimated by the CBO at being 10–15 percent of the gross product in the year 2000.[9]

The impact on welfare program expenses would also be considerable. A

1989 study of the Congressional Research Service shows that 62.4 percent of Puerto Ricans live below poverty level. Of persons 65 and over in Puerto Rico, 63.8 percent live below poverty level, as compared to 14.8 percent in the United States. Almost 70 percent of children in Puerto Rico live in poverty, compared to 16 percent in the United States.[10]

The Supplemental Security Income (SSI) program, which is not available in Puerto Rico, provides federal cash assistance to low-income elderly, blind, and disabled persons. Instead of SSI, Puerto Rico operates a program of Aid to the Aged, Blind and Disabled (AABD), under which federal funds are subject to a cap and the Commonwealth is required to pay 25 percent of the benefits. Under statehood, SSI would apply instead of the AABD program, the cap would be removed, and the maximum benefit levels would increase from $32 a month to $368. As the authors of the report commented: "A jump of this magnitude undoubtedly would expand the population eligible, increase payments to program participants 8- to 11-fold, and could potentially affect persons other than SSI recipients. The elderly in Puerto Rico tend to live in extended households and a large increase in the income of one household member might create a work disincentive for other household members."[11]

The application of the United States tax system to Puerto Rico as a consequence of statehood would mean, among other things, that the earned income tax credit (EITC) would extend to Puerto Rico. The EITC is a tax credit for households with earned income below a certain level and dependent children. An estimate indicates that in 1979 almost two-thirds of all Puerto Rican families with children would have been eligible under statehood for the EITC. In a 1996 report, the U.S. Government General Accounting Office (GAO) considers that the extension of the EITC to Puerto Rico would entail about a $574 million credit. In the absence of EITC, Puerto Rico's aggregate federal tax liability would have been about $623 million in 1995. This means that under statehood, Puerto Rican taxpayers would have a net aggregate federal tax liability of $49 million, which, however, would be wiped out, according to the report, if allowance is made for expansion of the filing population, in which the aggregate amount of EITC would be increased to about $638 million.[12] EITC alone would thus counteract the effect of extending federal income taxation to Puerto Rico and ensure the undisturbed enjoyment of the $4.1 billion in additional grants that Puerto Rico would receive under statehood.

The Nutrition Assistance Program (NAP) is the cornerstone of the Puerto Rican welfare system. Upon Puerto Rico becoming a state the Federal Food Stamp program would apply instead, which would increase the number of recipients by some 400,000 people, covering well above half of the population, and increase the present benefits by at least 20 percent.

The Aid to Families with Dependent Children (AFDC) program would also undergo substantial changes under statehood. The program now covers about 5 percent of the population, its funding is subject to a cap, and Puerto Rico has to pay 25 percent of the cost. Under statehood there would be no cap, benefits would increase by 75 percent to 83 percent, and a larger part of the population would be covered.

Medicaid presents a similar picture. Medicaid in Puerto Rico is also capped and Puerto Rico has to pay half of the costs. Under statehood, federal spending for this program in Puerto Rico would more than double. The Congressional Research Service study of the impact of statehood on welfare programs thus concluded: "Under the Statehood option for Puerto Rico, a sharp rise in welfare benefits could dramatically reconfigure the outline of the Island's income distribution. While, on the one hand, this could have salutary effects on the living standards of many low-income people, the effect on labor force participation and work disincentives in an economy in which unemployment is already very high (14.5 percent) is an issue of serious concern."[13]

Although statehood would thus involve dislocations to the island economy and greatly increased financial assistance from the United States, the immediate, short-term benefits to the enormous part of the population of Puerto Rico which lives in poverty would be considerable. It should indeed seem amazing to outsiders that, with all these bounties being continuously dangled before the Puerto Rican electorate, statehood should still be a minority movement in Puerto Rico, but by a slim margin and perhaps not for long.

The economic consequences of statehood pose additional questions to the United States. Should statehood be offered, if at all, subject to Puerto Rico attaining certain levels of prosperity, equal or at least much closer to the national average or even to those of the poorest state of the Union? Would it be enough to provide a ten- or fifteen-year transition period? Should a second referendum be required after the transition period and before actual admission to make sure that Puerto Ricans really want statehood and that the conditions then clearly indicate that it is in the best interests of the United States?

Another factor that should be considered, linked to the cultural issue, is the possible effect of statehood on the island's political stability. To a great number of Puerto Ricans, statehood is unacceptable under any circumstances. To many within that group, statehood entails the death of the fatherland. Given past history, the possibility of their resort to violence cannot be easily discounted. From

1975 to 1982, when the Statehood party was in power most of the time, 200 bombs went off in Puerto Rico and 140 in the United States mainland, all admittedly placed by Puerto Rican terrorists. The *New York Times* once quoted the head of the FBI antiterrorist section as calling the various Puerto Rican terrorist groups "the most active and violent groups operating in this country."[14] Since the mid-1980s things have been quieter, but will they remain that way if statehood is presented as an impending reality?

Still, Puerto Ricans are American citizens, and it is understandable that a great many of them, possibly an eventual strong majority, consider it their right to achieve statehood at some point. There are signs of a gradual, though serious erosion of the autonomist movement in the past three decades. The United States should realize that it may soon be faced with a petition for statehood from the people of Puerto Rico. An answer must be made ready. If the United States should decide that the economic problems can be waived or an adequate transition period devised, and that the cultural difficulties can be surmounted, it should immediately offer statehood, subject to such conditions as are deemed necessary, together with the options of enhanced Commonwealth status and independence, for the people of Puerto Rico to choose. Should Congress resolve that conditions are not ripe for such a momentous decision, it should frankly indicate what changes should occur for statehood to be granted or turn to other decolonizing options. What is indefensible is the present stance of smiling coyly whenever statehood is mentioned and coquettishly encouraging further advances from the famished suitor, without making up one's mind as to whether this mating dance can ever blossom into conjugal happiness.

As respects Commonwealth status, in the fifties it was the product of desperation. Finding closed the paths to independence and statehood, Puerto Ricans turned, as at other times in the past, to autonomy. Full autonomy, however, has not yet been achieved. Some United States officials mistakenly equate autonomy and independence.

Decolonization by way of a developed Commonwealth would not be difficult. There are precedents for all the necessary principal moves. A new compact of association or of "permanent" union should make clear beyond question that it may not be amended except by mutual consent.

The silly debates about sovereignty and the retention of plenary powers, which marred the negotiations with the Marianas, but not with the Free Associated States of other parts of Micronesia, should also come to an end. After all, the Supreme Court of the United States has already decided that Puerto Rico is "sovereign over matters not ruled by the United States Constitution."[15] The compact should be drafted on the basis that the United States should exercise in Puerto Rico only such powers or functions as are delegated to it by the people of Puerto Rico in the compact and are essential to the association.

The easiest way to solve the old problem concerning the indiscriminate application of federal laws is the traditional Statute of Westminster formula, also employed in the case of the British Associated States. United States laws should only apply to Puerto Rico if Congress specifically so decides, at the request or with the consent of the people of Puerto Rico. If so agreed, laws relating to the functions or powers delegated to the United States, such as selective service legislation, could automatically apply.

Puerto Rico should be able to apply for membership in international organizations, as is the case with the Netherlands Antilles and the Free Associated States of Micronesia. The Northern Marianas provision would be clearly insufficient. Puerto Rico should also be able to enter into international trade agreements. Proper consultation procedures should be agreed upon to make sure that agreements negotiated by Puerto Rico or the United States do not run counter to the interests of the association.

Assistance programs would apply to Puerto Rico only to the extent that the compact or United States legislation may provide. How this question is handled could greatly influence future events. If it is determined that there should not be any discrimination among American citizens in that respect, the statehood movement in Puerto Rico would possibly be seriously hurt, as its reliance on an additional torrent of grants would disappear. On the other hand, United States interests may be held to dictate that statehood be chosen mainly because of patriotic considerations and not because of economic necessity. In any event, greater participation by Puerto Rico in aid programs could be made subject to appropriate contributions by Puerto Rico to the United States treasury, increasingly so as its economy may permit.

The task of negotiating a revised compact between Puerto Rico and the United States should ideally be done in one step. In the course of the past forty-odd years the various issues have been studied at length. It could also, however, be done in two steps. A short, simple document would comprise the basic decolonizing principles. The details, such as the distribution of functions and the applicability of certain laws, could continue to be negotiated and could be the subject of supplementary agreements.

No matter what most autonomistas say because of their fixation with the notion of "permanence," it is in the nature of Commonwealth status that it does not close the door to independence or statehood, should the parties later decide that movement in either direction is desirable. Properly divested of its present colonial features, it could serve the interests of both the United States and Puerto Rico long into the future.

Puerto Rico, as remarked by the Supreme Court of the United States, "occupies a relationship to the United States that has no parallel in our history."[16] It should be kept so, unless the United States resolves that Commonwealth status no longer serves its best interests and decides to encourage statehood or independence at this time. If Commonwealth is seen otherwise by the United States, the development of such a unique relationship should not be limited by making it analogous to either a State of the Union or a territory. The value of Commonwealth status lies in its flexibility and its appeal to a broad band of opinion, having elements that make it resemble a State of the Union and others that are closer to nationhood. It occupies a large space in the center, a buffer zone between the extremes of complete integration and total separation from the United States. If its space is constricted by too close a semblance to the territorial or state models, the center may not hold and polarization may return, as in the thirties, with its load of sorrows. Commonwealth status has so far proved to be a sturdy species, but it would most probably continue to lose favor with the electorate in the near future and become irretrievably damaged if kept in colonial garb, wearing territorial knee-pants.

It would thus appear that the traditional policies toward Puerto Rico have run their course. Colonialism is no longer a viable alternative in the present world. The new policy should be clear and forthright, one that serves the interests of the United States while achieving full decolonization and settling the status debate for as long as possible, at least a generation or two.

All three status options are consistent with United States interests in varying ways. The interest mix may change in ways now unforeseeable, a fact that may call for a policy that allows the United States increased flexibility. The constituencies of political parties in Puerto Rico have been subject to particularly deep changes in the last third of the twentieth century. The economic model relied upon by the PDP, primarily based on the grant by the federal government of special tax privileges to stateside corporations investing in Puerto Rico, for example, was cast aside in 1996 by Congress.

In the forties and fifties the divisions seemed simpler. The PDP presented a Manichaean view of the world which made headway. On one side, its side, there were the poor and underprivileged, led by a selfless intelligentsia which would deliver them into modernity. On the dark side there lurked the scheming rich, the conservatives, the opponents of change. Such a Weltanschauung no longer holds.[17] To a large extent, class identification within the parties is much more complex. Underrepresentation and alienation are more the order of the day. The unattached voters, called *realengos* in Puerto Rico, have greatly increased their numbers. There are signs of increasing pluralism. The crumbling of the economic model, built on production for external markets and dependent on foreign capital and on fragile tax privileges extended by the United States, adds to the call for caution.[18] Unless significantly strengthened, Commonwealth status will in all probability soon lose its support. The competing set of values emphasized by other status alternatives are sufficiently attractive to outweigh those of a weakened Commonwealth.

The 1993 plebiscite favored improved Commonwealth. United States tradition calls for a response, a step that does not and should not preclude attention to other options. Although the policy of self-determination does not specify how to respond to a petition for statehood or for enhanced Commonwealth, its minimum content is that such a petition is entitled to consideration. The United States should consequently enter into negotiations for enhancement with representatives of the Commonwealth option, but making clear that any revision to the present compact shall not enter into effect unless approved by the people of Puerto Rico at a referendum. It should further require that in this referendum the people of Puerto Rico should be afforded the opportunity to express also their preference for independence or statehood over the enhanced Commonwealth status. Likewise, should the United States be ready now to admit Puerto Rico into the Union after a suitable transition period, it can require that at the referendum to be held for acceptance or rejection of the necessary enabling act, the people of Puerto Rico should be able to indicate their desire to enter instead into negotiations for enhanced Commonwealth or independence.

In fairness to the people of Puerto Rico, if the statehood option is to be offered in any of the above alternatives or in any other way, the United States should be as candid as possible concerning the conditions, if any, attached to it. It should be stated whether the option should be favored by a supermajority, in order to make sure that, in the present shifting winds of public opinion, Puerto Ricans have no second thoughts about statehood after attaining it; whether statehood would be subject to the achievement of specified levels of economic development; and whether English must be the language of public school instruction and of government. It should further be made clear to the Puerto Rican people that under statehood Puerto Rican athletes must naturally march with the United States flag and be part of the United States team. For the good of all concerned, present fanciful Puerto Rican interpretations of what statehood means should not be encouraged. Conditions to independence, if any, should also be clearly spelled out, as should the nature of enhanced or perfected Commonwealth. Many Commonwealth leaders are notoriously vague about the exact meaning of "enhanced" Commonwealth or hold wildly differing ideas.

The 1993 plebiscite thus opens up many alternatives, and it does not foreclose other choices the United States may want to bring before the people of Puerto Rico. The plebiscite may also be, uncharacteristically and unwisely, ignored, in which case the procedure would be different, but the substance would suffer little change. The procedure in such case would entail either a binding plebiscite along the lines of the one unsuccessfully sought in 1989–1991, or a call for negotiations with the committee that may be selected by a constitutional convention or at a referendum, whatever the people of Puerto Rico may decide.

The greatest need in any case is for the United States to determine what it is really prepared to do in shaping or helping to shape its relationship with Puerto Rico. The important thing is to bring to an end the present policy of dawdle and drift. The urgency of squarely meeting this issue has been brought to the attention of United States Presidents for a long time now. In the late seventies, Zbigniew Brzezinski, then National Security Adviser, wrote to President Carter: "The political status of Puerto Rico will be one of the most difficult and important issues that the American people will face in the 1980s. One only has to think of Northern Ireland and Quebec to appreciate the potentially explosive implications."[19]

What the United States privately determines to be its preferred relationship with Puerto Rico would naturally influence events to come. After the end of the Cold War, a new look—a reassessment of what the United States really wants from Puerto Rico, if anything—is in order. Is it in its best interests to have Puerto Rico become now a State of the Union? Should the decision be postponed until it becomes clearer whether a stable majority of Puerto Ricans truly desire and are ready for such a step, or should it be offered now, to attempt to settle matters once and for all? And would an independent Puerto Rico, with appropriate and continuing ties to the United States, if that path is chosen, be somehow a threat to its security or any other of its interests? Should the United States, contrary to its past policy, encourage independence?

And about Commonwealth, how does it serve at present the interests of the United States? Is it in the best interests of the United States to help it grow stronger or should it be purposefully weakened further and be done away with to facilitate movement towards either independence or statehood? Can an improved Commonwealth help Puerto Rico attain greater economic self-sufficiency and at least contribute to quiet the status debate for a reasonable period? Does the United States really need, finally, to keep Puerto Rico in a state of dependency, subject to its sovereign and unencumbered will, or does the reality of United States power allow it to decolonize Puerto Rico, in any of the many possible ways, without fear of disaster?

To sum up:

- There is no reason for continuing to back the status quo. Puerto Rico should cease being considered by so many a colony of the United States, a mere unincorporated territory or possession subject to the plenary powers of Congress.
- The term *colony* is not employed here in the usual, vituperative sense applied in the past to the dependencies of the European imperial nations. Economic exploitation of Puerto Rico was never an aim of the United States government. The charge rests, rather, on the unnecessary retention of excessive power over Puerto Rico, the consequent limitations to self-government, and the lack of proper attention to the requirements of a relationship based on equality and full, specific consent, be it under any of the status formulas under discussion.
- The United States should not carry the sole responsibility for the prolongation of the present untenable situation. With their petty squabbles, often garbled language, and shortsightedness, all Puerto Rican political parties also bear a significant part of the blame.
- It is clear that the present self-determination policy alone has not been effective in solving the status dilemma.
- The United States government should at the highest levels take a new, hard look at Puerto Rico, define its actual interests there as of this time and the foreseeable future, and devise a new policy.
- Part of this policy should be the recognition of the fact that decolonization can proceed separately from determining how to handle the results of the decolonization process.
- Any further plebiscites or referenda of the Puerto Rican people on matters of status should take into full account the views of all parties concerned. The consultation should present a level playing field. Nonbinding consultations have proved to be ineffectual. Congress should clearly state what status options are available and under what conditions and stand ready to honor the choice of the Puerto Rican people.
- On the part of Puerto Ricans there is also need for a new look at ourselves. As a minimum basis for developing a civilized discourse and

structuring a much-needed consensus, the following premises should
be agreed upon, without need for anyone to cast aside her or his personal preferences:

a. All three status formulas, although requiring different conditions,
   are respectable and feasible, from the point of view both of Puerto
   Rico and of the United States.

b. Preconceptions about the history of the relationship between the
   United States and Puerto Rico should be cast aside. This is no
   story about the misdeeds of an evil empire. There has been good
   faith and good will on both sides, although misunderstandings
   and lack of effective communication have on occasion marred the
   relationship.

c. The Puerto Rican political parties need to put aside their history
   and view one another fairly. The demonization of the statehood
   leaders by their opponents, portraying them as un-Puerto Rican
   and servile lackeys of imperialism, has served no constructive
   purpose, as has the charge of un-Americanism hurled by the
   statehooders against their adversaries. It is also wrong to see the
   autonomist parties as the main representation of the poor and
   destitute, pitted against the agents of the rich. Except for occasional periods, the wealthy have had little trouble in finding
   friends within the main parties. The cause of the destitute has
   been championed by all parties (the people placed special trust in
   Barbosa, Iglesias, and Muñoz Marín, to speak only of dead statesmen), but by and large the historical truth is that they have for
   long periods been underrepresented. The rewriting of parts of
   Puerto Rico's history by new generations of historians, who are
   delving into the plight of the poor and powerless through the centuries in the island and reevaluating the role of the traditional parties and the sayings and doings of their leaders, deserves special
   attention. Such leaders have too often been depicted as dauntless,
   unerring Gullivers. The trials and tribulations of the Lilliputians
   merit deeper study and understanding.

d. For the greater viability of whatever decolonization formula is
   chosen, Puerto Ricans must endeavor to operate within a climate
   of greater respect for each other and greater tolerance of dissent.

In all, independence, statehood, and enhanced Commonwealth each have
the potential of providing a happy ending to what so far has been a horror story.

Continuation of the present policy of inattention and inaction is the only alternative that should be scratched. Such a do-nothing policy will lead to further exacerbation of the virulent status debate in Puerto Rico, contraction of the center, and possible polarization and violence. Continuation of the present policy will mean that over five hundred years of subjection and despair are considered not to be enough, that further penance need be done for Puerto Rico to purge whatever sins account for its present wretchedness. The United States and Puerto Rico, together, can forge a better ending than that.

In spite of the exasperating slowness of the process of decolonizing Puerto Rico, for which there is no excuse, and of the long-standing confusion about how to go about it, there are encouraging signs. Most Puerto Ricans desire strong ties with the United States. The United States clearly harbors nothing but good will toward Puerto Rico. It is just a question of taking a hard look at a past about which there are quite a few things to regret, on both sides, and making the decision to forge a brave new beginning.

Notes

Introduction

1 For a thoughtful history of the granting of United States citizenship to Puerto Rico, see: Cabranes, José A., *Citizenship and the American Empire*, New Haven, Yale University Press, 1979.

2 "Puerto Rico, datos básicos sobre su historia, economía y sociedad," Departamento de Estado y la Administración de Fomento Económico, 1990, p. 20. Junta de Planificación, *Informe económico al Gobernador*, 1994, Table A-1.

3 Freyre, Jorge F., *External and Domestic Financing in the Economic Development of Puerto Rico*, Río Piedras, University of Puerto Rico Press, 1969, p. 94; Junta de Planificación, *Informe económico al Gobernador*, 1972, table 25; Junta de Planificación, *Informe económico al Gobernador*, 1994, p. 10.

4 Committee to Study Puerto Rico's Finances, James Tobin, chairman, "Report to the Governor," December 11, 1975, p. 8.

5 Junta de Planificación, *Apéndice estadístico, Informe económico al Gobernador*, 1990, table 29; Junta de Planificación, *Apéndice estadístico, Informe económico al Gobernador*, 1994, table 29.

6 Junta de Planificación, *Apéndice estadístico, Informe económico al Gobernador*, 1990, table 21. Freyre, *External and Domestic Financing in the Economic Development of Puerto Rico*, p. 94.

7 See: Curet, Eliezer, *Development by Integration to the United States*, Río Piedras, Editorial Cultural, 1986, pp. 79–81; Andic, Fuat, *El desarrollo económico y la distribución del ingreso en Puerto Rico*, San Juan, Banco Gubernamental de Fomento, 1964, p. 40; U.S. Department of Commerce, *Census of Population*, 1980, Washington, D.C., Government Printing Office, 1983.

8 Junta de Planificación, *Informe económico al Gobernador*, 1994, Table 31.

9 On the migration phenomenon, consult: Nieves Falcón, Luis, *El emigrante puertorriqueño*, Río Piedras, Editorial Edil, 1970; Senior, Clarence, *Puerto Rican Emigration*, Río Piedras, University of Puerto Rico Press, 1947; Torruellas, Luz M., *El movimiento migratorio de retorno en el período 1965–1970 y su impacto en el mercado laboral*, Río Piedras, University of Puerto Rico Press, 1982; Alvarez Curbelo, Silvia, "Coartadas para la agresión: Emigración, guerra y populismo," in Rivera Nieves, Irma, and Gil, Carlos, eds., *Polifonía salvaje*, San Juan, Editorial Postdata, 1995, p. 91.

10 Kurlansky, M., *A Continent of Islands*, Reading, Mass., Addison-Wesley, 1992, pp. 297–99.

11 For a short history of the non-Hispanic Caribbean, see: Trías Monge, José, *Historia constitu-*

cional de Puerto Rico, Río Piedras, University of Puerto Rico Press, 1994, vol. V, chapters 8, 9, and 10.

12 Gibraltar, with its less than three square miles claimed by two countries, represents no exception. In 1462 Spain reconquered it from the Moors and made it part of its national territory, the English captured it in 1704, and Spain ceded it to England in 1713. It has been a British Crown colony since.

Chapter 1: Puerto Rico Under Spanish Rule

1 See, for further details, Alegría, Ricardo, "La población antillana y su relación con otras áreas de América," in Caro, Aida, *Antología de lecturas de historia de Puerto Rico (siglos xv–xviii),* 3d ed., Río Piedras, University of Puerto Rico Press, 1977, pp. 47–63; Picó, Fernando, *Historia general de Puerto Rico,* Río Piedras, Ediciones Huracán, 1986, chapter 2; Chanlatte Baik, Luis, *La Hueca y sorcé (Vieques, Puerto Rico): Primeras migraciones agroalfareras antillanas: Nuevo esquema para los procesos culturales de la arqueología antillana,* Santo Domingo, 1981; Sued Badillo, Jalil, *Los caribes: Realidad o fábula,* Río Piedras, Editorial Antillana, 1978; Díaz Soler, Luis, *Puerto Rico: Desde sus orígenes hasta el cese de la dominación española,* Río Piedras, University of Puerto Rico Press, 1994, chapter 3.

2 Morales Carrión, Arturo, ed., *Puerto Rico: A Political and Cultural History,* New York, W. W. Norton, 1983, p. 45.

3 Caro Costas, Aida, "The Outpost of Empire," in Morales Carrión, ed., *Puerto Rico: A Political and Cultural History,* p. 14.

4 On the institutions of this period see, generally: Ots, J. M., *Manual del derecho español en las Indias y del derecho propiamente Indiano,* Buenos Aires, Editorial Lasada, 1945; Haring, C. H., *The Spanish Empire in America,* New York, Oxford University Press, 1947; Trías Monge, J., *Historia constitucional de Puerto Rico,* Río Piedras, University of Puerto Rico Press, vol. I, 1980, chapter 2.

5 *Recopilación de las Leyes de Indias,* Lib. (book) 3, Tít. (title) 3, L. (law) 61. The Laws of the Indies were compiled in 1681. Annotated editions, with information as to later laws, appeared in 1841 and 1846.

6 *Recopilación de las Leyes de Indias,* Lib. 5, Tít. 12, L. 2.

7 Trías Monge, J., *El sistema judicial de Puerto Rico,* Río Piedras, University of Puerto Rico Press, 1978, pp. 2ff.

8 Labra, J. M., *La autonomía colonial en España,* Madrid, Imp. Sucesores de Cuesta, 1892, pp. 39–40.

9 Labra, J. M., *América y la constitución española de 1812,* Madrid, Imp. Sindicato de Publicidad, 1914, p. 114.

10 García Gallo, A., *Metodología histórico-jurídica: Antología de fuentes del derecho español.* Madrid, Manual de Historia del Derecho Español, 1967, vol. 2, p. 145.

11 Santamaría de Paredes, V., *Curso de derecho político,* Madrid, Establecimiento Tipográfico de R. Fe, 5th ed., 1893, appendix.

12 A copy of the decree can be consulted in Cruz Monclova, Lidio, *Historia de Puerto Rico,* Río Piedras, University of Puerto Rico Press, 2d ed., 1970, vol. I, pp. 182–83.

13 Quiñones, F. M., *Historia de los partidos reformista y conservador,* Madrid, Imprenta de J. F. Morete, 1889, p. 9. On the formation of a liberal front against the dominant classes, see: Negrón Portillo, Mariano, *El autonomismo puertorriqueño: Su transformación ideológica (1895–1914): La prensa en análisis social: La Democracia de Puerto Rico,* Río Piedras, Edi-

ciones Huracán, 1981, p. 65. On the impact of class conflicts, see: Quintero Rivera, Angel G., *Conflictos de clase y política en Puerto Rico,* Río Piedras, Ediciones Huracán, 1976.

14 Cruz Monclova, *Historia,* vol. II, 1970, pp. 142–46.

15 See: Negrón Portillo, *El autonomismo puertorriqueño,* for an account of the forces behind the autonomist movement and its ideological changes from 1895 to 1914.

16 Cruz Monclova, *Historia,* vol. III, 1971, p. 264.

17 The revolution threatened the holdings of American sugar companies in Western Cuba. Picó, *Historia general de Puerto Rico,* pp. 218–19.

18 Portell Vilá, H., *Historia de Cuba en sus relaciones con Estados Unidos y España,* Havana, J. Montero, 1939, vol. III, p. 32.

19 On the complicated monetary system in effect before 1898, see: di Venuti, B., *Money and Banking in Puerto Rico,* Río Piedras, University of Puerto Rico Press, 1950, pp. 1–14.

20 For a detailed account of the antecedents and development of the autonomist movement, see: D'Alzina Guillermety, Carlos, *Evolución y desarrollo del autonomismo puertorriqueño, siglo xix,* San Juan, Universidad Politécnica de Puerto Rico, 1995.

21 See: López Cantos, Angel, *Fiestas y juegos en Puerto Rico (siglo xviii),* San Juan, Centro Avanzado de Estudios de Puerto Rico y el Caribe, 1990.

22 For further materials on Puerto Rican culture at the time and the development of a distinct Puerto Rican identity, see: Babín, María Teresa, *The Puerto Rican Spirit: Their History, Life and Culture,* New York, Collier Books, 1971; Picó, Fernando, and Rivera Izcoa, Carmen, *Tierra adentro y mar afuera: Historia y cultura de los puertorriqueños,* Río Piedras, Ediciones Huracán, 1991. On class divisions at the end of the nineteenth century, see: Quintero Rivera, Angel G., *Patricios y plebeyos: Burgueses, hacendados, artesanos y obreros: Las relaciones de clase en el Puerto Rico de cambio de siglo,* Río Piedras, Ediciones Huracán, 1988; Fernández Méndez, Eugenio, *Historia cultural de Puerto Rico, 1498–1968,* San Juan, Ediciones El Cemí, 1970; Morris, Nancy, *Puerto Rico: Culture, Politics and Identity,* Westport, Conn., Praeger, 1995.

23 For those further interested in the history of Puerto Rico under Spain and the social, economic, and political forces that shaped it, see: Picó, *Historia general de Puerto Rico;* González Vales, Luis E., *Alejandro Ramírez y su tiempo,* San Juan, University of Puerto Rico Press, 1978; Picó, Fernando, *Libertad y servidumbre en el Puerto Rico del siglo xix,* San Juan, Ediciones Huracán, 1979; Picó, Fernando, *Al filo del poder: Subalternos y dominantes en Puerto Rico (1739–1910),* Río Piedras, Ediciones Huracán, 1993; Morales Carrión, ed., *Puerto Rico: A Political and Cultural History,* chapters 1–7; Díaz Soler, *Puerto Rico: Desde sus orígenes hasta el cese de la dominación española;* and the selected bibliography at the end of this book.

Chapter 2: The Annexation

1 Callcott, W. H., *The Caribbean Policy of the United States, 1890–1920,* Baltimore, Johns Hopkins University Press, 1942, p. 1.

2 Portell Vilá, H., *Historia de Cuba en sus relaciones con Estados Unidos y España,* Havana, J. Montero, 1938, vol. I, pp. 234ff.

3 Ibid., p. 226.

4 Ibid., pp. 266, 268; Callcott, *Caribbean Policy,* p. 12.

5 Pratt, J. W., *America's Colonial Experiment,* New York, Prentice-Hall, 1950, p. 5; Perkins, Baxter, *The United States and the Caribbean,* Revised ed., Cambridge, Harvard University Press, 1966, pp. 92–93.

6 Callcott, *Caribbean Policy*, p. 19.

7 Ibid., p. 36.

8 Weinberg, A. K., *Manifest Destiny*, Baltimore, Johns Hopkins University Press, 1936, pp. 325, 392–93.

9 On the very early relations between the United States and Puerto Rico, see: Morales Carrión, Arturo, "Orígenes de las relaciones entre los Estados Unidos y Puerto Rico, 1700–1815," *Historia II*, no. 1 (1952).

10 Pratt, *America's Colonial Experiment*, p. 2.

11 Ibid., pp. 4–5.

12 Ibid., p. 7.

13 Ibid., p. 16.

14 Callcott, *Caribbean Policy*, p. 66; Pratt, *America's Colonial Experiment*, p. 25.

15 Pratt, *America's Colonial Experiment*, p. 186.

16 Kirk, Grayson L., *Philippine Independence*, New York, Farrar and Rinehart, 1936, pp. 4–5.

17 31 *Cong. Rec.*, 3702, 44th Cong., 2d Sess., April 11, 1898.

18 Ibid., p. 4100.

19 Callcott, *Caribbean Policy*, p. 103; Pratt, *America's Colonial Experiment*, pp. 231, 327.

20 Portell Vilá, *Historia de Cuba*, vol. III, p. 500.

21 Picó, Fernando, *1898: La guerra después de la guerra*, Río Piedras, Ediciones Huracán, 1987. On the Spanish-American War and some of its effects on Puerto Rico, see: Rosario Natal, Carmelo, *Puerto Rico y la crisis de la guerra hispanoamericana (1895–1898)*, Hato Rey, Ramallo Bros., 1975.

22 *Papers Relating to the Foreign Relations of the United States* (1898), Washington, D.C., Government Printing Office, 1901, pp. 822–23.

23 Ibid., p. 824.

24 *Cong. Rec.*, 55th Cong., 3rd. Sess., p. 2518.

25 Millis, Walter, *The Martial Spirit: A Study of Our War with Spain*, Boston, Houghton Mifflin, 1931, pp. 382–84; Portell Vilá, *Historia de Cuba*, vol. III, pp. 525–26.

26 Kirk, *Philippine Independence*, p. 15.

27 30 Stat. 1754.

28 8 Stat. 200 (1803).

29 8 Stat. 252.

30 30 Stat. 750.

31 *Fleming v. Page*, 9 How. 603, 613–14 (1850).

Chapter 3: Military Government

1 In English the island was called Porto Rico and the islanders Porto Ricans, following long-standing English usage. The word *Porto* is derived from Latin, which in Spanish turned into *Puerto*. The failure to use the Spanish term so irked the local people that in 1932 Congress changed the official English name of the island from Porto Rico to Puerto Rico.

2 Documents on the Constitutional History of Puerto Rico, Office of Puerto Rico in Washington, D.C., 1964, p. 55.

3 See: General Orders No. 101, U.S. Congress, House of Representatives, *Laws, Ordinances, Decrees and Military Orders*, 60th Cong., 2d Sess., House Document (hereafter H. Doc.) 1484, Part 4, Washington, D.C., Government Printing Office, 1909, p. 2177.

4 Berbusse, Edward J., *The United States and Puerto Rico, 1898–1900,* Chapel Hill, University of North Carolina Press, 1966, p. 90.

5 Ibid., p. 88.

6 Díaz Soler, Luis, *Rosendo Matienzo Cintrón,* Río Piedras, Instituto de Literatura Puertor-riqueña, 1960, p. 178, n. 44.

7 General Orders No. 101.

8 Negrón Portillo, Mariano, *Las turbas republicanas, 1900–04,* Río Piedras, Ediciones Huracán, 1990, pp. 215–16.

9 Davis, G. W., *Report on Civil Affairs in Porto Rico,* 56th Cong., 1st Sess., H. Rept. 2, p. 481.

10 Ibid., p. 549.

11 Ibid., p. 551.

12 Negrón Portillo, *Las turbas,* pp. 81 ff.

Chapter 4: The Shaping of a Colonial Policy

1 Carroll, Henry K., *Report on the Island of Porto Rico,* Washington, D.C., Government Print-ing Office, 1899, pp. 56–58.

2 *Report of the Insular Commission to the Secretary of War Upon Investigations Made into the Civil Affairs of the Island of Porto Rico,* Washington, D.C., Government Printing Office, 1899, p. 61.

3 U.S. Congress, *Senate Hearings before the Committee on Pacific Islands and Porto Rico of the United States Senate on S. 2264,* 56th Cong., 1st Sess., Senate Document (hereafter S. Doc.) 147, Washington, D.C., Government Printing Office, 1900, p. 96.

4 Ibid., 97.

5 Davis's views are expressed in U.S. Congress, House of Representatives, *Reports of Brig. Gen. George W. Davis on Civil Affairs in Porto Rico,* 56th Cong., 1st Sess., H. Doc. 2.

6 U.S. Congress, Senate, *Report of the Hawaiian Commission,* 56th Cong., 3rd Sess., S. Doc. 16, Washington, D.C., Government Printing Office, 1898.

7 U.S. Congress, House of Representatives, *Report of the Secretary of War, 1899,* 56th Cong., 1st Sess., H.R. Doc. 21, pp. 26–29.

8 Ibid., 24.

9 Sumner, W. B., "The Conquest of the United States by Spain," 8 *Yale L. J.* 176–77 (1899).

10 Thayer, J. B., "Our New Possessions," 12 *Harv. L. Rev.* 464, 475 (1899).

11 Baldwin, S. E., "The Constitutional Questions Incident to the Acquisition and Government by the United States of Island Territory," 12 *Harv. L. Rev.* 392, 415 (1899).

12 S. 2016, 56th Cong., 1st Sess. The later version, on which hearings were held, was S. 2264.

13 H.R. 6883, 56th Cong., 1st Sess.

14 U.S. Congress, House of Representatives, *Hearings on H.R. 6883,* House Committee on In-sular Affairs, January 8 and 10, 1900, Washington, D.C., Government Printing Office, 1900, p. 103.

15 S. Rep. 249, 56th Cong., 1st Sess., pp. 8–9.

16 31 Stat. 77.

17 Porter, K. H., and Johnson, D. B., *National Party Platforms (1840–1964),* Urbana, Univer-sity of Illinois Press, 1966, pp. 112–13.

18 Morison, S. E., and Commager, H. S., *The Growth of the American Republic,* New York, Ox-ford University Press, 1962, vol. 2, p. 430.

19 Langdell, C. C., "The Status of Our New Possessions," 12 *Harv. L. Rev.* 365, 386 (1899).

20 See, for example, Adams, E. B., "The Causes and Results of Our War with Spain from a Legal Standpoint," 8 *Yale L. J.* 119 (1899); Randolph, C. F., "Constitutional Aspects of Annexation," 12 *Harv. L. Rev.* 291, 314–15 (1898).

21 Lowell, A. L., "The Status of Our New Possessions—A Third View," 13 *Harv. L. Rev.* 155 (1899).

22 182 U.S. 244 (1901).

23 *Plessy v. Ferguson*, 163 U.S. 537, 551–52 (1896).

24 Freund, Sutherland, Howe, Mark and Brown, *Constitutional Law*, 4th ed., Boston, Little, Brown, 1967, vol. I, p. xlv.

25 Ibid., pp. xlv, xlvi.

26 Watts, J. F., Jr., in L. Friedman and F. L. Israel, *The Justices of the United States Supreme Court, 1789–1969*, vol. III, pp. 1471, 1479.

27 182 U.S. 244, 279–80 (1901).

28 Ibid., pp. 311–12.

29 Ibid., p. 306.

30 Ibid., pp. 341–42.

31 Ibid., p. 373.

32 Ibid., p. 369.

33 Ibid., p. 380.

34 *Hawaii v. Mankichi*, 190 U.S. 197 (1903).

35 *Rasmussen v. United States*, 197 U.S. 516 (1905).

36 *Balzac v. People of Porto Rico*, 258 U.S. 298 (1922).

Chapter 5: Life Under the Foraker Act

1 Barbosa, José Celso, *Orientando al pueblo*, San Juan, Imprenta Venezuela, 1939, vol. 4, p. 68. On public opinion in Puerto Rico as respects the Foraker Act and the period of military government, see: Luque de Sánchez, María Dolores, *La ocupación norteamericana y la ley Foraker: Raíces de la política colonial de los Estados Unidos. La opinión pública puertorriqueña*, Río Piedras, University of Puerto Rico Press, 1980; see also: Rafucci de García, Carmen, *El gobierno civil y la ley Foraker*, Río Piedras, University of Puerto Rico Press, 1981.

2 *La Democracia*, May 2, 1900.

3 Muñoz Rivera, Luis, *Campañas políticas*, Madrid, Editorial Puerto Rico, 1925, vol. I, pp. 279ff.

4 Ibid., pp. 1–2.

5 *First Annual Report of the Governor of Porto Rico*, Washington, D.C., Government Printing Office, 1901, pp. 45, 48–49.

6 41 *Cong. Rec.* 4467, 55th Cong., 2d Sess.

7 See: Negrón Montilla, Aida, *Americanization of Puerto Rico and the Public School System (1900–1930)*, Río Piedras, Editorial Edil, 1971.

8 *First Annual Report of the Governor of Porto Rico*, 1901, pp. 97–98.

9 *Second Annual Report of the Governor of Porto Rico*, Washington, D.C., Government Printing Office, 1902, p. 13.

10 *Third Annual Report of the Governor of Porto Rico*, Washington, D.C., Government Printing Office, 1903, p. 13.

11 Muñoz Rivera, *Campañas políticas*, vol. II, p. 168 (speech of January 30, 1908).

12 See: Trías Monge, J., *El choque de dos culturas jurídicas en Puerto Rico*, Orford, N.H., Equity
    Publishing, 1991.

13 *President's Annual Message*, Washington, D.C., U.S. Government Printing Office, 1902, p. 35;
    idem., 1903, p. 19.

14 Pagán, Bolívar, *Historia de los partidos políticos puertorriqueños (1898–1956)*, San Juan, Li-
    brería Campos, 1959, vol. I, pp. 99–102.

15 *Annual Report of the Governor of Porto Rico*, 1903–04, Washington, D.C., Government Print-
    ing Office, 1904, p. 32.

16 See: Negrón Portillo, Mariano, *El autonomismo puertorriqueño: Su transformación ideológica,
    1895–1914: La prensa en análisis social*, Río Piedras, Ediciones Huracán, 1981.

17 *Annual Message of the President to Congress*, Washington, D.C., Government Printing Office,
    1905, p. 51.

18 Muñoz Rivera, *Campañas políticas*, vol. II, p. 138.

19 The message is printed in 44 *Cong. Rec.* 1866 et seq., 61st Cong., 1st Sess.

20 See: 36 Stat. 11, ch. 4, July 15, 1909.

21 48 *Cong. Rec.* 2855.

22 *Annual Message of the President to Congress*, Washington, D.C., Government Printing Office,
    1912, pp. 11–12.

23 H. Rep. 341, 62d Cong., 2d Sess., p. 1.

24 *Annual Report of the Secretary of War*, Washington, D.C., Government Printing Office, 1913,
    vol. 1, p. 41.

25 De Diego, J., *Nuevas campañas*, Barcelona, Sociedad General de Publicaciones, 1916,
    pp. 133–35.

26 For a history of the ideological changes at this time of the autonomist movement, see: Ne-
    grón Portillo, *El autonomismo puertorriqueño*, pp. 90ff.

27 For the history of the labor movement in Puerto Rico, see: García, Gervasio I., and Quintero,
    A. G., *Desafío y solidaridad: Breve historia del movimiento obrero puertorriqueño*, Río Piedras,
    Ediciones Huracán, 1982.

Chapter 6: The Jones Act

1 Wilson, W., *The State*, Boston, D. C. Heath, 1918, p. 357.

2 Walworth, Arthur, *Woodrow Wilson*, 2d ed., Boston, Houghton Mifflin, 1965, vol. II, p. 45.

3 Archives of the Governor's Office, La Fortaleza, file marked "Correspondence on the Organic Act."

4 H.R. 24961, 62d Cong., 2d Sess.

5 McNeill, R. L., "The United States and Self-Government for Puerto Rico, 1898–1952,"
   Ph.D. diss., Fletcher School, Tufts University, 1956, p. 56.

6 House Hearings on H.R. 8501, 64th Cong., 1st Sess. (January 1916).

7 Letter of May 19, 1916, La Fortaleza Archives, file on the Jones Act.

8 H.R. 13979, 63rd Cong., 2d Sess.

9 Muñoz Rivera, L., *Campañas políticas*, Madrid, Editorial Puerto Rico, 1925, vol. II,
   pp. 274–76.

10 Ibid. vol. III, p. 160.

11 For the full text of this document, see: 53 *Cong. Rec.* 443.

12 53 *Cong. Rec.* 6412–13.

13 54 *Cong. Rec.* 3655.

14 Barbosa, J. C., *Orientando al pueblo*, San Juan, Imprenta Venezuela, 1939, vol. 4, pp. 129–34.

15 See: Córdova, Gonzalo F., *Resident Commissioner: Santiago Iglesias and His Times*, Río Piedras, University of Puerto Rico Press, 1993.

16 H.R. 13818, 63rd Cong., 2d Sess. (February 24, 1914).

17 S. 4604, 63rd Cong., 2d Sess. (February 25, 1914).

18 S. 5845, 63rd Cong., 2d Sess. (June 13, 1914).

19 *Hearings on S. 4604, before the Committee on Pacific Islands and Porto Rico*, U.S. Senate, 63rd Cong., 2d Sess., p. 4.

20 Ibid., p. 6.

21 Ibid., p. 8.

22 Ibid., p. 16.

23 See: H.R. 8501, soon modified by H.R. 9533, and S. 1217, 64th Cong., 1st Sess.

24 H.R. 8501, p. 9571.

25 See: S. Rep. 579, 64th Cong., 2d Sess.

26 53 *Cong. Rec.* 1327, 2250, 2258–59, 64th Cong., 2d Sess.

27 Ibid., p. 3009.

28 Ibid., p. 2250.

Chapter 7: The Jones Blues

1 *Annual Report of the Governor of Porto Rico, 1917–18*, Washington, D.C., Government Printing Office, 1918, p. 2.

2 57 *Cong. Rec.* 3210, 65th Cong., 3rd Sess.

3 See: the report of the Bureau of Insular Affairs in the *Annual Report of the Secretary of War*, Washington, D.C., Government Printing Office, 1916, p. 18. In this report the bureau makes also clear that the basic reason for extending American citizenship to Puerto Rico was to signal its intention to permanently keep the island within its sovereignty.

4 On the Puerto Rican Supreme Court decision, see: *Muratti v. Foote*, 25 D.P.R. 568 (1917). On the U.S. Supreme Court reversal, see: *Porto Rico v. Muratti*, 245 U.S. 639 (1917) and *Porto Rico v. Tapia*, 245 U.S. 639 (1917). A full opinion on the subject was rendered in *Balzac v. People of Porto Rico*, 258 U.S. 298 (1922).

5 H.J. Res. 144, 66th Cong., 1st Sess., presented by L. C. Dyer from Missouri.

6 See: H.R. 11119, 66th Cong., 2d Sess. (1920), and H.R. 6647, 67th Cong., 1st Sess. (1921).

7 58 *Cong. Rec.* 6718, 66th Cong., 1st Sess.

8 See: McNeill, R. L., "The United States and Self-Government for Puerto Rico, 1898–1952," Ph.D. diss., Fletcher School, Tufts University, 1956, p. 139.

9 H.R. 9995, 67th Cong., 2d Sess. A similar bill was filed in the Senate, S. 3137.

10 H.R. 9934, 67th Cong., 2d Sess.

11 H.J. Res. 471/2, Leyes de Puerto Rico, 1923, p. 785.

12 S. 913, 68th Cong., 1st Sess.

13 See: *Civil Government of Porto Rico, Hearings on S. 2448, S. 2571, S. 2572, and S. 2573, before the Committee on Territories and Insular Possessions*, U.S. Senate, 68th Cong., 1st Sess.

14 Ibid., p. 30.

15 Ibid., p. 82.

16 65 *Cong. Rec.* 8601, 68th Cong., 1st Sess.

17 H.R. 9847, 70th Cong., 1st Sess.

18 See: Muñoz Morales, L., *El status político de Puerto Rico*, San Juan, Tipografía El Compás, 1921.

19 H.R. J. Res. 68, 61 *Cong. Rec.* 575, 67th Cong., 1st Sess.

20 H.R. 12173, 70th Cong., 1st Sess.

21 Pagán, Bolívar, *Historia de los partidos políticos puertorriqueños (1898–1956)*, San Juan, Librería Campos, 1959, vol. I, pp. 268–306.

22 See: Roosevelt, Theodore, Jr., *Colonial Policies of the United States*, Doubleday, Doran, 1937; Muñoz Marín, L., "The Sad Case of Puerto Rico," *American Mercury*, vol. 16, No. 62, 1929, pp. 136–41.

23 Diffie, Bailey W., and Diffie, Justine W., *Porto Rico: A Broken Pledge*, New York, Vanguard Press, 1931, p. 220.

24 Ibid., p. 166.

25 Ibid., p. 220.

26 Clark, Victor S., *Porto Rico and Its Problems*, Washington, D.C., Brookings Institution, 1930, p. xxi.

27 Ibid., pp. 106–7.

28 Ibid., p. 105.

29 *Annual Report of the Governor of Porto Rico*, 1929–30, Washington, D.C., Government Printing Office, 1930, pp. 15–16.

30 Roosevelt, Jr., *Colonial Policies*, p. 120.

31 Ibid., p. 115.

32 Ibid., pp. 117–18.

33 Ibid., p. 85.

34 Ibid., p. xiii.

35 Quintero Rivera, A. G., "La ideología populista y la institucionalización universitaria de las ciencias sociales," in Alvarez Curbelo, Silvia, and Rodríguez Castro, María Elena, eds., *Del nacionalismo al populismo: Cultura y política en Puerto Rico*, Río Piedras, Ediciones Huracán, 1993, pp. 108ff.; Silvestrini, Blanca G., ed., *Politics, Society and Culture in the Caribbean: Selected Papers of the Fourteenth Conference of Caribbean Historians*, San Juan, University of Puerto Rico, 1983, pp. 113ff.; Bergad, Laird W., "Agrarian History of Puerto Rico, 1870–1930," 13 *Latin American Research Rev.* 63–94 (1978).

Chapter 8: The Troubled Thirties

1 64 Stat. 319, 81st Cong., 1st Sess. (1950).

2 7 Op. Proc. Gen. de Puerto Rico, 242 (1917).

3 44 Stat. 1421, amending section 48 of the Jones Act.

4 *Díaz v. González*, 261 U.S. 102 (1923).

5 *Bonet v. Texas Co. (P.R.), Inc.*, 308 U.S. 463 (1940).

6 See: Trías Monge, J., *El choque de dos culturas jurídicas en Puerto Rico*, Orford, N.H., Equity Publishing, 1991.

7 H.R. 9831, 73rd Cong., 2d Sess. (1934).

8 There is an abundant literature on Muñoz Marín. Some of the books in English are Tugwell, R. G., *The Arts of Politics as Practiced by Three Great Americans: Franklin Delano Roosevelt, Luis Muñoz Marín, and Fiorello La Guardia*, Garden City, N.Y., Doubleday, 1958; Aitken, T., *Poet in the Fortress: The Story of Luis Muñoz Marín*, New York, New American Library, 1964; Mathews, Thomas G., *Luis Muñoz Marín: A Concise Biography*, New York, American RRDM Corp., 1967.

9 See: Albizu Campos, Pedro, *La conciencia nacional puertorriqueña*, ed. Manuel Maldonado Denis, Mexico, Siglo Veintiuno, 1972.

10 For an account of this period, see: Picó, Fernando, *Historia general de Puerto Rico*, Río Piedras, Ediciones Huracán, 1986, pp. 249–52.

11 See: Ickes, H., *Secret Diary*, New York, Simon and Schuster, 1953–54, vol. 1, pp. 547–48.

12 Ibid. S. 4549, 74th Cong., 2d Sess.

13 H.R. 12611, 74th Cong., 2d Sess.

14 S.J. Res. 270, 74th Cong., 2d Sess., approved: 80 *Cong. Rec.* 8460.

15 H.R. 1992, 75th Cong., 1st Sess.

16 See: Mathews, Thomas G., *Puerto Rican Politics and the New Deal.* Gainesville, University of Florida Press, 1960, p. 119.

17 48 Stat. 55, 73rd Cong., 1st Sess.

18 *Annual Report of the Governor of Puerto Rico, 1934–35*, San Juan, Bureau of Supplies, Printing and Transportation, 1935, p. 9.

19 Introduction, Hanson, Earl P., *Transformation: The Story of Modern Puerto Rico*, New York, Simon and Schuster, 1955, pp. xi–xii.

20 Tugwell, Rexford G., *The Stricken Land: The Story of Puerto Rico*, New York, Doubleday, 1947, pp. 42–43.

21 Alvarez Curbelo, Silvia, "La casa de cristal: El ejercicio senatorial de Luis Muñoz Marín, 1932–1936," in *Senado de Puerto Rico, 1917–1992; Ensayos de historia institucional*, San Juan, Senado de Puerto Rico, 1992; Alvarez Curbelo, Silvia, "Coartadas para la agresión: Emigración, guerra y populismo," and "Populismo y autoritarismo: Reflexiones a partir de la experiencia muñocista," in Rivera Nieves, Irma, and Gil, Carlos, eds., *Polifonía salvaje*, San Juan, Editorial Postdata, 1995, pp. 91–107 and pp. 319–27.

22 See: Alvarez Curbelo, "Populismo y autoritarismo," pp. 319, 321; Morris, Nancy, *Puerto Rico: Culture, Politics, and Identity*, Westport, Conn., Praeger, 1995, pp. 168–69.

Chapter 9: The Elective Governor Act

1 In addition to the publications and reports of the Planning Board, other statistical sources for the period are Descartes, Sol L., *Basic Statistics on Puerto Rico*, Washington, D.C., Office of Puerto Rico, 1946; Perloff, H., *Puerto Rico: Economic Future*, Chicago, University of Chicago Press, 1950; and Blanco, Ana T., *Nutrition Studies in Puerto Rico*, University of Puerto Rico Social Research Center, 1946.

2 See Ferrao, Luis Angel, "Nacionalismo, hispanismo y la élite intelectual en Puerto Rico en los años treinta," in Alvarez Curbelo, Silvia, and Rodríguez Castro, María Elena, eds., *Del nacionalismo al populismo: Cultura y política en Puerto Rico*, Río Piedras, Ediciones Huracán, 1993.

3 See: Baldrich, Juan José, "Class and the State," Ph.D. diss., Yale University, 1981. A typescript is available at the Colección Puertorriqueña of the University of Puerto Rico library.

4 See: Alvarez Curbelo, Silvia, "La conflictividad en el discurso de Luis Muñoz Marín: 1926–1936," in Alvarez Curbelo and Rodríguez Castro, eds., *Del nacionalismo al populismo*, pp. 13–35.

5 For the history of the birth of the PDP see: Muñoz Marín, Luis, *Memorias, 1898–1940*, San Germán, Universidad Interamericana de Puerto Rico, 1982.

6 For specifics, see: Capalli, R. B., *Federal Aid to Puerto Rico*, mimeograph, Instituto de Derecho Urbano, 1970.

7 On the military role played by Puerto Rico and the Caribbean, see: Rodríguez Beruff, Jorge, *Política militar y dominación: Puerto Rico en el contexto latinoamericano*, Río Piedras, Edi-

ciones Huracán, 1988, and *El Caribe en la post-Guerra Fría,* Santiago de Chile, Facultad Latinoamericana de Ciencias Sociales, 1994.

8 For text and background, see Brinkley, D., and Facey-Crowther, D., *The Atlantic Charter,* New York, St. Martin's Press, 1994.

9 For the minutes of the Presidential Commission see: President's Committee to Revise the Organic Act for Puerto Rico—*Appendix to Hearings on S. 1407 before a Subcommittee on Territories and Insular Affairs*—U.S. Senate, 78th Cong., 1st Sess., Washington, D.C., 1943, cited hereafter as Minutes, President's Committee.

10 Trías Monge, J., *Historia constitucional de Puerto Rico,* Río Piedras, University of Puerto Rico Press, vol. II, 1981, pp. 281–82.

11 Minutes, President's Committee, p. 357.

12 Ibid., p. 502.

13 89 *Cong. Rec.* 7842, 78th Cong., 2d Sess. (1943).

14 Tugwell, Rexford G., *The Stricken Land: The Story of Puerto Rico,* New York, Doubleday, 1947, p. 538.

15 S. 1407, 78th Cong., 2d Sess.

16 90 *Cong. Rec.* 1664, 78th Cong., 2d Sess. (1944).

17 Letters from Muñoz to Ickes, November 13, 1944, from Ickes to Muñoz on November 30, 1944, and from Muñoz to Ickes on January 22, 1945; Muñoz-Ickes correspondence file, Luis Muñoz Marín Library, Trujillo Alto, Puerto Rico.

18 H.R. 3309 and S. 1184, 80th Cong., 1st Sess.

19 H. Rep. 455, 80th Cong., 1st Sess., 1947 Cong. Code and Administrative News 1588.

20 Public Law 362, 61 Stat. 770, 80th Cong., 1st Sess., cap. 490.

Chapter 10: The Establishment of the Commonwealth

1 For the Alianza demands see: the remarks of the Resident Commissioner in 63 *Cong. Rec.* 861, 68th Cong., 1st Sess. (1924). The 1928 bill is H.R. 9847, 70th Cong., 1st Sess. The Foraker debates can be found in 33 *Cong. Rec.* 2472, 56th Cong., 1st Sess., Part 3. Towner's remarks are in 53 *Cong. Rec.* 8457, 64th Cong., 1st Sess.

2 64 Stat. at L. 319, 48 U.S.C.A. §731b et seq. (1950).

3 Pacheco Padró, A., *Puerto Rico, nación y estado,* San Juan Montalvo, 1955, p. 24.

4 H.R. 3237, 79th Cong., 1st Sess.

5 See: Wheare, K. C., *The Statute of Westminster and Dominion Status,* Oxford, Clarendon Press, 1938.

6 For a fuller discussion of the drafting process of Public Law 600 and the relations with the Division of Territories, see: Fernós Isern, A., *Estado Libre Asociado de Puerto Rico: Antecedentes, creación y desarrollo hasta la época presente,* Río Piedras, University of Puerto Rico Press, 1974, pp. 81ff; Trías Monge, J., *Historia constitucional,* Río Piedras, University of Puerto Rico Press, vol. III, 1982, pp. 23ff.

7 1 Stat. at L. 51, f.(a). The Northwest Ordinance provided a government for the territory lying to the northwest of the Ohio River which covered the present states of Ohio, Indiana, Illinois and Michigan.

8 H.R. 7674, 81st Cong., 2d Sess.

9 Ibid., p. 7.

10 *Hearing before the Committee on Public Lands,* House of Representatives, 81st Cong., 2d Sess., March 14, 1950, p. 18.

11 *Hearings before the Committee on Public Lands,* House of Representatives, 81st Cong., 2d
Sess., on H.R. 7674 and S. 3336, Serial No. 35, Washington, D.C., Government Printing
Office, 1959, pp. 49–50.

12 *Hearing before the Subcommittee on Interior and Insular Affairs,* U.S. Senate, 81st Cong., 2d
Sess., on S. 3336, May 17, 1950, p. 4.

13 See S. Rep. 1779 and H. Rep. 2275 on the respective bills.

14 For an account of the attack, see: Aponte Vázquez, Pedro, *El ataque a La Fortaleza,* San Juan,
Publicaciones René, 1993.

15 Resolution 23 of the Constitutional Convention.

16 Muñoz Marín Library, Public Law 600, and archives of the author, University of Puerto
Rico Law School Library.

17 H. Doc. 435, 82d Cong., 2d Sess., p. 4.

18 H. Rep. 1832, 82d Cong., 2d Sess., April 30, 1952, *Approving the Constitution of the Commonwealth of Puerto Rico which was adopted by the People of Puerto Rico on March 3, 1952.*

19 *Hearings before the Committee on Interior and Insular Affairs,* U.S. Senate, 82d Cong., 2d
Sess., on S.J. 151, f. 32, pp. 12, 13, 18.

20 98 *Cong. Rec.* 6184–86, 82d Cong., 2d Sess.

21 Public Law 447, 82d Cong., 2d Sess., ch. 567, 66 Stat. 327.

22 These years, as well as the immediately preceding and following, have produced a significant
literature. For some of the texts, see: Díaz Quiñones, Arcadio, *La memoria rota,* Río Piedras,
Ediciones Huracán, 1993; González, José Luis, *El país de cuatro pisos y otros ensayos,* Río
Piedras, Ediciones Huracán, 1980; Rivera Medina, Eduardo, and Ramírez, Rafael I., *Del
cañaveral a la fábrica: Cambio social en Puerto Rico,* Río Piedras, Ediciones Huracán, 1985;
Alvarez Curbelo, Silvia, and Rodríguez Castro, María Elena, eds., *Del nacionalismo al pop-
ulismo: Cultura y política en Puerto Rico,* Río Piedras, Ediciones Huracán, 1993: Navas
Dávila, Gerardo, ed., *La transformación ideológica del PPD,* Río Piedras, University of Puerto
Rico Press, 1980. Wells, Henry, *The Modernization of Puerto Rico: A Political Study of
Changing Values and Institutions,* Cambridge, Harvard University Press, 1969; Weiskoff,
Richard, *Factories and Food Stamps: The Puerto Rican Model of Development,* Baltimore,
Johns Hopkins University Press, 1985.

Chapter 11: The Big Sleep

1 Resolution 222 (III), November 3, 1948.

2 Photocopies of these drafts are available at the author's archives at the University of Puerto
Rico Law School.

3 The full story, with the appropriate quotations, can be consulted in Trías Monge, J., *Historia
constitucional de Puerto Rico,* Río Piedras, University of Puerto Rico Press, vol. III, 1982, pp. 12ff.

4 *Department of State Bulletin,* April 20, 1953, U.S./U.N. press release, March 21, 1953.

5 United States Mission to the United Nations, Press Release 1741, August 28, 1953.

6 *Report by Hon. Frances P. Bolton and Hon. James P. Richards on the Eighth Session of the General Assembly of the United Nations,* April 26, 1954, printed for the use of the Committee on
Foreign Affairs, 83rd Cong., 2d. Sess., Washington, D.C., U.S. Government Printing Office,
1954, p. 241.

7 *Official Records of the General Assembly,* Eighth Session, plenary meeting 459, November 27,
1953, p. 10.

8 Ibid., pp. 319–20. Mexico, Guatemala, and Canada were among the countries that voted

against the resolution. Argentina, Venezuela, the United Kingdom, the Netherlands, and France were among those that abstained.

9 H.J. Res. 252, 80th Cong., 1st Sess.

10 See Resolution 21 of the Legislative Assembly of Puerto Rico, January 1954.

11 See: Friedrich, C. J., *Puerto Rico: Middle Road to Freedom*, New York, Rinehart, 1959.

12 For a full account of this story, see: Wells, Henry, *The Modernization of Puerto Rico: A Political Study of Changing Values and Institutions*, Cambridge, Harvard University Press, 1969.

13 *Diario de sesiones de la asamblea legislativa*, 1959, vol. 12, part 1, p. 425.

14 See: H.R. 5926, 86th Cong., 1st Sess., March 23, 1959, and S. 2023, 86th Cong., 1st Sess., May 1, 1959.

15 *Hearing before the Committee on Interior and Insular Affairs*, U.S. Senate, 86th Cong., 1st Sess., on S. 2023, June 9, 1959, p. 29.

16 *Hearings before a Special Subcommittee on Territorial and Insular Affairs, House of Representatives*, 86th Cong., 1st Sess., H.R. 9234, Serial 14, Washington, D.C., 1960, p. 15.

17 Ibid., p. 810.

18 Photocopies of complete minutes of these meetings and of the memoranda and draft bills exchanged between the parties can be consulted at the Luis Muñoz Marín Library and in the author's papers at the University of Puerto Rico Law School.

19 Ibid., p. 18 of the memo.

20 H.R. 5945, 88th Cong., 1st Sess.

21 *Hearings before the Subcommittee on Territorial and Insular Affairs*, House of Representatives, 88th Cong., 1st Sess., on H.R. 5945, May 15 and 16, 1963.

22 Public Law 88-271, 78 Stat. 17.

23 *Status of Puerto Rico,* Report of the United States–Puerto Rico Commission on the Status of Puerto Rico, August 5, 1966, pp. 6–7.

24 See: *Presidential Report for Puerto Rico: Report of the Ad Hoc Advisory Group on the Presidential Vote for Puerto Rico,* Washington, D.C., Government Printing Office, 1971.

25 Letter dated May 12, 1975, from A. Mitchell McConnell, Acting Assistant Attorney General, Legislative Affairs, President Gerald R. Ford Library, Ann Arbor, Mich., Norman E. Ross Files, Ad Hoc Committee, files 2–3.

26 Ibid., letter dated May 2, 1975, from Monroe Leigh, principal legal adviser to the State Department.

27 President Ford Library, White House Special Files—P.R. Compact of Permanent Union, letter dated October 30, 1975, from Brooks, Military Assistant, to James E. Connor, Secretary to the Cabinet.

28 President Ford Library, letter from the Secretary of the Interior to Connor, dated November 7, 1975.

29 President Ford Library, James M. Cannon files, Puerto Rico, May 2, 1975, memorandum.

30 *Compact of Permanent Union Between Puerto Rico and the United States—Report of the Ad Hoc Advisory Group,* 1975, also containing the Spanish version.

31 President Ford Library, James Cannon files, "Puerto Rico."

32 Ibid., letter from Connor to Cannon, March 2, 1976.

33 H.R. 11200 and 11201, 121st Cong., 1st Sess.; S.J. Res. 215.

34 President Ford Library, White House Central Files, ST 51-52, F6-6, memorandum dated December 21, 1976.

35 "Text of Statement by Ford," *New York Times,* January 1, 1977.

36 *New York Times,* January 21, 1977.
37 This and other documents mentioned in this section can be consulted in the three-volume compilation prepared by the Puerto Rico Federal Affairs Administration: *Political Status Referendum, 1989–91.*
38 Ibid., vol. II, pp. 1ff., report entitled *Potential Economic Impacts of Changes in Puerto Rico's Status under S. 212.*
39 H.R. 4765, 101st Cong., 2d Sess.

Chapter 12: Puerto Rico and the United Nations from 1960 to the Present

1 A/Res./145. For secondary sources which include the full text of the major resolutions cited in these notes see: the U.N. Year Books; Gautier Mayoral, C., *Puerto Rico y la ONU,* Río Piedras, Editorial Edil, 1978; Mari Bras, Juan, *El otro colonialismo,* Comisión Central, Partido Socialista Puertorriqueño, 1982.
2 For the report of the Fourth Committee, which was the subject of the vote, see: A/4651.
3 Resolution 1654 (XV).
4 A/BUR/SR 192, September 23, 1971.
5 A/AC 109/L. 833.
6 Resolution 2908 (XXVII), November 2, 1972.
7 The general pattern of such resolutions was set by A/AC 109/900 of August 29, 1973.
8 A/AC 109/PV. 1125, August 28, 1978.
9 A/AC 109/574.
10 93 Stat. 1420, August 2, 1979.
11 A/Res. 35/118, December 14, 1980.
12 Tom Wicker, "In the Nation: An American Colony?" *New York Times,* August 14, 1981.
13 A/AC 109/107, August 4, 1982.
14 *Washington Post,* September 25, 1982.
15 A/AC 109/PV 1357, September 7, 1989.
16 A/AC 109/PV 1357, September 26, 1991.

Chapter 13: Decolonization in the Caribbean and in Micronesia

1 For a detailed consideration of the history of the British West Indies, see: Ragatz, I. V., *Guide to the Study of British Caribbean History, 1763–1864,* Washington, D.C., Octagon Books, 1963; Burns, A., *History of the British West Indies,* London, George Allen and Unwin, 1954; Lewis, Gordon K., *The Growth of the Modern West Indies,* New York, Monthly Review Press, 1968; Williams, Eric, *From Columbus to Castro: The History of the Caribbean,* New York, Random House, 1970; and Trías Monge, J., *Historia constitucional de Puerto Rico,* Río Piedras, University of Puerto Rico Press, vol. V, 1994, chapter 8, and authorities cited therein.
2 For its technical definition and other characteristics, see: Interpretation Act of 1889 (52 & 58 Vict. 63) sec. 18 (2); the Colonial Laws Validity Act of 1865 (28 & 29 Vict. c. 63) s. 2; 10 *Halsbury's Statutes of England,* 1st ed., 1909, par. 862 et seq. and par. 909 et seq., as well as other statutes included in this last collection.
3 The British Caribbean Federation Act of 1956, 4 & 5 Eliz. 2 c. 23, 4 *Halsbury's Statutes of England,* 3rd ed., pp. 597ff.
4 See: West Indies Act of 1967, c. 4, 4 *Halsbury's Statutes,* 3rd ed., p. 610.
5 See: O'Neil, L., "The European Community and the Caribbean: A Caribbean Perspective," in Sutton, P., ed., *Europe and the Caribbean,* London, Macmillan Caribbean, 1991, pp. 187ff.

6 For a series of general articles on the subject see: Pluchon, P., *Histoire des Antilles et de la Guyane,* Toulouse, Privat, 1982.

7 Useful books on the subject are: Lémery, H., *La révolution française à la Martinique,* Paris, 1936; Saint-Ruf, G., *L'épopée Delgrès: La Guadeloupe sous la révolution française, 1789–1802,* Paris, Editions l'Harmattan, 1977.

8 For an English translation, see: Blaustein, Albert P., ed., *Constitutions of the Dependencies and Special Sovereignties,* New York, Oceana Publications, 1988, p. 13.

9 For a detailed study of the status of overseas departments, see: Luchaire, G., and Conac, G., *La constitution de la république française,* Paris, Economica, 2d ed., 1987.

10 Ibid., pp. 1262–63.

11 Hintjens, H., "France in the Caribbean," in Sutton, ed., *Europe and the Caribbean,* p. 7.

12 For an English translation, see: Blaustein, ed., *Constitutions.*

13 On the origins of Papiamento, see: Ferrol, O., *La cuestión del origen y de la formación del Papiamento,* The Hague, Smit Drukkers-Uitgevers BU, 1982.

14 Bureau of the Census, U.S. Department of Commerce, *1990 Census of the Population.* Washington, D.C., Government Printing Office.

15 Congress approved the Trusteeship Agreement for the former Japanese Mandated Islands on that date. See: 61 Stat. 3301, T.I.A.S. No. 1665, 8 U.N.T.S. 189.

16 "Legal Problems Arising from the United Nations Trusteeship System," 42 *Am. J. Int. L.* 262, 271 (1948).

17 *People of Saipan v. Department of Interior,* 502 F.2d 90, 95 (9th Cir. 1974), cert. den. 420 U.S. 1003 (1975); *Commonwealth of the Northern Mariana Islands v. Atalig,* 723 F.2d 682 (9th Cir. 1984). For a discussion of cases on the territorial similarity doctrine, see: Ullman, Carl, "New Players in the Public Borrowing Game: Tax and Sovereignty Considerations as Free Associated States and Indian Tribes approach Wall Street," 11 *U. of Hawaii L. Rev.* 111, 115–19 (1989).

18 S. Rep. 94-956 to accompany H.J. Res. 549 (Foreign Relations and Armed Services Committee), U.S. Code and Cong. Adm. News, 94th Cong., 2d Sess. 1976, vol. 2, p. 451.

19 Secretarial Order 2882, 29 Fed. Reg. 13, 613 (1964), superseded by Secretarial Order 2918, 34 Fed. Reg. 159 (1969).

20 Public Law 94-241, 90 Stat. 263, 48 U.S.C.A. sec. 1681.

21 S. Rep. 94-956, p. 449, n.5.

22 Leibowitz, Arnold H., *Defining Status,* Dordrecht, Martinus Nijhoff Publishers, 1989, p. 546. Leibowitz's book provides a well-researched, panoramic view of the history of each area under the rule of or associated with the United States.

23 Section 105. The Court of Appeals for the First Circuit has repeatedly decided that Congress may not legislate internally for Puerto Rico: *Córdova & Simonpietri Ins. v. Chase Manhattan Bank,* 649 F.2d 36 (1981); *United States v. Quiñones,* 758 F.2d 40 (1985); *Camacho v. Autoridad de Teléfonos de Puerto Rico,* 868 F.2d 482 (1st Cir. 1989).

24 See: Leibowitz, *Defining Status,* p. 568.

25 Herald, Merybeth, "The Northern Mariana Islands: A Change of Course Under Its Covenant with the United States," 71 *Ore. L. R.* 127, 140 (1992).

26 Ibid., p. 564.

27 McHenry, D. F., *Micronesia: Trust Betrayed,* New York, Carnegie Endowment for Peace, 1975, p. 225; Prince, Henry G., "The United States, the United Nations, and Micronesia: Questions of Procedure, Substance and Faith," 11 *Mich. J. of Int. L.* 11, 35 (1989).

28 Comments, "International Law and Dependent Territories: The Case of Micronesia," 50 *Temple L. Q.* 58, 84 (1976); Gale, Roger W., *The Americanization of Micronesia: A Study of the Consolidation of United States Rule in the Pacific,* Washington, D.C., University Press of America, 1979, p. 293.

29 Leary, Paul M., *The Northern Marianas Covenant and American Territorial Relations,* Berkeley, Institute of Governmental Studies, University of California, 1980, pp. 33–35; Bergsman, Peter, "The Marianas, the United States and the United Nations: The Uncertain Status of the New American Commonwealth," 6 *Cal. W. Int. L. J.* 382, 409–10 (1976); Prince, "The United States, the United Nations, and Micronesia," n24, p. 83.

30 Leibowitz, *Defining Status,* p. 593.

31 King, Victoria, "The Commonwealth of the Northern Marianas' Rights Under United States and International Law to Control Exclusive Economic Zone," 13 *U. of Hawaii L. R.* 477, 500 (1991).

32 See, for example, S. Rep. 94-596, n. 5, pp. 8–9.

33 S. Rep. 94-596, Jan. 27, 1976, Foreign Relations and Armed Services Committee (to accompany H.J. Res. 599), 94th Cong., 2d Sess., p. 8, U.S. Code and Cong. Admin. News, vol. 2, 1976, p. 455..

34 King, "The Commonwealth of the Northern Marianas' Rights," n. 28, p. 500.

35 Public Law 99-239, 99 Stat. 1800 (1986).

36 *Daily Yomiuri,* November 17, 1993.

37 See: *Proclamation 5564, November 3, 1986,* 51 F.R. 40399 and *Proclamation 6728, September 27, 1994,* 59 F.R. 49777.

38 *Morgan Guaranty Trust v. Republic of Palau,* 639 F. Supp. 706, 716 (S.D.N.Y., 1986); Ullman, "New Players in the Public Borrowing Game," 111, 131.

39 Section 121 (a) of the RMI and FAS compact. The corresponding provision of the Palau compact will not as a rule be cited. The compacts may be consulted at 48 U.S.C.A. §1681.

40 Leibowitz, *Defining Status,* 675.

41 *House Report 99-188 to accompany H.J. Res. 187,* 99th Cong., 1st Sess., 1985, pp. 5, 8.

42 Ibid., p. 5.

43 Ullman, "New Players in the Public Borrowing Game," pp. 111, 123ff.

44 *House Report 99-188 to Accompany H.J. Res. 187,* 99th Cong., 1st Sess., 1985, p. 31. The separate agreements can be consulted in the appendix to the report.

45 Gale, *Americanization of Micronesia,* pp. 294ff.

46 Smith, Gary, *Decolonization and United States Military Interests in the Trust Territory of the Pacific,* Canberra, Research School of Pacific Studies, Australian National University, 1991, p. 3; McHenry, *Micronesia,* p. 224.

47 Smith, *Decolonization,* p. 3 n.62.

48 McHenry, *Micronesia,* p. 224.

49 Smith, *Decolonization,* pp. 3, 41, 77.

50 Hinck, J., "The Republic of Palau and the United States: Self-Determination Becomes the Price of Free Association," 78 *Calif. L. R.* 959 (1990).

51 Rodríguez Orellana, M., "In Contemplation of Micronesia: The Prospects for the Decolonization of Puerto Rico Under International Law," 18 *Univ. of Miami Inter-American L. R.* 457, 484, 488–90; Slocum, Ruth C., "The Last Trusteeship: Palau's Struggle for Self-Determination Under the United Nations International Trusteeship System," 10 *Boston*

C. Third World J. 165 (1990); "Self-Determination and Free Association: Should the United States Terminate the Pacific Islands Trust?" 21 *Harv. J. International L.* 1, 83–84 (1980).

52 Larmour, Peter, "Cook Islands," in Unesco Supported Series on Social Sciences in the Pacific, *Decentralization in the South Pacific*, University of the South Pacific, 1985, pp. 255ff.; Smith, *Decolonization*, p. 100.

Chapter 14: Clearing the Way for a Second Look

1 *San Juan Star*, February 24, 1996.
2 *San Juan Star*, December 13, 1995. Figures taken from *Crime in the United States, 1994*, Federal Bureau of Investigation.
3 Vales, Pedro A., Ortiz, Astrid A., and Mattei, Noel E., *Patrones de criminalidad en Puerto Rico: Apreciación histórica, 1898–1980*, Puerto Rico, W. Serra Deliz, 1982.
4 *San Juan Star*, July 2, 1995.
5 General Accounting Office, *GAO Report NSIRD-96-119*, April 17, 1996.
6 Leibowitz, Arnold H., *Defining Status*, Dordrecht, Martinus Nijhoff, 1989, pp. 642–43.
7 See: Cabranes, José A., "Puerto Rico: Out of the Colonial Closet," 33 *Foreign Policy* 66 (Winter 1978–79).

Chapter 15: Possible Paths to Decolonization

1 At the request of Governor Muñoz Marín, President Kennedy decided to rein in the Department of Defense plans to occupy the whole of Vieques and Culebra and prod the government of Puerto Rico to resettle its inhabitants. Kennedy Library, National Security Files, box 155A, letter dated January 16, 1962, from the President to the Governor; ibid., Oral History, January 11, 1965, interview of Muñoz Marín by Lee White.
2 Fernández, Ronald, *The Disenchanted Island: Puerto Rico and the United States in the Twentieth Century*, New York, Praeger, 1992, pp. 206ff.
3 San Juan, *El Nuevo Día*, June 12, 1996.
4 2 Stat. 641–43, February 20, 1811.
5 36 Stat. 557, June 20, 1910 (enabling act for New Mexico), and 36 Stat. 568, June 20, 1910 (enabling act for Arizona).
6 34 Stat. 267–78, June 16, 1906.
7 U.S. Bureau of the Census, *1980 Census of Population*. General Social and Economic Characteristics, Washington, D.C., Government Printing Office, 1984, p. 24.
8 Congressional Budget Office Papers, *Potential Economic Impacts of Changes in Puerto Rico's Status Under S. 712*, April 1990, p. 7.
9 Loc. cit.
10 Congressional Research Service, August 1, 1989, letter to Senator Daniel P. Moynihan, Political Status Referendum, 1989–1991, *Reports and Studies on the Puerto Rico Status and Related Issues*, Puerto Rico Administration of Federal Affairs, n.d., vol. II, p. 126. See also family poverty data cited in the introduction.
11 Ibid., p. 185.
12 General Accounting Office, *Tax Policy: Analysis of Certain Potential Effects of Extending Federal Income Tax to Puerto Rico*, August 1996, Report 96-127, Washington, D.C., pp. 4, 10.
13 Ibid., p. 187. The date of the study is November 15, 1989.

14 As quoted by Alex Maldonado, *San Juan Star,* April 23, 1995, p. V46.

15 *Posadas de Puerto Rico Association v. Tourism Co.,* 478 U.S. 328 (1986); *Rodríguez v. Popular Democratic Party,* 457 U.S. 1 (1982).

16 *Examining Board v. Flores de Otero,* 426 U.S. 572 (1976).

17 See: Díaz Quiñones, Arcadio, "La vida inclemente," in his *La memoria rota,* Río Piedras, Ediciones Huracán, 1993, pp. 17–66. In the course of the past three decades, new generations of Puerto Rican historians have been producing valuable insights on this and other aspects of Puerto Rican history. The selected bibliography at the end of this book contains a representative sample of significant works written on these themes in recent years.

18 Dietz, James L., "La reinvención del subdesarrollo: Errores fundamentales del proyecto de industrialización," in Alvarez Curbelo, Silvia, and Rodríguez Castro, María Elena, eds., *Del nacionalismo al populismo: Cultura y política en Puerto Rico,* Río Piedras, Ediciones Huracán, 1993, pp. 179–205.

19 James Carter Presidential Library, Atlanta, Stuart Eizenstat Papers, box 264.

Glossary

Agregado Sharecropper.

Alcalde Mayor.

Alianza The Alliance party. Successor to the Unión de Puerto Rico and composed of remnants of the Unión and a dissident branch of the Republican party. Supported autonomy.

Audiencia or *Audiencia Territorial* The highest court in a Spanish colony.

Autonomistas Members of the Autonomist party. Believers in self-government in association with the metropolitan country. Opponents of independentistas, incondicionales, and estadistas.

Cabildo Municipal council.

Capitán General A high military rank normally held by the Governor of Puerto Rico in Spanish times.

Caribes Warlike Arawak Indians inhabiting some of the smaller Antilles.

Chamorros Native inhabitants of the Mariana Islands.

Coalición A coalition of the Unión Republicana and the Socialist parties that won the 1932 and 1936 elections, the second time in the century when statehood parties held power.

Cortes The Spanish Parliament.

Criollo Native.

Diputación Provincial Advisory body to the Governor.

Estadistas Believers in statehood.

Incondicionales Believers in union with Spain as a province thereof.

Independentistas Believers in independence.

Jíbaro A Puerto Rican from a rural area.

Nacionalista A member of the Nationalist party.

NPP New Progressive party.

Omnímodas The grant of absolute power to the Governor in Spanish times.

Partido Federal The Federal party. Short-lived party founded by Luis Muñoz Rivera during the military government period. Supported statehood.

Partido Incondicional Español The Unconditionally Spanish party, which favored union with Spain.

Partido Independentista Puertorriqueño The Puerto Rican Independence party, founded in 1946. Its forerunners date from 1912.

Partido Liberal When the Alianza broke up, the Liberal party represented the branch that favored independence. It was the strongest single party in Puerto Rico from 1932 to 1940.

Partido Liberal Reformista The Liberal Reformist party. Early autonomist party in Spanish times, less outspoken than its successor, the Autonomist party.

Partido Nacionalista Supports attaining independence by violent means.

Partido Obrero. A short-lived workers' party founded by Santiago Iglesias in 1899.

Partido Popular Democrático Founded by Luis Muñoz Marín in 1938. Supports Commonwealth status.

Partido Republicano Founded by Barbosa, this party supported statehood and had many successors, including the Partido Estadista, the Unión Republicana, and the present New Progressive party.

Partido Republicano Puro The segment of the old Republican party that did not join the Alianza and later became part of the Unión Republicana.

PDP Popular Democratic party. See *Partido Popular Democrático*.

Peninsulares Spaniards.

Peón, peones Laborer(s).

Populares Members of the Popular Democratic party.

Presidio A garrison.

Real y Supremo Consejo de Indias Chief advisory body to the Spanish king in ruling Spanish America.

Regidor Municipal councilman.

Situado A yearly subsidy sent by Mexico to Puerto Rico in the early centuries.

Taínos Peaceful Arawak Indians inhabiting Puerto Rico when the Spanish arrived.

Teniente a guerra Mayor of a small town.

Unión de Puerto Rico Political party founded in 1904 by Luis Muñoz Rivera, José De Diego, and others. Supported fuller self-government and eventual independence or statehood, especially independence.

Unión Republicana Composed of the statehood branch of the Alianza and the Partido Republicano Puro.

Selected Bibliography

Albizu Campos, Pedro. *La conciencia nacional puertorriqueña*, ed. Manuel Maldonado Denis. Mexico: Siglo Veintiuno, 1972.

Alegría, Ricardo. "La población antillana y su relación con otras áreas de América," in Aida Caro, *Antología de historia de Puerto Rico (siglos xv–xviii)*, 3d ed. Río Piedras: University of Puerto Rico Press, 1977, pp. 47–63.

Alvarez Curbelo, Silvia. *Senado de Puerto Rico, 1917–1992: Ensayos de historia institucional*. San Juan: Senado de Puerto Rico, 1992.

Alvarez Curbelo, Silvia, and Rodríguez Castro, María Elena, eds. *Del nacionalismo al populismo: Cultura y política en Puerto Rico*. Río Piedras: Ed. Huracán, 1993.

Anderson, Robert W. *Party Politics in Puerto Rico*. Stanford, Calif.: Stanford University Press, 1965.

Azize, Yamila. *La mujer en la lucha*. Río Piedras: Editorial Cultural, 1985.

Babín, María Teresa. *The Puerto Rican Spirit: Their History, Life and Culture*. New York, 1971.

Baldrich, Juan José. *Class and the State: The Origins of Populism in Puerto Rico, 1934–52*. Ann Arbor, Mich. (microfilm), 1981.

———. *Sembraron la no siembra: Los cosecheros de tabaco puertorriqueños frente a las corporaciones tabacaleras, 1920–34*, Río Piedras: Ediciones Huracán, 1988.

Banco Santander. *Puerto Rico desde el cielo*. 1995.

Berbusse, Edward J. *The United States and Puerto Rico, 1898–1900*. Chapel Hill: University of North Carolina Press, 1966.

Bergad, Laird W. *Coffee and the Growth of Agrarian Capitalism in Nineteenth-Century Puerto Rico*. Princeton: Princeton University Press, 1983.

Bhana, Surendra. *The Development of Puerto Rican Autonomy under the Truman Administration, 1944–52*. Ann Arbor, Mich. (microfilm), 1972.

———. *The United States and the Development of the Puerto Rican Status Question, 1936–68*. Lawrence: University of Kansas, 1975.

Cabranes, José A. *Citizenship and the American Empire*. New Haven: Yale University Press, 1979.

———. "Puerto Rico: Out of the Colonial Closet." 33 *Foreign Policy* 66 (Winter 1978–79).

Callcott, W. H. *The Caribbean Policy of the United States, 1890–1920.* Baltimore: Johns Hopkins University Press, 1942.

Carr, Raymond. *Puerto Rico: A Colonial Experiment.* New York: Vintage Books, 1984.

Chanlatte Baik, Luis. *La Hueca y sorcé (Vieques, Puerto Rico): Primeras migraciones agroalfareras antillanas: Nuevo esquema para los procesos culturales de la arqueología antillana.* Santo Domingo, 1981.

Clark, Victor S. *Porto Rico and Its Problems.* Washington, D.C.: Brookings Institution, 1930.

Córdova, Gonzalo F. *El ideal estadista en Barbosa y Martínez Nadal.* Puerto Rico, 1988.

Cruz Monclova, Lidio. *Historia de Puerto Rico (siglo XIX).* Río Piedras: University of Puerto Rico Press, 6th ed., 6 vols., 1970–79.

Curet Cuevas, Eliezer. *Development by Integration to the United States.* Río Piedras: Editorial Cultural, 1986.

D'Alzina Guillermety, Carlos. *Evolución y desarrollo del autonomismo puertorriqueño, siglo xix.* San Juan: First Book Publishing, 1995.

Delano, Jack. *From San Juan to Ponce on the Train.* Río Piedras: Puerto Rico University Press, 1990.

———. *Puerto Rico Mío: Four Decades of Change.* Washington, D.C.: Smithsonian Institution Press, 1990.

Delgado Cintrón, Carmelo. *Derecho y colonialismo: La trayectoria histórica del derecho puertorriqueño.* Barcelona: Editorial Edil, 1988.

Díaz Quiñones, Arcadio. *La memoria rota.* Río Piedras: Ediciones Huracán, 1993.

Díaz Soler, Luis. *Puerto Rico: Desde sus orígenes hasta el cese de la dominación española.* Río Piedras: University of Puerto Rico Press, 1994.

Dietz, James. *Economic History of Puerto Rico: Institutional Change and Capitalist Development.* Princeton: Princeton University Press, 1986.

Diffie, Bailey W., and Diffie, Justine Whitfield. *Porto Rico: A Broken Pledge.* New York: Vanguard Press, 1931.

Fernández Méndez, Eugenio. *Historia cultural de Puerto Rico, 1498–1968.* San Juan: Ediciones El Cemí, 1970.

Fernández, Ronald. *The Disenchanted Island: Puerto Rico and the United States in the Twentieth Century.* New York: Praeger, 1992.

Fernós Isern, Antonio. *Estado Libre Asociado de Puerto Rico: Antecedentes, creación y desarrollo hasta la época presente.* Río Piedras: University of Puerto Rico Press, 1974.

———. *Puerto Rico libre y federado.* San Juan: Biblioteca de Autores Puertorriqueños, 1951.

Figueroa Díaz, Wilfredo. *El movimiento estadista en Puerto Rico*. Hato Rey: Editorial Cultural, 1979.

Friedrich, Carl J. *Puerto Rico: Middle Road to Freedom*. New York: Rinehart, 1969.

Gale, Roger W. *The Americanization of Micronesia: A Study of the Consolidation of United States Rule in the Pacific*. Washington, D.C.: University Press of America, 1979.

García Passalacqua, Juan M. *La alternativa liberal: Una visión histórica de Puerto Rico*. Río Piedras: University of Puerto Rico Press, 1974.

————. *La crisis política en Puerto Rico*. San Juan: Editorial Edil, 1983.

García, Gervasio, and Quintero, Angel G. *Desafío y solidaridad: Breve historia del movimiento obrero puertorriqueño*. Río Piedras: Ediciones Huracán, 1982.

Gautier Mayoral, Carmen. *Puerto Rico y la ONU*. Río Piedras: Editorial Edil, 1978.

González, José Luis. *El país de cuatro pisos y otros ensayos*. Río Piedras: Ediciones Huracán, 1980.

González Vales, Luis E. *Alejandro Ramírez y su tiempo*. Río Piedras: University of Puerto Rico Press, 1978.

González, Lydia M., and Quintero, Angel G. *La otra cara de la historia: La historia de Puerto Rico desde su cara obrera*. Vol. I, 1800–1925. Río Piedras: CEREP, 1984.

Goodsell, Charles T. *Administration of a Revolution: Executive Reform in Puerto Rico under Governor Tugwell, 1941–46*. Cambridge: Harvard University Press, 1965.

Hanson, Earl P. *Transformation: The Story of Modern Puerto Rico*. New York: Simon and Schuster, 1955.

Haring, C. H. *The Spanish Empire in America*. New York: Oxford University Press, 1947.

Heine, Jorge, ed. *Time for Decision: The United States and Puerto Rico*. Lanham, Md.: North-South, 1983.

Johnson, Roberta Ann. *Puerto Rico: Commonwealth or Colony?* New York: Praeger Special Studies, 1980.

Kirk, Grayson L. *Philippine Independence*. New York: Farrar & Rinehart, 1936.

Las ideas anexionistas en Puerto Rico bajo la dominación norteamericana. Río Piedras: Ediciones Huracán, 1981.

Leibowitz, Arnold H. *Defining Status*. Dordrecht: Martinus Nijhoff, 1989.

Lewis, Gordon K. *Freedom and Power in the Caribbean*. New York: Monthly Review Press, 1963.

Lewis, Oscar. *La Vida: A Puerto Rican Family in the Culture of Poverty in San Juan and New York*. New York: Random House, 1966.

Lidin, Harold. *History of the Puerto Rican Independence Movement*, vol. 1: Nineteenth Century. Río Piedras, 1981.

López, Adalberto, and Petras, James, eds. *Puerto Rico and the Puerto Ricans*. New York: John Wiley and Sons, 1974.

Luque de Sánchez, María Dolores. *La ocupación norteamericana y la Ley Foraker:*

Raíces de la política colonial de los Estados Unidos. La opinión pública puertor-riqueña. Río Piedras: University of Puerto Rico Press, 1969.

Maldonado Denis, Manuel. *Puerto Rico: A Socio-Historic Interpretation.* New York: Vintage Press, 1972.

Marqués, René. *El puertorriqueño dócil y otros ensayos.* Río Piedras: Editorial Antillana, 1977.

Martínez Fernández, Luia. *El Partido Nuevo Progresista: Trayectoria hacia el poder y los orígenes sociales de sus fundadores (1967–68).* Santurce: Editorial Edil, 1986.

Mathews, Thomas G. *Puerto Rican Politics and the New Deal.* Gainesville: Florida University Press, 1960.

McHenry, D. F. *Micronesia: Trust Betrayed.* New York: Carnegie Endowment for Peace, 1975.

Meléndez, Edgardo. *El movimiento anexionista en Puerto Rico.* Río Piedras: University of Puerto Rico Press, 1979.

Morales Carrión, Arturo. "Orígenes de las relaciones entre los Estados Unidos y Puerto Rico 1700–1815." *Historia* 2, no. 1 (1952).

Morales Carrión, Arturo, ed. *Puerto Rico: A Political and Cultural History.* New York: W. W. Norton, 1983.

Muñoz Marín, Luis. *Memorias, 1898–1940.* San Juan: Universidad Interamericana, 1982; and *Memorias, 1940–52,* 1992.

Negrón Portillo, Mariano. *El autonomismo puertorriqueño; Su transformación ideológica, 1895–1914: La prensa en análisis social.* Río Piedras: Ediciones Huracán, 1981.

———. *Las turbas republicanas, 1900–04.* Río Piedras: Ediciones Huracán, 1990.

———. *Reformismo liberal, reformismo conservador: Dos etapas del reformismo puertorriqueño (1895–1914).* Río Piedras: Centro de Investigaciones Sociales, University of Puerto Rico.

Nieves Falcón, Luis. *Diagnóstico de Puerto Rico.* Río Piedras: Editorial Edil, 1970.

———. *El emigrante puertorriqueño.* Río Piedras: Editorial Edil, 1975.

O'Toole, G. J. A. *The Spanish War: An American Epic, 1898.* New York: W. W. Norton, 1984.

Pagán, Bolívar. *Historia de los partidos políticos puertorriqueños (1898–1956).* San Juan: Librería Campos, 2 vols., 1959.

Perkins, Baxter. *The United States and the Caribbean.* Cambridge: Harvard University Press, rev. ed., 1966.

Perloff, Harvey. *Puerto Rico: Economic Future.* Chicago: University of Chicago Press, 1950.

Perusse, Roland I. *The United States and Puerto Rico: The Struggle for Equality.* Malabar, Fla.: Krieger, 1990.

Picó, Fernando. *1898: La Guerra después de la Guerra.* Río Piedras: Ediciones Huracán, 1987.

————. *Al filo del poder: Subalternos y dominantes en Puerto Rico (1739–1910)*. Río Piedras: Ediciones Huracán, 1993.

————. *Historia general de Puerto Rico*. Río Piedras: Ediciones Huracán, 1986.

Picó, Fernando, and Rivera Izeda, Carmen. *Tierra adentro y mar afuera: Historia y cultura de los puertorriqueños*. Río Piedras: Ediciones Huracán, 1991.

Pratt, J. W. *America's Colonial Experiment*. New York: Prentice-Hall, 1950.

Quintero Rivera, Angel G. *Conflictos de clase y política en Puerto Rico*. Río Piedras: Ediciones Huracán, 1976.

————. *Lucha obrera: Antología de grandes documentos en la historia obrera puertorriqueña*. Río Piedras: CEREP, 2d ed., 1972.

————. *Patricios y plebeyos: Burgueses, hacendados, artesanos y obreros: Las relaciones de clase en el Puerto Rico de cambio de siglo*. Río Piedras: Ediciones Huracán, 1988.

Raffucci de García, Carmen. *El gobierno civil y la ley Foraker*. Río Piedras: University of Puerto Rico Press, 1981.

Rivera Medina, Eduardo, and Ramírez, Rafael I. *Del cañaveral a la fábrica: Cambio social en Puerto Rico*. Río Piedras: Ediciones Huracán, 1985.

Rodríguez Orellana, Manuel. "In Contemplation of Micronesia: The Prospects for the Decolonization of Puerto Rico Under International Law." 18 *Univ. of Miami Inter-American L. Rev.* 457.

Roosevelt, Theodore, Jr. *Colonial Policies of the United States*. New York: Doubleday, Doran, 1937.

Rosario Natal, Carmelo. *Puerto Rico y la crisis de la guerra hispanoamericana, 1895–98*. Hato Rey: Ramallo Bros., 1975.

Sánchez Torniello, Andrés. *El plebiscito de los anexionistas*. Río Piedras: Editorial Bayoán, 1993.

Senior, Clarence. *Puerto Rican Emigration*. Río Piedras: University of Puerto Rico Press, 1947.

Silvestrini, Blanca G. *Violencia y criminalidad en Puerto Rico, 1898–1973: Apuntes para un estudio de historia social*. Río Piedras: Editorial Universitaria, 1980.

Silvestrini, Blanca G., ed. *Politics, Society and Culture in the Caribbean: Selected Papers of the Fourteenth Conference of Caribbean Historians*. San Juan: University of Puerto Rico, 1983.

Silvestrini, Blanca G., and Luque de Sánchez, María Dolores. *Historia de Puerto Rico: Trayectoria de un pueblo*. San Juan: Cultural Puertorriqueña, 1987.

Smith, Gary. *Decolonization and the United States Military Interests in the Trust Territory of the Pacific*. Canberra, Research School of Pacific Studies, Australian National University, 1991.

Suárez, Manuel. *Requiem for Cerro Maravilla*. Maplewood, N.J.: Waterfront, 1987.

Sued Badillo, Jalil. *Los caribes: Realidad o fábula*. Río Piedras: Editorial Antillana, 1978.

Torruella, Juan R. *The Supreme Court of the United States and Puerto Rico: The Doctrine of Separate and Unequal*. Río Piedras: University of Puerto Rico Press, 1985.

Trías Monge, José. *El choque de dos culturas jurídicas en Puerto Rico*. Orford, N.H.: Equity Publishing, 1991.

———. *Historia constitucional de Puerto Rico*. Río Piedras: University of Puerto Rico Press, 5 vols., 1980–83, 1994.

Tugwell, Rexford G. *The Stricken Land: The Story of Puerto Rico*. New York: Doubleday, 1947.

Tumin, Melvin M., and Feldman, Arnold S. *Social Class and Social Change in Puerto Rico*. Princeton: Princeton University Press, 1961.

United States Department of Commerce. *Economic Study of Puerto Rico* (the Kreps Report). Washington, D.C.: Government Printing Office, 2 vols., 1979.

Wagenhem, K. *Puerto Rico: A Profile*. New York: Praeger, 1974.

Weinberg, A. K. *Manifest Destiny*. Baltimore: Johns Hopkins University Press, 1936.

Weiskoff, Richard. *Factories and Food Stamps: The Puerto Rican Model of Development*. Baltimore: Johns Hopkins University Press, 1985.

Wells, Henry. *The Modernization of Puerto Rico: A Political Study of Changing Values and Institutions*. Cambridge: Harvard University Press, 1969.

Williams, Eric. *From Columbus to Castro: The History of the Caribbean*. New York: Random House, 1970.

Index